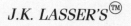

J.K. LASSER'S™

NEW RULES FOR ESTATE AND TAX PLANNING

Fourth Edition

Look for these and other titles from J.K. Lasser™—Practical Guides for All Your Financial Needs

J.K. Lasser's Small Business Taxes by Barbara Weltman
J.K. Lasser's 1001 Deductions and Tax Breaks by Barbara Weltman
J.K. Lasser's Real Estate Tax Edge by Scott Estill and Stephanie Long
J.K. Lasser's The New Bankruptcy Law and You by Nathalie Martin and
    Stewart Paley

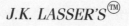

NEW RULES FOR ESTATE AND TAX PLANNING

Fourth Edition

Stewart Welch III
Harold Apolinsky
Craig M. Stephens

WILEY

John Wiley & Sons, Inc.

Published by John Wiley & Sons, Inc., Hoboken, New Jersey.
Published simultaneously in Canada.

For general information about our other products and services, please contact our Customer
Care Department within the United States at (800) 762-2974, outside the United States at
(317) 572-3993 or fax (317) 572-4002.

Wiley also publishes its books in a variety of electronic formats. Some content that appears in
print may not be available in electronic books. For more information about Wiley products,
visit our web site at www.wiley.com.

Library of Congress Cataloging-in-Publication Data

Welch, Stewart H.
    J.K. Lasser's new rules for estate and tax planning : keep more today, leave more to your
heirs tomorrow / Stewart H. Welch, III, Harold I. Apolinsky, Craig Stephens. – 4th ed.
        p. cm. – (J.K. Lasser–practical guides for all your financial needs)
    Includes index.
        ISBN 978-1-118-11355-4 (pbk.); ISBN 978-1-118-16644-4 (ebk);
ISBN 978-1-118-16645-1 (ebk); ISBN 978-1-118-16646-8 (ebk)
    1. Inheritance and transfer tax–Law and legislation–United States.   2. Estate
planning–United States.   I. Apolinsky, Harold I.   II. Stephens, Craig M.   III. Title.
IV. Title: New rules for estate and tax planning revised.
    KF6585.A66 2012
    343.7305′3–dc23
                                                                            2011029302

Printed in the United States of America.

10 9 8 7 6 5 4 3 2 1

Contents

Acknowledgments

Harold Apolinsky, Esq., Estate Tax Law Specialist

It would not have been possible to write a book of this magnitude without the support, assistance, and encouragement of our law firm, Sirote & Permutt. We owe a special thank you to the 13 other members of our Estate and Probate Department: Katherine N. Barr, Elizabeth Hutchins, Shirley Justice, Leigh Kaylor, Melinda Mathews, Joel Mendler, Sandy Mullins, Tanya Shunnara, Melissa May, Peter Wright, Mike Thomas, John Baggette, and George Gaston—bright and gifted lawyers who believe in top-quality legal care, outstanding service to clients, and innovation.

We are all constantly seeking and studying new estate planning ideas to help clients not only accumulate wealth, but keep wealth within their families. I want to acknowledge the encouragement of my wife, Marissa Levine Apolinsky, who exhibited unlimited patience as I spent time writing. Also, the years of encouragement from my children, Steve Apolinsky, Felice Apolinsky, and Craig Apolinsky, who convinced me that with hard work and determination nothing was impossible to achieve. Finally, without the help of our loyal assistants, Marsha Self and Beverly Stradford, and our top estate planning associates Tanya Shunnara, Esq., and Melissa May, Esq., the demanding publishing deadlines could never have been met. The most fun for me has been to work with Stewart Welch, a most gifted individual and innovative financial advisor.

Craig Stephens, Esq.

I would like to thank my wife, Jenna S. Stephens, who provided me with un-interrupted time working on this book. Juggling this book revision, a blessed practice, teaching Estate Planning at Cumberland School of Law, and parenting two-year-old twins required significant support from my loving wife, and I thank her for it.

I would also like to thank Harold Apolinsky and Stewart Welch III for providing me with the opportunity to be a part of the fourth edition of this book and a coauthor of the fourth edition. I am fortunate to have worked with Harold and Stewart on many projects, and our collaborative efforts will hopefully lead many families to produce a lasting legacy for decades to come.

Stewart Welch III, Accredited Estate Planner, Certified Financial Planner℠

This book would have never happened without help and moral support from many people. First and foremost, I want to thank my coauthors, Harold Apolinsky and Craig Stephens. Harold is not only a true scholar but a true gentleman as well. He has been generous with both his time and his talents. Thanks, Harold. I also want to thank Craig Stephens for his insightful contributions to this revision. Craig is a rising star in the legal profession.

Bob Holman, CPA, is a senior partner with the accounting firm of Sellers, Richardson, Holman & West, LLP., in Birmingham, Alabama. I have had the distinct pleasure of working with Bob for more than two decades. He is unques-tionably one of the brightest people I have ever met.

As most of you are aware, insurance can be a very confusing product to understand. I am fortunate to have had the assistance of two of the coun-try's top insurance specialists. I would like to thank my father, Stewart H. Welch Jr., CLU, who has been a top professional in the business for more than 50 years. He never ceases to amaze me with his energy and creative ideas. I have truly been blessed to have had his guidance throughout my life. Babs Hart specializes in long-term care insurance, and her input regarding that section of the text was invaluable.

I could not have considered attempting this project without the assistance and moral support of my associates. Greg Weyandt, CPA, is a member and the Chief Operating Officer and Chief Compliance Officer of both of my financial advisory companies and runs the day-to-day operations with near flawlessness which allowed me to concentrate on this project. Michael Wagner, CPA, CFP® and Kimberly Reynolds, MS, CFP® are Senior Advisors at The Welch Group. Their expertise and diligence in preparing for our client meetings has made my life much easier and enjoyable. Their efforts are ably supported by Associate Advisor, Foster Hyde. Jeff Davenport, Wendy Weber, and Ramona Boehm can always be counted on to make certain our administration operations run smoothly. Roxie Jones is our receptionist and always makes everyone feel well taken care of. Woodard Peay, CFP®, MBA, is a member in Fee-Only Planning Professionals, LLC, a financial advisory firm in which I am the principal owner. Woodard is extraordinarily bright and a seasoned professional. I am grateful to Woodard and his key associates; Beth Moody, MS; and Melissa Erikson for running their company so well. I owe a special thanks to Hugh Smith, CPA, CFP®, CFA, for his expert support of this project. Hugh is a member at The Welch Group and the Chief Investment Officer for both companies.

I feel very fortunate to have the opportunity to work with the prestigious publishing house of John Wiley & Sons, Inc., a traditional "blue blood" firm whose roots can be traced back to 1807. I could not mention John Wiley & Sons, Inc., without thanking Editorial Director Debra Englander, a longtime friend of mine who has become as much my sister as a trusted colleague.

Writing a book of this type is a full-time job in and of itself. Because running my company is also a full-time job, my family ends up paying a large price for my commitments. The biggest price by far was paid by my wife, Kathie. She endured many weeknights and most weekends alone while I spent much of my nonwork time writing. Throughout the entire time she remained very supportive, and I love her even more for it. I especially want to thank my mother, Sally Welch, for her constant prayers and support. She is a fine person who has been a guiding light all of my life. I also have two wonderful sisters, Jean Watson and Babs Hart, who have always been cheerleaders for all my endeavors.

There is no way to express how grateful I am for the wonderful clients I have the pleasure of serving. Each, in their own way, has contributed to my own learning and therefore to this book.

Finally, Harold, Craig, and I would like to thank two people for their special assistance with this book project. Kimberly Bernard is Development Editor at John Wiley & Sons, Inc. Kim helped keep this project on schedule and provided valuable assistance to the editing process.

In addition Professor Jeffrey A. Cooper is a professor of law at Quinnipiac University School of Law in Hamden, Connecticut. While using our book as a resource for his classes, Professor Cooper offered invaluable suggestions for improving the content for this revision.

Introduction

Writing a book of this magnitude requires a tremendous amount of time and emotional energy. I agreed to take on this project only under the condition that I could convince one of the country's best legal minds to join me as a coauthor. To my great delight, Harold Apolinsky agreed to my proposal. Harold is one of the country's most respected estate tax lawyers. He testified before Congress and spent innumerable hours in Washington lobbying influential senators and representatives. He served as general counsel for the American Family Business Institute. The American Family Business Institute is the premiere trade association educating members of Congress on the need for major reform of the estate tax. Dick Patten serves as the president and CEO of the American Family Business Institute in Washington, D.C. For more information, please visit www.nodeathtax.org. I am also delighted that Harold convinced his protégé, Craig Stephens to also coauthor this book. Craig is both highly intelligent and resourceful and has been a pleasure to work with on this project.

I own a fee-only wealth management firm serving a nationwide clientele, Harold is the senior tax and estate planning member of Sirote Permutt, one of Alabama's largest law firms along with Craig Stephens, who is a partner in the same law firm. Together, we have had the opportunity to work with many affluent individuals throughout the United States. The common characteristic that we find among them is that they take pride in both their financial success and in their ability to handle their finances. But this book was not written just for the affluent but for the many people who want to *become* affluent.

What does it take? Although you may already have accumulated a sizable estate and feel comfortable handling your investments, chances are you haven't paid sufficient attention to estate *planning*. This is the reason we wanted to write this book. The purpose of *J.K. Lasser's New Rules for Estate and Tax Planning, Fourth Edition* is to make certain that you have taken steps to make sure your estate is in order and that you have a specific strategy in place. Whether you are just getting your financial feet on the ground or you are a millionaire many times over, this book offers valuable strategies you can use today and in the future.

As you read this book, we encourage you to keep your parents' situation in mind because some of the more advanced strategies may be more appropriate for them than for yourself. You may want to discuss these issues with them or lend this book to them. After all, you should all share the goal of maximizing the amount of money that you can transfer to your heirs and charitable organizations.

The book begins with an overview of the most important aspects of the 2010 Tax Relief Act. You will be able to use this chapter as a reference tool for reviewing significant estate and income tax laws affecting you.

Next, you will need to assess the adequacy of your current estate plan. What is the value of your total estate? You will learn how to determine your *estate* net worth. This is vital because knowing its value will let you define the resources available to your family to provide for their income needs should you die prematurely. You will also be able to determine approximately how much in estate taxes your heirs might owe.

It is also important to assess whether you are on track toward retirement—are you accumulating enough investment assets to provide you with a worry-free retirement? Studies indicate that the average working American is saving less than one-third of what he or she needs to have enough assets to maintain the same lifestyle during retirement. In many cases, this shortfall will be made up from inheritances. If you find out that you're lagging behind, this book will help you figure out how much you need to be investing to get on track, and you'll learn how to devise an appropriate investment plan.

Another key aspect of estate planning is, of course, having a will. Research indicates that as many as 80 percent of adult Americans either don't have a will or their will is out-of-date. If you fall into this group, you should stop procrastinating. It really does matter if you die without a will! We'll outline the perils of dying without one. The resulting chaos will surprise you. You'll learn how to prepare yourself so that you can minimize the time and expense of working with an attorney.

The use of trusts is a vital part of most estate plans. You can use them to protect your children from themselves, to protect you from possible future creditors, or to save on income and estate taxes. These are powerful weapons in the war to protect your assets for yourself as well as future heirs. It is our experience that many people carry large amounts of life insurance, including their employer's group life. Utilizing some type of trust is often an invaluable estate planning tool. You'll learn about the irrevocable life insurance trust, living trust, and other types of trusts.

Many of you face the difficult task of funding your children's education. You'll learn how to effectively use qualified tuition plans and education individual retirement accounts as well as custodial accounts and minors' trusts. You'll also learn about how grandparents can be willing partners in assisting with your children's educational expenses.

If you are interested in providing financial support to a religious organization, an educational institution, or a favorite charity, you'll gain insights on the best ways to maximize the effectiveness of your donations. Often, gifts to tax-exempt organizations can solve a financial dilemma such as how to convert low-basis non-income-producing property into income-producing property while avoiding a large tax bill.

Once you have accumulated enough assets for your retirement years, you may want to shift your focus to transfer strategies for your children and other heirs. We'll outline strategies that will allow you to transfer to heirs significant wealth at a fraction of its market value while maintaining control of your property.

People who own a family business or farm often face a perilous future; this is especially worrisome because many of these individuals desperately want to ensure that the business or farm remains in the family so that it can be continued by future generations of family members. Obstacles to this goal include estate taxes and lack of liquidity. The solution is a well-developed transition plan, which is also fully explained in this book.

In today's litigious society, many people fear the threat of a lawsuit that results in financial ruin. Feeling helpless, we may cross our fingers and hope it does not happen to us. A preferable approach is to be proactive. If you consider yourself a likely target, you can do many things to protect your assets. Some solutions are as simple as transferring assets to a spouse who is less at risk. Other solutions include the use of trusts, family limited partnerships, and even more exotic options such as domestic or foreign asset protection trusts. For entrepreneurs, we extensively review the pros and cons of the various entity choices you have for operating your business.

As you develop and implement your estate plan, you'll almost certainly need the assistance of a qualified professional. Finding the right person, someone who is truly qualified, can be a daunting task. It is one of the reasons many people fail to establish their estate plan. To help support you with this process your coauthors will gladly help you find an advisor to assist you with your needs. In

Appendix A are tips on how to get the most out of your advisors while minimizing their fees.

As Americans, our limitations are constrained only by our own imagination, our willingness to take time to develop an appropriate strategy, and the self-discipline to execute our game plan. Picking up this book is an essential first step. Carefully reading it and implementing the strategies most appropriate to your situation will enable you to take a giant leap toward taking charge of your financial destiny. May God smile on your journey.

Stewart H. Welch III, CFP®, AEP

Tax Relief, Unemployment Insurance Reauthorization, and Job Creation Act of 2010

President Obama signed the Tax Relief, Unemployment Insurance Reauthorization, and Job Creation Act of 2010 (2010 Tax Relief Act) on December 17, 2010. With many tax provisions originally enacted under The Economic Growth and Tax Relief Reconciliation Act of 2001 set to expire or already expired, the 2010 Tax Relief Act was a necessity. Taxpayers needed stability, and Congress reached a compromise tax legislation bill with the 2010 Tax Relief Act.

Like previous tax acts, unfortunately, the stability will be short lived. Most of the provisions in the 2010 Tax Relief Act will, once again, expire after December 31, 2012. Therefore, we can expect a new tax act to be discussed, negotiated, and enacted sometime in late 2012. In the meantime, taxpayers should become familiar with an overview of the 2010 Tax Relief Act and its effect on income tax provisions, business tax provisions, education incentives, and transfer tax provisions.

Without a new tax act in 2012, income tax rates will rise, estate tax rates will rise, gift tax rates will rise, and generation-skipping tax rates will rise. Undoubtedly, these potential tax increases will become the subject of the 2012 election season. In 2012, there will be a presidential election and many seats in Congress will be up for re-election. Therefore, we can expect great debate on the future of our tax system as we approach the end of 2012. This debate will lead to *some* type of tax act that will likely be effective on January 1, 2013. Therefore, it will be important to remain in contact with your tax advisors to fully understand how the inevitable 2013 tax act will affect you. In the meantime, a short window exists for planning opportunities that will be discussed throughout this book.

Marginal Ordinary Income Tax Rates

Without the provisions of the 2010 Tax Relief Act, the marginal income tax rates were set to increase on January 1, 2011. The increase would have applied to both ordinary income tax rates and capital gains tax rates. Therefore, at the end of 2010, many taxpayers were contemplating transactions which would accelerate income tax recognition into 2010 since tax rates were set to increase on January 1, 2011. However, the 2010 Tax Relief Act extended the 2010 ordinary income tax rates and capital gains tax rates into 2011 and 2012.

Prior to enactment of the 2010 Tax Relief Act, the Obama Administration had pledged no new taxes on middle-class Americans. A similar pledge was not made for wealthy Americans. As a result of negotiations and compromise, the 2010 income tax rates were extended for all taxpayers, not just middle-class Americans and individuals making less than middle-class Americans. See Table 1.1 for a complete review of the schedule for joint and single tax filers.

Although the 2010 Tax Relief Act extended the income tax marginal rates, the predictability of income tax rates is somewhat short-lived. If Congress takes no action before January 1, 2013, the income tax rates will return to 15%, 28%, 31%, 36%, and 39.6%. Therefore, it is expected that many taxpayers will, again, consider acceleration of income tax recognition events into late 2012 unless Congress takes action before then that will address income tax rates starting on January 1, 2013.

TABLE 1.1 Schedule of Reduction of Individual Income Tax Rates

Year	$0–$17,000	$17,001–$69,000	$69,001–$139,350	$139,351–$212,300	$212,301–$379,150	$379,151+
Joint Filers						
2011–2012	10%	15%	25%	28%	33%	35%
Year	$0–$8,500	$8,501–$34,500	$34,501–$83,600	$83,601–$174,400	$174,401–$379,150	$379,151+
Single Filers						
2011–2012	10%	15%	25%	28%	33%	35%

Capital Gains Tax Rates

The Jobs and Growth Act–2003 provided significant capital gains tax relief. The law immediately dropped the maximum net capital gains rate by 5 percentage points from 20 percent to 15 percent. The 10 percent capital gains rate for lower-income taxpayers fell to 5 percent. The lower rates are expected to continue through December 31, 2012.

Tip

Review all assets where you have a long-term capital gain to determine if it is advisable to sell before the current capital gains tax (15% federal) reverts back to the old capital gains tax rate of 20% (January 1, 2013).

The 2010 Tax Relief Act also reduced the employee portion of social security taxes from 6.2% to 4.2%. This change is only in effect for 2011. The 2010 Tax Relief Act did not change the employer portion of the social security tax.

For self employed individuals, the 2010 Tax Relief Act reduced the self employment taxes from 12.4% to 10.4% for earned income in 2011 (no changes were made for post-2011 years).

Educational Provisions

The Tax Relief Act that was enacted in 2001 introduced many tax benefits for implementing an educational savings plan. With respect to the 2010 Tax Relief Act, additional benefits were enacted by extending the American Opportunity Tax Credit for Higher Education Expenses through 2012. This tax credit applies to all four years of an undergraduate college education. The amount of the tax credit is generally 100% of the first $2,000 in qualifying educational expenses. An additional 25% of the next $2,000 in qualifying educational expenses is allowed. The maximum credit is $2,500 (which assumes $4,000 in qualifying educational expenses). Qualifying educational expenses include tuition and related course materials, such as books, software, and lab supplies.

Education IRA

Under prior law, you could make a nondeductible contribution of up to $500 per year to an Education IRA, more commonly known as Coverdell Education Savings Accounts. Your earnings grew tax-free and the distributions, when used for qualified educational expenses, were taxed at the student beneficiary's tax bracket. While this Education IRA was beneficial, it was only a partial solution to the problem of funding today's education costs.

The Tax Relief Act of 2010 extended the benefits of the Coverdell Education Savings Accounts that were enacted by the Tax Relief Act of 2001. The most significant provisions of the benefits that were extended include the following:

- Increased the contribution limits from $500 per year to $2,000 per year.
- Provided that distributions, when used to pay for qualified education expenses, would be tax-free.
- Allowed tax-free withdrawals for elementary (including kindergarten) and secondary public, private, and religious school tuition and expenses.
- Included tuition, room and board, tutoring, uniforms, extended day program costs, computer technology hardware and software, Internet access, and special needs services for special needs beneficiary as qualifying expenses.
- Allowed HOPE Scholarship Credit and Lifetime Learning Credit for other expenses.
- Extended the time in which the contribution can be made to April 15 of the following tax year.
- Phased out your ability to contribute to an Education IRA above certain income levels. The 2010 Tax Relief Act extended the phase-out range for joint filers with adjusted gross income (AGI) of $190,000–$220,000. Also extended was the phase-out range for single tax filers with AGI of $95,000–$110,000.

The Coverdell Education IRA still provides a significant incentive to prefund education expenses. However, the $2,000 contribution amount is scheduled to drop to $500 after 2012. Unless the law is changed before that time, it is expected that Education IRAs will be a less attractive way to save for college expenses.

Tip

If you would like to make a contribution to an Education IRA for your child but you do not qualify because your AGI is too high, consider having your child contribute to his or her own account. Unlike other IRAs, a person does not have to have earned income to contribute to an Education IRA nor is there a minimum age requirement.

Section 529 Plans

While the 2010 Tax Relief Act did not modify the existing rules for Section 529 plans, because Section 529 plans have become a very flexible and taxpayer friendly way to save for education, we would like to retain the discussion of Section 529 plans in this new edition of the book.

WHAT IS A SECTION 529 PLAN?

A Section 529 plan is a program that allows individuals to (1) purchase tuition credits or certificates on behalf of a designated beneficiary, entitling the beneficiary to a waiver or payment of the beneficiary's higher education expenses; or (2) make contributions to an account that is established for the sole purpose of meeting qualified higher education expenses of the designated beneficiary of the account.

PLAN CONTRIBUTIONS

A Section 529 plan may only accept contributions in the form of cash and not in property. However, a Section 529 plan may accept payment by check, money order, credit card, or other similar methods.

There are no limits as to the amount of money that can be contributed to a Section 529 plan (unless limited by the plan sponsor); however, there are penalties for distributions not used for qualified education expenses. Most important, unlike the Education IRA, there are no income phase-out rules that prevent high-income taxpayers from contributing to a Section 529 plan.

TAX-FREE GROWTH

Earnings in a Section 529 plan grow tax deferred until distributions are made, at which time the distributions are tax free if used to pay qualified education expenses. For example, suppose you and your spouse contributed $100,000 to a Section 529 plan on behalf of a one-year-old grandchild. This $100,000 would grow tax-free until such time as it is distributed for higher education expenses, presumably beginning at the child's age 18. If your plan sponsor averaged a 9 percent return, the account value would exceed $400,000 by the time you are ready to begin drawing funds for your grandchild's college. When the funds are then used to pay for qualified education expenses, there will be no income taxes due on those distributions. Qualified higher education expenses include tuition, books, supplies, equipment, fees, expenses for special needs services, and room and board (within certain limits). The amount of qualified higher education expenses is reduced by scholarships and amounts paid by the beneficiary or others that qualify for the HOPE Scholarship or Lifetime Learning Credits.

> ### Tip
>
> If you are currently using a Uniform Gift to Minors Account (UGMA) or a Uniform Transfer to Minors Account (UTMA) as a funding vehicle for your child's education, consider the Section 529 plan or an Education IRA instead. By doing so, you'll not only avoid current taxation on earnings (remember the so-called kiddie tax?), but distributions used for education expenses will be tax-free.

PENALTIES ON NONQUALIFIED DISTRIBUTIONS

If distributions from a Section 529 plan are not used for qualified education expenses, a 10 percent penalty is imposed on the recipient of the funds. In addition, the *earnings portion* of the distribution is subject to ordinary income taxes. Usually, the tax will be triggered when distributions exceed the educational expenses of the designated beneficiary. According to some states' plans, any funds not distributed prior to the beneficiary attaining the age of 30 will be deemed a nonqualifying distribution (some exceptions apply for a special needs beneficiary). Exceptions to this penalty apply for payments made due to the beneficiary's death, disability, or receipt of a scholarship.

INVESTMENT OPTIONS

One potential downside of Section 529 plans is that you are unable to direct the investments of the plan. The investment accounts are operated as blind pools where you have no input over specific investment decisions. Most plan sponsors do, however, indicate the general investment approach they use. Often, contributors have the ability to select from a variety of investment strategies, with some Section 529 plans offering as many as 10 options. An important feature added under the old Tax Relief Act–2001 is the ability to switch from one state-sponsored program to another every 12 months. This significantly increases your ability to change your broad investment strategy to meet your particular needs.

GIFT TAX CONSEQUENCES

A contribution to a Section 529 plan is considered a completed gift from the account owner to the designated beneficiary at the time of the contribution and is thus eligible for the annual gift tax exclusion (currently $13,000 or $26,000 in the case of a joint gift by spouses). If the contribution exceeds the annual gift tax exclusion, the amount not exceeding five times the current annual exclusion may be applied pro rata to annual exclusions over five years.

For example, you could make an initial contribution of $65,000 for each designated beneficiary without incurring gift tax liability for the contribution. The $65,000 contribution would be treated as if you made a $13,000 contribution in each of the next five years. Note that this presumes that no other gifts are made to the beneficiary during this five-year period. Any additional gifts would be subject to gift taxes. However, because the annual exclusion amount is indexed for inflation, this amount could increase in future years. Married couples can join together in making gifts, thus increasing the potential contribution to $130,000 without incurring gift taxes.

ESTATE TAX CONSEQUENCES

Even though the donor retains the right to change the designated beneficiary (to another member of the donor's family) and to receive distributions from the account if no other person is designated, funds invested in the Section 529 plan are not included in the donor's gross estate unless the funds are in fact returned to the donor. Thus, once you contribute an amount to a Section 529 plan, that amount is out of your estate(s), as is the future appreciation on that amount. However, if a contribution exceeding the annual exclusion is applied pro rata to the annual exclusion over five years but the donor dies before the fifth year, that portion of the contribution that has not yet been applied to the annual exclusion for the years following the donor's death will be included in the donor's estate.

For example, suppose Mr. Leonard contributes $65,000 to a Section 529 plan and elects to have this applied pro rata over the next five years to the annual exclusion. Furthermore, assume Mr. Leonard passes away in the fourth year following the contribution. The amount of the annual exclusion to be applied in the fifth year ($13,000) would be brought back into Mr. Leonard's estate.

Tip

Creditor Protection for Section 529 Plans?
Funds held in a Section 529 plan may be subject to the claims of creditors and divorce proceedings. Typically, state law will prevail. If you are concerned about creditor protection, consider using a Section 529 plan sponsored by a state that has strong creditor protection laws.

For more information on Section 529 plans go to the Resource Center at www.welchgroup.com; then click on "Links".

SOME FINAL THOUGHTS ON SECTION 529 PLANS

Note that under the Section 529 plan, you are able to change your beneficiary. This is important because one child may choose not to attend college or may attend a relatively inexpensive college while another child may attend a very expensive college. A Section 529 plan allows you to move your funds around as needed. The former Tax Relief Act–2001 included "cousins" in the definition of family member. However, be sure to check the applicable plan's rules and restrictions for changing beneficiaries.

2010 Tax Relief Act—Miscellaneous Provisions Relating to Education

Several other provisions of the 2010 Tax Relief Act are worth noting:

- Employers can still offer education assistance programs providing up to $5,250 per year for an employee. The payment is deductible by the employer and not includable in the income of the employee. Undergraduate and graduate courses qualify, and the courses do not have to be related to the employee's job-related field. This benefit is extended through 2012.

- The 2010 Tax Relief Act continues to allow for deductibility of student loan interest of up to $2,500 (with phase-out limitation) through 2012.

Business and Corporate Tax Relief

The 2010 Tax Relief Act extended certain business and corporate tax relief provisions that were previously enacted by the 2001 Tax Act and the Jobs and Growth Act of 2003. For business property placed in service in 2011, the business taxpayer can immediately deduct (rather than depreciate) up to $500,000 under Section 179 of the Internal Revenue Code.

For certain new property (instead of used property that may be new to the business), there may be an available 100% bonus depreciation depending on the type of property involved. This deduction is scheduled to end after 2012.

Estate, Gift, and Generation-Skipping Transfers

The 2010 Tax Relief Act provided sweeping changes to the estate, gift, and generation-skipping tax system. (See Table 1.2) The former 2001 Tax Relief Act repealed the estate and generation-skipping taxes for 2010. Prior to 2010, it was unclear whether the one-year repeal would take place, and if it took place, whether it would be extended for additional years. The 2010 Tax Relief Act confirmed that the estate and generation-skipping taxes were, in fact, repealed for 365 days during 2010. However, the estate and generation skipping taxes were reenacted on January 1, 2011, and, along with the gift tax, they became unified with a uniform $5 million exemption and a maximum tax rate of 35%. Uncertainty remains a planning hurdle in the transfer tax arena because the provisions of the 2010 Tax Relief Act are only in place until December 31, 2012. At that time, if Congress does nothing, the transfer tax laws will revert to pre-2001 provisions.

While the 2010 Tax Relief Act did provide *some* certainty with respect to a potential estate tax liability, uncertainty still exists for deaths occurring after December 31, 2012. The uncertainty is highlighted by the question in the following box.

Under the 2010 Tax Relief Act, what amount of federal estate tax will be owed on an estate of $5,000,000?

    a. $675,000

    b. $0

    c. $2,045,000

TABLE 1.2 Potential Estate (Death) Tax Savings under Tax Relief Act–2001 as Compared to Death in 2011 and 2012

	$5 Million Estate	$10 Million Estate	$20 Million Estate	$50 Million Estate	$100 Million Estate
2011–2012	$0	$1,750,000	$7,000,000	$15,710,000	$33,250,000
2013 tax	$2,045,000	$4,795,000	$10,654,200	$27,154,200	$54,654,200
Savings	$2,045,000	$3,045,000	$3,654,200	$11,444,200	$21,404,200

The 2013 data assumes Congress allows the 2010 Tax Relief Act to 'sunset' and revert back to prior tax law.

Give up? The answer is that both (b) and (c) are correct! The answer b, is correct if you die in 2011–2012. The answer c is correct if you die in 2013 and the exemption reverts to $1.0 million. We hope you are beginning to see the importance of carefully developing your estate plan.

Please don't misunderstand, the 2010 Tax Relief Act does provide potentially significant tax relief, assuming that death occurs prior to January 1, 2013. Table 1.2 illustrates the estate tax savings under current law versus what taxes will be if the current law reverts to prior law on January 1, 2013 under the sunset provision.

Following is a list of select provisions that could affect your estate planning:

- The 2010 Tax Relief Act lowered the maximum estate, gift, and generation-skipping rates, and it raised the amount of assets that are not subject to estate, gift, and generation-skipping taxes. Table 1.3 outlines the new rates and applicable exclusion amounts.

- The new law enacted portability provisions. A decedent's applicable exclusion amount is now the basic exclusion amount of $5 million plus, in the case of a surviving spouse, the deceased spouse's *unused* applicable exclusion amount.

- For decedents who died in 2010, their estate was allowed to elect to have no estate tax apply for 2010, along with a carry-over basis system. Or, the estate could elect for an estate tax to apply in 2011 (with a $5 million exemption amount) and receive a step-up in basis.

- For 2011, the maximum generation-skipping tax rate became 35%.

TABLE 1.3 2010 Tax Relief Act Applicable Exclusion Amount

Year	Applicable Exclusion Amount	Maximum Estate Tax Rate (%)
2011–2012	$5,000,000	35
2013	$1,000,000[1]	55

[1] 2010 Tax Relief Act is automatically repealed unless Congress extends the law.

Estate Planning Issues under the 2010 Tax Relief Act

Because of the uncertainty surrounding the current status of the estate tax laws, everyone with a net worth of more than $1,000,000 (the exclusion amount in 2013 if Congress does nothing) should review their estate plan. An approach we favor is for the client to contact one of their professional advisors on the estate planning team, whether the estate planning lawyer, financial planner, life insurance agent, accountant, or trust officer. Authorize that team member to assemble the team in a preliminary meeting to review the listing of the assets and liabilities (financial x-ray), review the current documents, and then meet with the client and the client's spouse to make team recommendations. This approach maximizes the creative input and communication and often aids in identifying important new alternatives to consider. The financial x-ray would show what assets are titled in the name of each spouse; what, if any, assets are titled in joint names; and, ideally, what assets are in the children's names.

As has been said previously, what will be the estate or death tax is really elective. By making annual gifts during your lifetime, then transferring the maximum tax-free amount (applicable exclusion amount) to your children and grandchildren at death, and finally bequesting your remaining estate to a family charitable foundation, your estate tax would be zero.

Here are two areas to focus your attention:

1. Despite so-called portability provisions of 2011 and 2012, does each spouse have the new tax-free amount in his or her separate name? The first and simplest step of estate planning is to obtain two tax-free amounts for the family instead of one. This requires, however, not only the proper words in the documents, but that the first spouse to die have titled in his or her name (not jointly) assets with a fair market value (other than qualified retirement plans or IRAs) equal to the tax-free amount ($5,000,000 in 2011 and 2012). This step can basically save the family up to $3,461,600 in taxes.

2. The client should also focus on what is currently to be done with the tax-free amount at the client's death. Will it simply go in trust for the surviving spouse? Will it go in trust for the benefit of the surviving spouse, children, and grandchildren? Will it go outright to children and grandchildren?

In summary, you should take the following three steps as you undertake your estate planning review based on 2011 and 2012 estate tax laws and the possible changes in 2013 when the current law expires:

1. Contact your advisor(s) and request a review of your current estate plan in view of the range of changes most likely. Your plan will need to be flexible enough to deal with a variety of possible outcomes.

2. The most prudent assumption for you to make, considering the changes scheduled for 2013, is that the amount of assets that you will be able to

pass to nonspousal heirs will be $1,000,000. By providing adequate liquidity under this circumstance, you assure your heirs that you will have adequate resources to pay estate taxes no matter what year you die.

3. Let your voice be heard! Congressional indecisiveness makes it practically impossible to properly plan your estate. Contact your congressional representatives and request resolution to the question mark surrounding the current estate tax law. Go to the Resource Center at www.welchgroup.com; then click on 'Links'; then click on "Congressional Representatives Contact List".

Planning Considerations Under 2010 Tax Act

In 2011 and 2012, you have an opportunity to revisit your own estate plan in light of a recently passed estate tax law that offers many opportunities for business owners, wealthy families, as well as the 'not yet wealthy.' The reason your 'opportunity' is time-sensitive is that this new law is set to expire December 31, 2012. Here's a quick review of the major provisions of the new law as well as several planning strategies worth considering:

- *Up to $5 million exempt from estate taxes.* **Planning point:** Many wills use a formula that states that the maximum amount allowed under law first goes to fill up the family trust with the balance going either outright or in trust for the surviving spouse. With this higher limit, it means that in many cases all of the assets will go to the family trust and none to the surviving spouse either outright or in the marital trust. For many families, this is an unintended consequence. Have your attorney review your documents to determine if changes are warranted.

- *Portability of Exemption Amount.* **Planning point:** Theoretically, the activity of equalizing the estates between spouses is no longer necessary since the surviving spouse now "inherits" the deceased spouses' unused exemption. However, if the surviving spouse were to remarry and that new spouse die, the exemption of the first deceased spouse would be lost forever. When you review your estate documents, decide if assets need to be transferred between spouses to make certain the full exemption is available to both of you. Transfers between spouses during life or at death are not subject to either gift or estate taxes.

- *Make Gifts During Your Lifetime.* **Planning point:** If you are a small business owner who would like to make certain the business stays in the family, 2011 and 2012 may be an excellent time to gift some of your business ownership to children. You may get a double benefit, due to timing the gift at the end of the recent Great Recession whereby business valuations are low. Then as the economy recovers the appreciation of the transferred business interests will accrue to the new owners, which helps you reduce your future estate as well. And this is not for just business owners. If you have an estate that significantly exceeds the exemption amount, you may want to consider making tax-free gifts to family members using assets that you believe will appreciate in value in the years ahead. This may be a disappearing opportunity since this $5 million tax-free gift is set to expire. If Congress takes no action, this limit will drop to $1 million on January 1, 2013.

- *Heirs receive a new tax basis for transfers at death.* (This is not new but is a point worth making.) **Planning point:** You face a trade off in deciding whether to make transfers during your lifetime versus transfers at death. The recipient of a gift during your lifetime gets your same tax basis so that a future sale would be potentially subject to capital gains taxes.

- *Lower transfer tax rates now.* **Planning point:** If you have a very large estate and would consider making gifts that exceed the $5 million lifetime gift limit, you'll likely never have a chance to do so at a lower gift tax rate—35%.

If you feel your estate is large enough to take advantages of any of these strategies, be clear that, at a minimum, you need at least a basic estate plan, which would include a will, durable power of attorney, and an advanced healthcare directive.

In this chapter we have provided an overview of both the complications surrounding the current uncertainty regarding estate tax laws as well as actions you should consider taking now. In our next chapter, we will delve deeper into the importance of developing your estate plan and planning opportunities under the 2010 Tax Relief Act.

Estate Planning

You Need It—Here's Why

What Is Estate Planning?

Estate planning is the process of controlling your assets, both during your life and after your death, with three primary objectives in mind. First, you want to ensure that your assets will always be sufficient to provide for you and your family's lifestyle needs. Second, you want to make certain that your assets go to the people and/or organizations of your choosing. Finally, you want to minimize the amount of taxes, fees, and court interference associated with settling your estate. This definition is broad, as well it should be. A properly designed estate plan encompasses the landscape of financial issues.

Investment Planning

Your investment plan should focus on providing enough assets to meet your retirement needs, the cost of funding your children's education, and expenses such as financial assistance for elderly parents. It should be designed so that your expected long-term returns will meet your financial objectives. Your risk tolerance should be examined to ensure that your portfolio is not too aggressive for your personality.

Tax Planning

As you're managing all your finances, you should pay close attention to tax efficiency. Consider the following question. How can you best use tax-deferred or tax-free investment vehicles? Are there ways to accomplish some of your goals by shifting income from yourself to another family member who is in a lower tax bracket? Can you make a gift to a charity in such a way that you receive long-term economic benefits? Is it possible to convert ordinary income, which is taxed at your highest tax bracket, to long-term capital gains?

Protecting Your Family

How long will you live? Of course, you cannot answer this question. Your estate plan should address the possibility of a premature death as well as the possibility that you will live "too long." Simple solutions to "dying too soon" include the use of life insurance. Issues of "living too long" are often handled through use of trusts, living trusts, a power of attorney, or long-term care insurance.

Protecting Your Assets

Given our litigious society, if you have accumulated significant assets, your estate plan should include an asset protection plan. You can employ simple strategies such as liability insurance or more exotic strategies such as foreign asset protection trusts.

Carrying out Your Personal Goals and Wishes

Do you have a deep desire to protect our environment? Have you considered making gifts to your alma mater? Do you have a relative who may need financial support? Outline all your goals and then design your estate plan to carry them out.

Gathering and Drafting Appropriate Documents

A vital part of your estate plan will consist of developing appropriate legal documents to ensure that your wishes are carried out. The most basic of the documents will be your will. Other documents include deeds, mortgages, and trusts and property titles. Part of your estate plan should include gathering and organizing all vital documents. This has two important advantages. First, your documents will be easy for you to locate and retrieve when they need to be reviewed. Second, your survivors won't have to search for documents needed to settle your estate after your death. Believe us, your loved ones will think kindly of you for having done this for them.

As you can see, estate planning consists of much more than simply avoiding taxes. The right planning will not only give you and your family great peace of mind but will also help you accumulate wealth faster and more effectively.

The Benefits of Estate Planning

Developing your estate plan is perhaps the most important financial step you can take. It creates focus and puts you in charge of many aspects of your finances. Let's look at the benefits to your immediate family.

If you are single, your estate plan will provide for the orderly transfer of your assets to those people or organizations you specify, thus reducing or eliminating the hassle for those who will assist in settling your estate. If you are married and have children, the issues will usually be more complex, but the benefits of planning will also be more profound. Make certain that your surviving family has immediate access to cash to cover ongoing living expenses while your estate is being settled. Although it may be hard to imagine that this would be a problem, it is not unusual for the courts to freeze assets for weeks or even months while trying to determine the proper disposition of the estate. The surviving spouse is then forced to apply to the court for needed cash to pay current living expenses. You can imagine the additional stress caused by this difficulty.

In your estate plan, you may also want to address issues regarding funding for your children's education. If you have young children, you may want your surviving spouse to have the option of not being employed so that he or she can devote more attention to your children.

If your spouse lacks knowledge or experience in financial matters, your estate plan should provide for assistance with financial management, such as setting up trusts. Also, your estate plan should consider the consequences of both you and your spouse dying simultaneously. If you have minor children, you will want to select someone to manage your assets for their benefit. You don't want the court to make this decision for you. In this situation, your estate plan should also address when your children will receive your assets free of trust. When children receive substantial assets before they are mature enough to handle them properly, the results can be devastating.

There was a case involving a child movie star. Because he was a minor, his earnings were held in trust until he was legally an adult (age 18 in his state of residence). We are sure you can imagine what happened when he turned 18. Fast cars and late-night parties consumed a small fortune in less than 24 months.

Even more pressing than financial matters is the issue of who will raise your children if you and your spouse die prematurely. Give very careful thought to your choice of a legal guardian. Remember it is this person's values that are likely to be instilled in your children. In developing your estate plan, you will also want to give consideration to the age and financial condition of a potential guardian. Some guardians may lack the child-rearing skills you feel are necessary. Make sure that your plan does not create an additional financial burden for the guardian.

Do you have a favorite cause, charity, or religious organization? You can use your estate plan to provide financial assistance either during your life or at your death. This is one of the instances in which our government actually provides you with incentives to do so.

During your lifetime and at your death, your estate plan should focus on how best to reduce taxes and expenses. For when you're alive, the primary focus is on income tax issues. At death, there may also be estate tax issues and administrative fees as well as other expenses to consider. Plan well and you can minimize costs, thus allowing more money to pass to your family.

Your estate plan can also be used to provide assistance and help for members of your extended family. Consider carefully, for example, whether you may need to provide financial support for a parent, sibling, niece, or nephew. If the answer is yes or maybe, there may be solutions that also provide you with tax benefits.

The ultimate benefit of a well-crafted estate plan is that it provides you with a compass for managing your finances. It will lessen not only your own stress but that of your loved ones as well. It is the right thing for you to do, and it's worth the time, effort, and expense.

The Nightmares of Poor Planning

All too often, people procrastinate and neglect their estate planning. The results can be devastating. Take a moment to review the following list and determine whether any of the examples could apply to you or your family. If the answer is yes, let this serve as your wake-up call to get started now!

- You are sued, which results in an exceedingly high judgment against you. Your estate plan should include asset protection strategies.

- You become disabled and are unable to handle your finances. Part of an appropriate estate plan includes a power of attorney designating who will take control of your finances should you become incompetent.

- You die without naming the guardians of your child or children. This mistake forces the courts to make this decision for you, possibly resulting in your children being raised by someone you would not have chosen.

- Your children inherit money at an age that destroys both their ambition and their work ethic. We have seen this happen often. Setting up a trust that provides for their needs without overindulging them can solve this problem.

- You own a business or real estate that must be sold at fire sale prices in order to pay your estate taxes. We've seen cases where property had to be sold for a fraction of its true value because the taxes were due but real estate prices were depressed. You must determine your potential estate tax liability and determine where the cash would come from to pay that liability.

- You or your spouse move to a nursing home, and the bills consume all of your assets. One potential solution to this problem is to own a long-term care insurance policy.

- You fail to provide for a child with a disability or special needs. In such a case the child may become a ward of the state. If your child has special needs, you need to consider specialized trust planning.

- Your family must pay excessive legal fees and court costs to settle your estate. You may not be able to eliminate these costs, but you can significantly reduce them through proper planning.

Each of these nightmares has a solution that can be addressed through your estate plan.

The Myths of Estate Planning

You may still not be convinced that estate planning is absolutely necessary. We often find that people have preconceived notions about estate planning that have no basis in reality. Let's examine a few of the more popular versions.

Myth #1: Estate Planning Is for Old People

You are a Baby Boomer, Generation Xer, or Generation Yer and have plenty of time to develop your estate plan, right? Wrong. Estate planning is an important consideration not only for older people but for everyone. Unless your family circumstances and finances are incredibly simple, you need to begin developing your estate plan *now*.

Myth #2: Estate Planning Is for the Rich

Be careful to distinguish between your *financial net worth* and your *estate net worth*. Adding life insurance death benefits to your other assets can easily place you in estate tax jeopardy! Additionally, there are many estate planning issues other than taxes. For example, consider the issue of financial management in the event you become incompetent owing to an accident or illness.

Myth #3: Estate Planning Focuses on Death

Many people avoid estate planning because it makes them think about death—either their own death or the death of someone they love. We have had many client meetings in which an individual broke out in tears at the thought of a loved one's death. Obviously, estate planning must deal with death, but many living issues are just as important. For example, what is the best way to fund your child's college education? Do you pay for it from cash flow or do you gift your child money and use a custodial account or a qualified educational trust? What is the best way to protect your hard-earned assets from a successful lawsuit? Your estate plan must address an array of living issues as well as death issues.

Guidelines for Successful Estate Planning

Get Organized

Pull all of your vital documents together and organize them so that you or the person(s) who will assist in settling your estate can easily locate each document. Consider setting up a designated file cabinet at your home or office. Essential documents include the following:

- Federal tax returns (for the last seven years)
- State tax returns (for the last seven years)
- Pay stubs (the two most recent ones)
- Financial statement
- Confirmation statements (brokerage accounts, mutual funds, etc.)
- Retirement plan statements (IRA, Keogh, pension, profit sharing, etc.)
- Insurance policies (life, disability, property and casualty, health, etc.)
- Amortization schedules (home, business, property, etc.)
- Business documents (partnership agreements, corporate papers, etc.)
- Corporate/partnership tax returns
- Wills (if you are married, for you and your spouse)
- Trust agreements
- Gift tax returns
- Employee benefits summary
- Notes, mortgages, deeds to real estate, termite bond, survey, appraisal
- Bank account statement(s) (for the last 12 months)
- Credit card statement(s) (for the last 12 months)
- Birth certificate(s)
- Car title(s)
- Marriage certificate
- Retirement plan beneficiary designations
- Loan agreement(s)

Determine Your Current Estate Net Worth

A detailed discussion of how to determine your current estate net worth is included in Chapter 3. Put simply, it is vital that you know where you are now. People often believe they have small estates, and therefore have little concern for estate planning. They are shocked to find that not only could they potentially owe estate taxes, but those taxes could run into the tens of thousands of dollars! When you include your life insurance, the dollars add up fast.

Establish Your Estate Planning Goals

Included in Chapter 6 is a discussion of how to establish your estate planning goals. There are many, many strategies available to accomplish a vast array of potential goals. By establishing your goals early, you bring order and focus to your estate plan while avoiding the hit-and-miss planning that most people use. Your goals should be divided into lifetime goals and death goals.

Hire Competent Professional Help

Most likely you will need a team of competent advisors from various fields to assist you in your estate planning, including attorneys, financial advisors, insurance representatives, accountants, and bankers. Many of these people specialize within their general fields. For example, some attorneys specialize in estate planning. Many financial advisors are now specializing in *Wealth Management*. Wealth Management focuses on wealth accumulation and multigenerational wealth transfers. You will find life insurance representatives who specialize in working with business owners and bankers who cater to high net worth clients. Putting together the right advisors and then working with them as a team will pay big dividends in your end results.

Monitor Your Progress

Estate planning is a dynamic process, not a static one. Your circumstances are constantly changing, as are our tax laws. Reviewing your estate plan every two to three years will keep you on the leading edge of the strategies and techniques available to meet your goals.

Case Study

Proper planning can make a significant difference even in a seemingly straight forward case. Bob and Alice are in their mid-forties. Bob is an orthopedic surgeon, and Alice sells real estate on a part-time basis. They have three young children, Bob, Jr., age 12, Randy, age 9, and Jenny, age 7. Both Bob and Alice want to be certain that if either of them (or both!) were to die prematurely the family would be financially secure. They are particularly concerned that they have the funds to send the children to the best possible college, and they also believe that at least one of their children will go to professional school. To address these issues, Bob has purchased a $6 million term life insurance policy on his life, making Alice the beneficiary. They have also bought $500,000 of term life on Alice's life, thinking that if Alice died prematurely Bob might need financial help to pay the costs of hiring a full-time nanny. Several years ago they had an attorney who was a friend

TABLE 2.1 Estate Tax Exemptions

Year	Estate Tax Exemption ($)
2011	5 million
2012	5 million
2013	1 million[1]

[1] The 2010 Tax Relief Act is automatically repealed in 2013 unless Congress extends the law.

of theirs draw wills for each of them. The wills state that all assets will be passed outright to the surviving spouse. Here's a snapshot of their financial picture:

$6,555,000	Assets
− 695,500	Total liabilities
5,860,000	Financial net worth
+6,000,000	Personal life insurance—Bob
+ 500,000	Personal life insurance—Alice
12,360,000	Taxable estate (estate net worth)

Do Bob and Alice have a tax problem? Under their current "simple" will structure, if Bob and Alice were killed in a common accident in 2011 or 2012, their heirs would owe $826,000. If death occurred in 2013, they would owe a whopping $3,343,000.

As you may imagine, Bob and Alice want to avoid taxes while maximizing transfers for the support of their children. There is a way to solve this potential problem. Using two simple strategies, an Irrevocable Life Insurance Trust and a Credit Shelter Trust, they could reduce this potential liability to zero for 2011 and 2012, and they could reduce it to $1.9 million for 2013. The specifics of these techniques will be discussed later in this book. While the amount of life insurance was higher than we typically see, it wasn't an inappropriate or unusual case. It's important for you to understand that what initially may appear to be a very simple problem can turn out to be far more complicated after you complete a detailed review. Identifying the issues early will enable you to implement the right strategies.

In the next chapter, we will review how the federal tax system works, and you'll learn how to develop *your* estate net worth statement, calculate your potential estate taxes, and outline a broad range of strategies you can use to reduce taxes and implement your estate plan.

CHAPTER 3

The Estate Tax System

How Much Are You Really Worth?

Determining Your Estate Net Worth

Although minimizing the amount of estate taxes you will owe should not be your only goal, it is certainly an important one. In our view, the estate tax system is nothing more than a wealth transfer system whereby the government takes a portion of your wealth and redistributes it to the masses. Under prior tax law, many middle-income Americans began to discover that they too faced the possibility of estate taxes. The 2010 Tax Relief Act refocuses on wealthy Americans but everyone should keep a close eye on what Congress does or doesn't do about allowing the estate tax exemption to revert back to $1 million. Table 3.1 outlines the current estate and gift tax limits.

Understanding the Estate Tax System

It seems like everything you do subjects you to another tax: Your earnings are subject to income taxes; your purchases are subject to sales tax; your real estate holdings are subject to property tax; your security sales are subject to capital gains taxes. It's hard to believe that you or your heirs are expected to pay taxes upon your death. The government does give you a break, but to receive the maximum benefits you must plan carefully. Here's how the system works:

First, you die. Ouch! Then your *executor* makes a list of all of your assets (called an estate inventory).

TABLE 3.1 Applicable Federal Gift and Estate Tax Exemption Amounts

Year of Death	Gift Tax Exemption ($)	Estate Tax Exemption ($)
2011	5,000,000	5,000,000
2012	5,000,000	5,000,000
2013	1,000,000	1,000,000[1]

[1] If Congress fails to take action, the current law will sunset on December 31, 2012 and we will automatically revert back to prior law.

> *Executor:* The person or institution that is legally responsible for settling an estate. He or she may also be referred to as the estate representative or administrator. Normally you appoint an executor by way of instructions in your will.

The executor then subtracts all of your liabilities, including notes, mortgages, funeral expenses, and the administrative costs of settling your estate (attorneys' fees, court costs, etc.). This net estate is called the *adjusted gross estate.* If you were married, any assets left to your spouse would not be subject to estate taxes at this time because of the *unlimited marital deduction.* The government waits until your spouse dies and then assesses the estate tax. If you leave money to qualified charities, you get to deduct that as well. You have now arrived at your taxable estate.

> *Unlimited marital deduction:* The legal provision that enables you to leave an unlimited amount of assets to a surviving spouse free of estate taxes. This has the effect of *postponing* the estate taxes until the death of that spouse.

Your executor then figures the tentative tax using the IRS tax tables (see Table 3.2).

From the tentative tax amount your executor subtracts the *Applicable Federal Gift and Estate Tax Credit.* This is a dollar-for-dollar deduction from the tentative tax amount (see Table 3.3).

> *Applicable Federal Gift and Estate Tax Credit:* The dollar credit amount allowed by the federal government that has the effect of making a certain portion of your estate not subject to taxes.

If the result of subtracting the Applicable Gift and Estate Tax Credit is a positive number, that is the amount of taxes that are due. Your executor must then raise the cash to pay the taxes out of your assets, usually within nine months

TABLE 3.2 Federal Gift and Estate Tax Rate Table (Tentative Tax)

Taxable Estate ($)	Tax Owed ($)	Plus (%)	On Amount in Excess of ($)
0–10,000	0	18	0
10,001–20,000	1,800	20	10,000
20,001–40,000	3,800	22	20,000
40,001–60,000	8,200	24	40,000
60,001–80,000	13,000	26	60,000
80,001–100,000	18,200	28	80,000
100,001–150,000	23,800	30	100,000
150,001–250,000	38,800	32	150,000
250,001–500,000	70,800	34	250,000
500,001–750,000	155,800	37	500,000

of your death. Once the taxes are paid, your executor distributes the balance of your assets according to the directions given in your will. If you do not have a will, your assets will be distributed according to state law (see Chapter 6). This process can take from six months to several years. Sound confusing? Let's walk through an example.

Case Study

Alfred and Jane McNemara want to develop a plan that will minimize taxes and set up trusts for their two daughters in case they die prematurely. Our first objective is to determine their current *estate net worth* as well as to identify how their assets are titled. We do this by completing Worksheet 3.1.

Estate net worth: The sum of all of your assets, including your share of any jointly owned assets, *plus life insurance on your life that is owned by you,* minus any debts you owe.

TABLE 3.3 Applicable Federal Gift and Estate Tax Credit and Exclusion Amounts

Year of Death	Applicable Credit Amount ($)	Applicable Exclusion Amount ($)
2011	1,730,800	5,000,000
2012	1,730,800	5,000,000
2013[1]	345,800	1,000,000

[1] If Congress fails to extend or change the current law.

WORKSHEET 3.1 Sample Estate Net Worth Statement

As of 2/20/XX
| Your name: | Alfred McNemara | Date of birth: | 6/29/XX |
| Spouse name: | Jane McNemara | Date of birth: | 5/20/XX |

	Ownership ($)			
	Alfred	**Jane**	**Joint**	**Family Total**
Assets				
Cash and cash equivalents:				
Checking and savings accounts			27,000	27,000
Other		250,000	163,000	413,000
Personal and household property:				
Automobiles	46,000	32,000		78,000
Furniture			95,000	95,000
Jewelry	5,000	45,000		50,000
Personal effects	23,000	19,000		42,000
Art			115,000	115,000
Coin collections				
Other				
Real estate (estimated current market value):				
Residence(s)			2,950,000	2,950,000
Other properties	650,000			
Investments (estimated current market value):				
Individual stocks				
Individual bonds				
Personal mutual funds			250,000	250,000
Other investments: Ltd. partnership	25,000			25,000
Retirement plans:				
Alfred's 401(k) and IRA	1,625,000		XX	1,625,000
Jane's IRA		25,000	XX	25,000
Equity interest in a business			XX	
Life insurance (face amount):				
Personal	4,750,000	250,000	XX	5,000,000
Employer group	125,000		XX	125,000
Total assets	7,249,000	621,000	3,600,000	11,470,000
Liabilities				
Short-term liabilities:				
Credit cards	21,500	9,750		31,250
Long-term liabilities:				
Mortgage(s)			490,000	490,000
Automobile loan(s)	14,000	7,000		21,000
Other loans: Home equity loan			57,000	57,000
Miscellaneous liabilities:				
Unpaid taxes				
Estimated funeral and administrative expenses[1]				
Total liabilities	35,500	16,750	547,000	599,250
Estate net worth (total assets less total liabilities)	7,213,500	604,250	3,053,000	10,870,750

[1] Funeral and administrative expenses can vary from 2 to 8 percent. For the sake of simplicity, they are ignored in this case study.

Next, we need to determine the McNemaras' potential estate tax liability. Let's assume that Alfred dies first. Alfred has named Jane as the beneficiary of all of his life insurance policies and his retirement plans. Most of their other assets, such as their home and personal property, are titled in both of their names (joint tenants with right of survivorship). So all of Alfred's assets would be transferred to Jane (see Worksheet 3.2).

Because of the unlimited marital deduction, there are no estate taxes due at Alfred's death. Our attention is drawn to the possible estate tax should Jane now die prematurely or if the combined estate of Jane and Alfred will likely grow to the point that it will become large enough to be subject to estate taxes in the future. And if this is the case, what can we do to minimize this risk while both Alfred and Jane are able to make changes to their estate plan?

Step 1	Determine the total value of Jane's assets (including her life insurance).	$11,470,000
Step 2	Determine Jane's liabilities.	−$599,250
Step 3	Subtract your answer in Step 2 from your answer in Step 1 to arrive at the adjusted gross estate.	$10,870,750
Step 4	Subtract the following:	
	a) Charitable contributions made through Jane's will	−$0
	b) Unlimited marital deduction (not applicable for Jane)	−$0
Step 5	This figure represents the taxable estate.	$10,870,750
Step 6	Compute the gross federal estate tax using Table 3.2 (see highlighted line).	$3,785,563
Step 7	Subtract the Applicable Credit Amount (for Jane) Table 3.3.	−$1,730,800
Step 8	Subtract Applicable Credit Amount (for Alfred).	$1,730,800
Step 9	This is the amount of tax due on Jane's estate.	$323,963

First, we should note (see Step 8 above) that under Tax Relief Act, the surviving spouse 'inherits' any unused Exclusion Amount from the deceased spouse which allows the heirs to apply two Applicable Credit Amounts towards any estate taxes. While the estate tax in our case study is not large, it could have been eliminated. What is significant is that we have identified a potentially costly problem in the form of rising estate costs as the value of the McNemara estate continues to grow with all future growth subject to higher and higher estate taxes. There are many strategies we can use to substantially reduce or eliminate the McNemaras' tax liability.

WORKSHEET 3.2 Jane's Estate Net Worth Statement after Alfred's Death

As of 2/20/XX
Your name: Jane McNemara   **Date of birth:** 5/20/XX

	Ownership ($)
	Jane
Assets	
Cash and cash equivalents:	
Checking and savings accounts	27,000
Other	413,000
Other: Proceeds from life insurance	4,875,000
Personal and household property:	
Automobiles	78,000
Furniture	95,000
Jewelry	50,000
Personal effects	42,000
Art	115,000
Coin collections	
Other	
Real estate (estimated current market value):	
Residence(s)	2,950,000
Other properties	650,000
Investments (estimated current market value):	
Individual stocks	
Individual bonds	
Personal mutual funds	250,000
Other investments: Ltd. partnership	25,000
Retirement plans: 401(k) and IRAs	1,650,000
Equity interest in a business	
Life insurance (face amount):	
Personal	250,000
Total assets	11,470,000
Liabilities	
Short-term liabilities:	
Credit cards	31,250
Long-term liabilities:	
Mortgage(s)	490,000
Automobile loan(s)	21,000
Other loans: Home equity loan	57,000
Miscellaneous liabilities:	
Unpaid taxes	
Estimated funeral and administrative expenses[1]	
Total liabilities	599,250
Estate net worth (total assets less total liabilities)	10,870,750

[1] Funeral and administrative expenses can vary from 2 to 8 percent. For the sake of simplicity, they are ignored in this case study.

Your Estate Tax Picture

Now, let's determine the value of *your* estate and *your* potential taxes. Remember, your estate net worth is equal to your financial net worth plus your life insurance death benefits.

Step 1

Add up the value of all your assets using Worksheet 3.3. Note that the dollar figure we are looking for is the *market value*, not what you paid for the asset.

Market value: The value of an asset if it were sold today, net of all selling expenses.

Let's start with the obvious: You own everything solely in your name. You must also include any assets of which you are a joint owner. For example, if you own a hunting lodge with your brother, your one-half interest would be included in your estate. The same is true, for example, if you own your home jointly with your spouse. Some care must be taken in allocating ownership of jointly held property. For example, in the case where you own the hunting lodge with your brother, if you paid for 90 percent of the purchase price, then 90 percent of the value would be included in your estate unless you made a gift to your brother. Also, do not overlook any life insurance you own. If the insurance is on your life, remember, it is the *death benefit* that will be included in your estate, not the cash value. If someone owes you money, the value of that note or accounts receivable should be included. Also, do not forget items of personal property like cars, boats, clothing, jewelry, and so on.

Death benefit: The proceeds your beneficiary would receive from the life insurance company upon your death.

Step 2

Still using Worksheet 3.3, add up all the money you owe, including debts, mortgages, and liens. If you owe money on jointly owned property, only your share of that debt counts. You also should include any unpaid property or income taxes, as well as the cost of funeral and administrative expenses. Funeral expenses can vary from $2,000 to $20,000 or more. Although administrative expenses can vary widely, a generous rule of thumb would be 5 percent of your gross estate.

Step 3

Using Worksheet 3.3, subtract your total liabilities (Step 2) from your total assets (Step 1). The result is your adjusted gross estate.

WORKSHEET 3.3 *Your* Estate Net Worth Statement

As of
Your name: Date of birth:
Spouse name: Date of birth:

	Ownership ($)			
	You	Spouse	Joint	Family Total

Assets
Cash and cash equivalents:
  Checking and savings account
  Other _____

Personal and household property:
  Automobiles
  Furniture
  Jewelry
  Personal effects
  Art
  Coin collections
  Other _____

Real estate (estimated current market value):
  Residence(s)
  Other properties: _____
    _____

Investments (estimated current market value):
  Individual stocks
  Individual bonds
  Personal mutual funds
  Other investments: _____
    _____

Retirement plans: _____			XX	
_____			XX	
_____			XX	
Equity interest in a business			XX	

Life insurance (face amount):

Personal			XX	
Employer group			XX	
Total assets				

Liabilities
Short term liabilities:
  Credit cards
Long term liabilities:
  Mortgage(s)
  Automobile loan(s)
  Other loans _____

Miscellaneous liabilities:
  Unpaid taxes
  Estimated funeral and administrative expenses[1]
    Total liabilities
    Estate net worth (total assets less total liabilities)

---

[1] Funeral and administrative expenses can vary from 2 to 8 percent. For the sake of simplicity, they are ignored in this case study.

Step 4

The government allows you two primary deductions:

- *The unlimited marital deduction.* If you are married, you can leave an unlimited amount of assets to your spouse free of any estate taxes! At first blush, this appears to be the perfect solution to your estate tax dilemma. But when planning your estate you must look beyond this rule for ways to reduce the amount of taxes that your *heirs* will ultimately pay.
- *Charitable contributions.* If you leave money or assets to qualified charitable organizations in your will, you will receive a deduction for estate tax purposes.

Adjusted gross estate (from Worksheet 3.3) $ _____

Minus marital deduction (either a "0" if there is no surviving spouse or 100% of assets left to your surviving spouse)   − _____

Minus charitable bequests in your will   − _____

    Your taxable estate $ _____

Tip

If you are married, instead of leaving a bequest to your favorite charity (or charities) in your will, consider leaving the bequest to your spouse. Then suggest in the will that your spouse give the bequest to the charity. Assuming your spouse complies with your request, in addition to receiving a charitable deduction, your spouse will also receive an income tax deduction. Two deductions for the same dollars!

Step 5

By taking the deductions from Step 4, you have arrived at your taxable estate. If you are married and using the marital deduction, you will have effectively postponed your estate taxes until your surviving spouse dies. To better understand the impact of estate taxes, let's assume you and your spouse die simultaneously or that you are not married.

Step 6

Calculate your gross federal estate tax. Apply the tax rates from Table 3.2 to determine the gross federal estate tax. This represents your *tentative tax.*

Step 7

From the gross federal estate tax, you now get to subtract the Applicable Estate Tax Credit. This credit allows you to give a certain amount of your estate to anyone without owing federal estate taxes (called the applicable exclusion amount). See Table 3.3 for details. Note that this credit is applied directly dollar-for-dollar against the tentative tax as calculated in Step 6. You may be able to use two credits under the portability provisions of the 2010 Tax Relief Act . . . one for you and for your deceased spouse if he or she has not already used his or her credit. This portability provision expires on December 31, 2012 unless Congress extends or changes the current law.

Your Future Estate

If your result in Step 7 is a positive number, that is the tax you would owe, and it is time for you to meet with your professional advisor(s) to develop a plan for tax minimization. If your answer is a negative number, then you currently would not owe any estate taxes.

In addition to federal estate taxes, many states impose their own death or inheritance taxes. Even if it appears now that no taxes will be owed on your estate, that may not be the case later, after you have accrued more assets. Table 3.4 shows future estate values based on various growth rates. Keep these figures in mind as you begin planning. Some of the growth rates in Table 3.4 may seem unrealistic, but if you are still working, in addition to growth of existing assets, you are hopefully accumulating new assets through contributions to retirement plans, personal investment programs, and acquisitions. In fact, these growth rates may be too conservative. It's a good idea to update your estate net worth worksheet annually so you can gain a sense of your estate's growth rate. This will indicate the kind of planning you will need to consider in the future. In reviewing your estate situation, it is also important to consider any potential inheritances that you are likely to receive.

Overview of Estate Planning Strategies

There are many techniques and strategies that can help you achieve your estate planning goals. Some of the more powerful ones include the following:

- *Wills.* A will forms the cornerstone of most people's estate plan. Wills can provide tremendous flexibility for controlling assets and avoiding taxes. Chapter 7 provides details for drafting your will.
- *Trusts.* You can use trusts during your lifetime or after your death to help implement your estate game plan. Various types of trust planning will be discussed throughout Chapter 8.
- *Retirement accounts.* Retirement plans are key to wealth accumulation. In Chapter 4 we will show you ways to increase their effectiveness tenfold.
- *Gifting.* One way to reduce your estate (and thereby your taxes) is to give part of your estate away. In Chapter 11 you will learn how to create leverage with a gifting program, as well as how to maintain a measure of control over gifted assets.

TABLE 3.4 The Future Value of Your Estate

Current Estate Value ($)	10 Years ($)	15 Years ($)	20 Years ($)
3% Growth Rate			
500,000	672,000	778,000	903,000
750,000	1,008,000	1,168,000	1,354,000
1,000,000	1,344,000	1,558,000	1,806,000
2,000,000	2,688,000	3,116,000	3,612,000
3,000,000	4,032,000	4,674,000	5,418,000
5% Growth Rate			
500,000	814,000	1,039,000	1,326,000
750,000	1,221,000	1,559,000	1,984,000
1,000,000	1,628,000	2,078,000	2,653,000
2,000,000	3,257,000	4,157,000	5,306,000
3,000,000	4,886,000	6,236,000	7,959,000
7% Growth Rate			
500,000	983,000	1,379,000	1,934,000
750,000	1,475,000	2,069,000	2,902,000
1,000,000	1,967,000	2,759,000	3,869,000
2,000,000	3,934,000	5,518,000	7,739,000
3,000,000	5,901,000	8,277,000	11,609,000
9% Growth Rate			
500,000	1,183,000	1,821,000	2,802,000
750,000	1,775,000	2,731,000	4,203,000
1,000,000	2,367,000	3,642,000	5,604,000
2,000,000	4,734,000	7,284,000	11,208,000
3,000,000	7,102,000	10,927,000	16,813,000

- *Charities*. There are several strategies, such as the charitable remainder trust, whereby you can improve your financial circumstances while helping your favorite charity. In Chapter 12 you will learn how you can benefit from charitable donations.

- *Family limited partnerships*. Using a family limited partnership can shift assets to family members at a significant discount from their current value. Family limited partnerships are reviewed in Chapter 13.

In this chapter, you have learned about our estate tax system and about your specific situation. Since money is the glue that holds an estate plan together, the next chapter will focus on investment strategies you can use to maximize your estate accumulation plan.

CHAPTER 4

Investment Strategies for Maximizing Estate Growth

Traditional investment philosophy suggests that as you get older you should invest more conservatively. Not long ago, commonly accepted wisdom employed the following investment allocation formula as a rule of thumb: *100 minus your age equals the percent of stocks you should have in your portfolio*. This means that a 70-year-old would only have a 30 percent allocation to stocks. While this strategy should reduce portfolio volatility, it also significantly reduces the long-term growth potential of your holdings. We believe this "old-age" way of approaching investing is out of touch with today's world. Advances in medicine and biotechnology have allowed scientists to better understand the aging process and develop methods for enhancing longevity. Some scientists now believe the average 50-year-old will live to age 120. Talk about a need for growth in your portfolio! One of retirees' greatest fears is that they will outlive their financial resources and become dependent on their children (or the government) for their financial support. In order to address the need for a portfolio that could provide significant long-term growth *and* income for retirees, coauthor Welch developed the Growth Strategy with a Safety Net®, which today represents one of the best solutions for the possibility of living too long. Here's how it works.

The goals of the Growth Strategy with a Safety Net® are as follows:

1. Protect your retirement income from market fluctuations.
2. Maximize your retirement income.
3. Produce an ever-increasing income stream that will more than offset the ravages of inflation.
4. Provide for significant portfolio growth, ultimately providing a legacy for your heirs or favorite charitable organizations.

Sound impossible? Well read on!

Growth Strategy with a Safety Net®

First, you determine how much annual income you need and multiply that number by the number of years that you want to protect your income. Be sure your annual withdrawal rate does not exceed your risk tolerance (see the section on withdrawal rates later in this chapter). Use the following scale:

Conservative: 6–10 years or more

Moderate: 4–5 years

Aggressive: 2–3 years

Next, add an amount of money that represents a generous emergency fund. Your total here will be invested as follows:

1. Emergency fund plus your first year's income need is invested in a high-yielding money market account. To find the highest money market yields, go to the Resource Center at www.welchgroup.com; then click on "Links"; then "Highest money market yields."
2. The money that represents your remaining two to ten years' income need will be invested in a bond ladder using bonds maturing every 12 months. This completes your Safety Net.
3. Implement your Growth Strategy by investing the balance of your money in a diversified portfolio of stocks or stock mutual funds. Periodically, you will sell a portion of your appreciated stocks and use the proceeds to replenish your bond ladder.

In a year when stocks do poorly, you postpone sales and wait for the market to recover. Historically, one to three years is sufficient time for this to occur.

For example, assume you have $2,000,000 available to meet your retirement income needs. You decide that a $20,000 emergency reserve account should be sufficient to cover any unforeseen financial emergencies and that initially you would like to draw $78,000 per year (a 4 percent withdrawal rate) from your investment portfolio in addition to your other income sources, which include Social Security and pension from your employer. You consider yourself

TABLE 4.1 Initial Safety Net

$20,000	Emergency reserves invested in a money market account
$78,000	First year's income need invested in a money market account
$78,000	Bond maturing in 1 year
$78,000	Bond maturing in 2 year
$78,000	Bond maturing in 3 year
$78,000	Bond maturing in 4 year
$78,000	Bond maturing in 5 year
$78,000	Bond maturing in 6 year
$78,000	Bond maturing in 7 year
$78,000	Bond maturing in 8 year
$78,000	Bond maturing in 9 year
$78,000	Bond maturing in 10 year
$800,000	Safety Net total (40% of portfolio)

a conservative investor and therefore decide to protect this income for 10 years. Table 4.1 outlines how your Safety Net is set up initially.

Each month you draw $6,500 from your money market account along with Social Security and pension to cover your normal living expenses. If you have a financial emergency, you have an additional $20,000 available in your money market emergency reserve account. Having your Safety Net in place guarantees that your income needs will be met for a total of ten years. Note that the interest earnings on your bonds can be either added to your money market account to provide an increasing income stream or reinvested as part of your Growth Strategy.

The balance of your portfolio ($1,200,000) is invested in a diversified portfolio of stocks or stock mutual funds and will provide you with needed long-term growth. In years when the stock market does well, you will sell $78,000 worth of stocks and buy another bond that matures in ten years to replace the $78,000 that you spent during the previous year. If the market does poorly in a given year, you will postpone selling stocks until there is a market recovery. You can take comfort in knowing that your income is totally secure for the next nine years no matter what happens to the stock market. Figure 4.1 provides a visual illustration of what the Growth Strategy with a Safety Net® looks like.

In an unprecedented historical occurrence, we have had two generational bear markets within a single decade: one that lasted from 2000 to 2003 and one that began in 2008 and ended in March of 2009. Both saw stock market indices drop more than 50 percent from the market peak to the market trough. More typically, you'll have a bear market, defined as a 20 percent decline within a 12-month period, once every three to ten years (a full market cycle). The

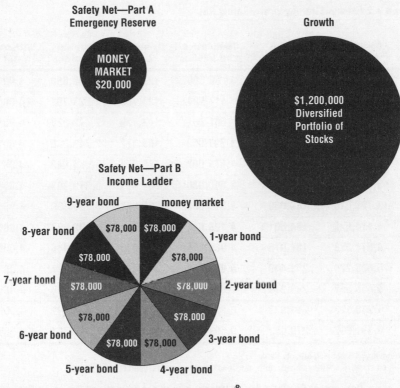

FIGURE 4.1 Growth Strategy with a Safety Net®

typical bear market lasts only about 14 months before recovery begins. Having a five- to ten-year Safety Net should be more than sufficient to get you through a bear market while allocating enough money to growth investments (stocks or stock mutual funds) to allow your portfolio the opportunity to grow and offset the ongoing ravages of inflation.

This strategy allows you to allocate a large portion of your money in the stock market, where it can grow, while your income is protected during periods of poor market performance. We should add that this strategy is relatively tax efficient for taxable accounts because you have a portion of your portfolio producing taxable income in the form of interest (your Safety Net) and a portion of your portfolio whose distributions are subject to the lower long-term capital gains tax (the growth portion). Table 4.2 illustrates the power of this strategy over time. Not only are you maximizing your current income, but the potential growth of your stock portfolio allows both your income and portfolio values to rise over time.

Table 4.3 profiles the volatility and return characteristics of conservative, moderate, and aggressive portfolios based on the Growth Strategy with a Safety Net®. It should be noted that while the one-year risk associated with investing in stocks or stock mutual funds is relatively high, that risk profile decreases

TABLE 4.2 Growth Strategy with a Safety Net®

Year	Beginning Balance	Annual Withdrawals	Cumulative Withdrawals	Growth at 6.4%	Ending Capital Account	Withdrawn Rate
1	2,000,000	80,000	80,000	122,880	2,042,880	4.00%
5	2,177,115	87,085	417,524	133,762	2,223,793	4.00%
10	2,420,727	96,829	881,767	148,729	2,472,627	4.00%
15	2,691,597	107,664	1,397,957	165,372	2,749,305	4.00%
20	2,992,777	119,711	1,971,907	183,876	3,056,942	4.00%
25	3,327,658	133,106	2,610,080	204,451	3,399,003	4.00%
30	3,700,011	148,000	3,319,662	227,329	3,779,339	4.00%
35	4,114,028	164,561	4,108,644	252,766	4,202,233	4.00%
40	4,574,373	182,975	4,985,910	281,049	4,672,448	4.00%
45	5,086,229	203,449	5,961,338	312,498	5,195,277	4.00%
50	5,655,359	226,214	7,045,914	347,465	5,776,610	4.00%
55	6,288,173	251,527	8,251,850	386,345	6,422,992	4.00%
60	6,991,797	279,672	9,592,725	429,576	7,141,701	4.00%

Assumptions: 6.4% blended rate of return.
8% ROR on stocks; 4% ROR on bonds. 60% stocks/40% bonds & money market.

TABLE 4.3 Retirement Portfolio Equity (Stock) Allocation Guidelines Based on Growth Strategy with a Safety Net™

	Conservative	Moderate	Aggressive
One-year downside risk[1]	−17%	−22%	−29%
10-year downside risk[1]	2%	1%	0%
20-year downside risk[1]	6%	6%	6%
Expected returns (10 years+)[2]	8.0%	8.5%	9.25%
Investment Mix:			
Equities (stocks)	60%	70%	85%
Fixed income (CDs, bonds, money market)[3]	40%	30%	15%

[1] One-year downside risks are based on historical returns from 1973–2010. 10-year and 20-year downside risks are based on historical returns from 1946–2010.
[2] Return assumptions are based as follows:
   Equities   10%
   Fixed Income 5%
Returns are approximated and based on net returns after estimated investment expenses but before taxes.
[3] The fixed income portion of the portfolio should be based on the Growth Strategy with a Safety Net®. See pages 33–37.
Note: These portfolios are for postretirement investment accounts and should be used only as general guidelines. Your actual retirement portfolio should be diversified into numerous asset classes. Consult with your financial advisor. Investment results are not guaranteed. Risks and returns are targets only. Statistics are based on historical data indicating possible calendar year losses for equities of 37% and losses for fixed income of 5%.

substantially over time. The basis of the Growth Strategy with a Safety Net® is allowing time for the market to recover. Table 4.3 indicates how market volatility dissipates over time.

As your retirement date approaches, you should begin to build your Safety Net ahead of time. For example, let's assume you plan to retire in seven years and you have decided that you want to protect six years' worth of your income (Safety Net). Continuing with our example, the next year you would sell $78,000 worth of stocks (assuming the market is up!) and buy a bond that matures just before your retirement date. This will fund your first year's income. The following year, you will do the same thing: Sell $78,000 of stocks and buy a bond that matures in five years. Using this strategy, by the time you retire, your Safety Net will be fully in place, and you will have maximized the growth potential of your investments until the time you need to begin drawing on them for your retirement income.

Withdrawal Rates

At this point it is important that you understand both the concept and the importance of the withdrawal rate (sometimes referred to as the withdrawal factor) as it relates to your portfolio.

Your withdrawal rate is equal to the percentage of dollars you are taking from your portfolio on an annual basis. For example, if you have $1,000,000 in your investment portfolio and you take out $50,000 in a given year, your withdrawal rate is 5 percent ($50,000 divided by $1,000,000). If your withdrawal rate is too high, you run the risk of depleting your investment account. Based on our experience, an appropriate withdrawal rate scale is as follows:

Conservative: 4 percent or less

Moderate: 5 percent

Aggressive: 6 percent or more

This scale is sometimes adjusted for age and health factors. For example, a 9 percent withdrawal rate might not be considered aggressive for someone who is 95 years old and in ill health. But for our purposes, we'll use the scale described above. How you determine the appropriate withdrawal rate for you will be based on your particular circumstances and risk tolerance.

Prioritizing Your Investment Dollars

How do you maximize the power of your estate accumulation program? We have already seen how retirees can use the Growth Strategy with a Safety Net® to increase their retirement income while maintaining long-term growth. You can also significantly magnify the power of your estate accumulation program by choosing the best investment environment. The investment environment relates to whether the investment is a retirement account, a tax-deferred account such as an annuity, or a personal investment account. Each environment has its advantages and disadvantages, but some are better than others, particularly for accumulating money for your estate and retirement. By prioritizing where your investment dollars go, you can significantly enhance your long-term accumulation results. Let's begin with a review of your best options.

Retirement Planning: Choosing the Best Investment Environments

Under most circumstances, the best method for accumulating money for your retirement is through a qualified retirement plan. This may seem obvious, but you would be surprised at how often we find that people fail to understand this. For example, a new client was very concerned about saving for retirement. Every month he contributed 6 percent of his salary to a 401(k) plan, 50 percent of which was being matched by his employer. The plan allowed him to contribute up to 15 percent of his pay. When asked why he was not investing more money in his 401(k), he said he could not afford to contribute more. It turned out that he was paying several hundred dollars each month toward a whole life insurance policy. Through some rearranging of his life insurance, he was able to maintain the insurance policy without further premium payments and divert those funds into his 401(k). Not only would those life insurance premium dollars grow faster in his 401(k), but he got a tax deduction to boot! This is actually an easy mistake to make. To avoid it, you must review where all your investment dollars are going. To get the most benefit, invest the *maximum* allowable into tax deductible retirement plans before you invest *any* money in personal investment programs. This is a very important concept. Look at the dramatic differences depicted in Table 4.4.

Retirement Plans

The power of retirement plans is created through one or more of the following:

- Tax deductibility of contributions
- Tax-deferred growth
- Tax-free growth (Roth IRA)

If your employer provides a contributory retirement plan such as a 401(k) plan, funding it should be your first priority, especially if the employer provides a matching contribution. If you are self-employed, you should consider starting your own retirement plan. You have numerous options available to you including the Simplified Employee Pension Plan (SEP), Single-Person 401(k), Profit Sharing Plan, SIMPLE plan, or Defined Benefit Plan, as well as a number of variations. If you have employees, they must be included in your plan. Which one is best for you will depend on your specific circumstances. You'll need the help of a professional advisor to assist you in setting up one of these plans to

TABLE 4.4 The Power of Retirement Plan Investing

Compare: $1,000 per month invested on a pretax basis in a retirement plan vs. paying the income tax on $1,000 per month and investing personally.

Retirement	vs.	Personal
$1,000 per month		$650 per month[1]
× 25 years		× 25 years
@10%		@9.8%[2]
$1,337,890		$840,422
Approximately 60% more!!		

[1]35% marginal tax bracket assumed. If your marginal tax bracket is higher (state income taxes, Medicare taxes, etc.) the results of investing personally worsen and vice versa.
[2]Assumes annual tax load of 0.20%.
Note: Retirement Plan distributions will be subject to ordinary income taxes. (Federal maximum, 35% for 2011 and 2012). Distributions from the personal investment program will likely be primarily subject to long-term capital gains taxes. (Federal maximum 15% for 2011 and 2012). If held until death, the personal account would receive a stepped-up cost basis and income taxes would be avoided. If the retirement plan were held until death, a beneficiary (under certain circumstances) could continue to defer a large portion of the gain.

make certain you maximize the benefits to you and that you follow the complex plan regulations.

Roth IRAs also require special consideration. With a Roth IRA, you don't receive an income tax deduction for your contribution, but your withdrawals are tax-free. Typically a Roth IRA is the best choice if your tax bracket is relatively low. Note that certain restrictions apply to tax-free withdrawals for Roth IRAs. Although contributions are *not* tax deductible, earnings are tax-deferred and withdrawals are tax-free under the following circumstances:

- Withdrawals are made at least five years after the Roth IRA was established and you are at least age 59 $^{1}/_{2}$.
- Withdrawals are made because of death or disability.

Tax-free withdrawals of up to $10,000 are allowed to cover the expenses of purchasing your first home.

Don't forget that the spouse of an employee who participates in a company retirement plan is eligible to contribute to a Roth IRA or a Traditional IRA even if that spouse has no earned income. The rules regarding the phase-out of deductibility of contributions are shown in Table 4.5.

Although you can contribute to both a Traditional IRA and a Roth IRA, your total combined contribution cannot exceed $5,000 (plus an additional $1,000 if you are age 50 or older).

If you are eligible for an IRA, you should invest in one. Are you better off with the deductible Traditional IRA or the nondeductible Roth IRA? For many people, the Roth IRA will produce better results. However, it is not the hands-down winner. Again, you will need to do your homework or seek the aid of a financial

TABLE 4.5 Phase-Out of Deductibility of Traditional IRA and Roth IRA Contributions[1]

Traditional IRA		
Single taxpayer and head of household	2011	$56,000 to $66,000
Married filing jointly	2011	$90,000 to $110,000
Roth IRA		
Single taxpayer and head of household	2011	$107,000 to $122,000
Married filing jointly	2011	$169,000 to $179,000

[1]Phase-out is adjusted annually based on changes in the CPI. Consult with your tax advisor for changes for 2012 or later.

advisor. Contributing to a Roth IRA is definitely better than contributing to a *nondeductible* Traditional IRA, because neither contribution is deductible, but future distributions from the Roth IRA will be tax-free if you follow the qualifying rules. Also, the Roth IRA is not subject to the *Required Minimum Distribution Rules*, which require that you to begin systematic withdrawals from retirement plans beginning after you turn age 70 $1/2$.

ROTH CONVERSIONS

The law allows you to convert your Traditional IRA to a Roth IRA. If you choose to do so, you will owe ordinary income tax on the conversion for the tax year the conversion occurs. Should you convert your existing Traditional IRA to a Roth IRA? There is no one right answer for everyone. What is best for you will depend on your particular circumstances. One thing that is clear is that it makes sense to convert only if you can pay the income taxes from proceeds outside of your IRA. Your financial advisor can help you run the numbers to see what is best for you, or do your own calculations at the Resource Center at www.welchgroup.com; then click on "Links"; and then click on "Roth Conversion Calculator."

Tip

The IRA to 401(k) to Roth IRA Conversion Strategy

Under the 2010 Tax Relief Act there is no longer an earned income limitation on converting to a Roth IRA for 2011 or 2012, so everyone has the opportunity to do this if it makes sense. When you convert your traditional IRA you must pay income tax now but all future growth and distributions are not subject to income tax for qualified withdrawals. Converting to a Roth IRA only makes sense if you have money held outside of the IRA to pay the taxes due. Here's a strategy that may allow you to postpone paying the conversion taxes: If you have an IRA with basis (i.e. a non-deductible IRA that has a profit) and a company 401(k) plan, then see if the 401(k) plan will allow you to roll part of your IRA into the 401(k) plan. With this strategy you can roll all of your tax deferred dollars into the

401(k) and leave only the basis (dollars that taxes has been paid on) in the traditional IRA. Now you can convert the remaining basis into a Roth IRA. You will pay zero tax on this conversion since you are only converting basis which is after-tax dollars. The benefit of this is to move this money into an account where you will pay no taxes on future growth. You should consult with your tax advisor before implementing this strategy.

Tip

The Roth Conversion "Two-Step" Strategy

Here's one more tax deferral strategy: If you are ineligible to make current contributions to either a deductible Traditional IRA or a Roth IRA because you fail the income test (i.e. you make too much money!), there's still a way to get money into a Roth IRA. We call it the Roth Conversion Two-Step Strategy because it requires that you complete a two-step process. First you contribute to a non-deductible traditional IRA (there is no income test qualifications), then you immediately "convert" to a Roth IRA. This is a little loophole in the tax law . . . so take advantage of it while you can! Remember, a non-working spouse can also use this strategy. This works best in conjunction with the Roth IRA to 401(k) Conversion Strategy discussed in the previous tip.

Retirement plans do have some disadvantages. First, if you take your money out before age 59 $\frac{1}{2}$, you will likely owe a 10 percent penalty in addition to ordinary income taxes on the proceeds. More important, retirement accounts (excluding Roth IRAs) convert what may have been long-term capital gains (taxed at a maximum rate of 15 percent in 2011 and 2012) to ordinary income, taxed at your highest personal tax bracket. These disadvantages are typically overcome based on the value of the immediate income tax deduction and the tax deferral of income until withdrawn.

Magnify the Power of Your Retirement Plan Tenfold

Receiving an immediate tax deduction and tax-deferred growth are two powerful reasons for using retirement plans in your investment program. Is there a way to magnify these results? Under certain circumstances, the answer is most definitely yes. The determining factor is who you designate as your beneficiary. For many reasons, your primary beneficiary should usually be your spouse. However, we often find that people either leave their *contingent beneficiary* blank or they name their estate. This can be a big mistake. Let's assume that you have named your spouse as your primary beneficiary and you leave your contingent beneficiary blank. If your wife dies before you do, your retirement plan assets will automatically go to your estate and be distributed according to the terms specified in your will. Let's assume your will leaves everything to your children. Because your estate is the beneficiary, the income taxes on your retirement plan assets must be paid by December 31st of the fifth year following the year of your death. In other words, the advantage of tax deferral ends five years after you die. We'll refer to this as Option #1. If, on the other hand, you had named your children as the contingent beneficiary, they would have the option to continue deferring the majority of the retirement plan assets over their own lifetime. This is Option #2. Under these circumstances, the law requires that your children begin mandatory distributions prior to December 31 of the calendar year following the year of death. However, the mandatory distributions are based on *their* life expectancy. This results in a reduced mandatory (taxable) distribution, thus allowing for a substantial continuation of deferral. There are two very important points here that you and your beneficiaries should be aware. First, Option #2 is by far the best income tax strategy for the beneficiaries since it will allow them to stretch the income taxes over their respective lifetimes. In order to qualify for Option #2, the beneficiaries must begin taking the mandatory distributions by the deadline. Second, if there is more than one beneficiary, they must elect to separate the inherited IRA in order to use their own life expectancy for the calculation of the mandatory distribution. If they fail to do this, the life expectancy of the oldest beneficiary will be used. This is clearly a disadvantage for younger beneficiaries. It is also important to note that if you do not name an individual or individuals as your beneficiary, Option #1 is the only option your heirs will have. Let's look at two examples.

For our first example, assume that you are age 45 and you are the named beneficiary under your father's IRA in the amount of $200,000. He dies and you elect to receive only the minimum required distributions. Based on IRS life expectancy tables, your life expectancy is 38.8 more years (see Appendix C for IRS Life Expectancy Table). By dividing 38.8 into $200,000 you determine that your mandatory withdrawal for the first year is $5,155 or about 2.6%. If you actually earned, say 6%, this means that you were able to continue to defer all of your $200,000 plus a portion of your earnings. Note that you must recalculate your required minimum distribution each year since your life expectancy changes each year. Over 38.8 years (your life expectancy according to the IRS) the combination of your mandatory withdrawals ($113,000) plus the remaining portfolio value ($889,000) exceeds $1,000,000!

For our second example, let's assume your father uses this strategy naming your 25-year-old son (instead of you) as the beneficiary. Your son's life expectancy is 58.2 years. Your father dies and your son now elects to take minimum distributions (first year = $3,436) while deferring any additional growth. If the account earns an average of 7 percent per year, the account value would have grown to almost $1 million by the time he reaches age 65. This is in addition to the $737,000 in mandatory distributions that he took out over that time period! This strategy allows you to leverage a modest retirement account into a million-dollar financial asset.

Personal Investment Accounts

By now you know that you should put the maximum amount allowable into your retirement plan(s) before you invest any money personally for your retirement. The main advantage of a personal investment program is that you have access to your money without penalties if you should need it. Doing so may trigger income taxes, but for investments held for more than 12 months, you will be taxed at the more favorable long-term capital gains rate (maximum federal tax rate of 15 percent for 2011 and 2012). Dividends paid on stocks of public corporations are also taxed at a maximum federal tax rate of 15%. This more favorable tax treatment of corporate dividends provides an incentive for investors to invest in dividend-paying stocks.

Still, the primary disadvantage of investing personally is the imposition of current taxation. For equities, the use of dividend-paying stocks or holding appreciated securities for long-term capital gains tax treatment will help reduce your tax bite. For fixed-income investments, you can invest in municipal bonds. The interest income from these bonds is not subject to federal income taxes and, in certain cases, is not subject to state, city, or county taxes either. However, you should use some caution here. We often find that people who have bought municipal securities are in a relatively low tax bracket. They would have been better off, after taxes, having bought taxable securities. Remember, it's the *net* jingle in your pocket that counts. The formula for comparing taxable verses tax-free investments is as follows:

$$\text{Taxable Yield} = \frac{\text{Tax Free Yield}}{1 - \text{Federal Tax Bracket}}$$

For example, if you are in the 28 percent federal tax bracket and you want to compare a tax-free bond yielding 4.5 percent to a taxable bond of similar quality and maturity yielding 7 percent, your calculation would be as follows:

$$\text{Taxable Yield} = \frac{.045}{1 - .28} = \frac{.045}{.72} = .0625 \text{ or } 6.25\%$$

From this example, obviously the taxable bond yielding 7 percent is preferable. Go to the Resource Center at www.welchgroup.com; then click on "Links"; and then click on "Tax Equivalent Yield Converter" for a financial calculator that can help you compare the net return on municipal versus taxable bonds.

It should be noted that all tax-free bonds are not entirely tax-free. Certain types of municipal bonds are subject to the *alternative minimum tax*. The Internal Revenue Service rules require you to first calculate your income taxes the usual way and then recalculate them the alternate way, which includes the interest income from certain municipal bonds. If the alternate method creates a larger tax, that is the tax you must pay. To avoid this potential problem you must either buy municipal bonds that are not subject to the alternative minimum tax or make certain that you will not be subject to the tax. Your tax advisor can help you determine the best course for you.

Tax-Deferred Investment Programs

Tax-deferred investment programs fall into two main categories: tax-deferred annuities and cash value life insurance. The obvious advantage to these programs is having your money grow without being subjected to current income taxes. However, the disadvantages are also significant. Let's start by looking at annuities. Annuities have four main disadvantages:

1. *High expenses*. Many annuities have relatively high expenses associated with their purchase. Annual expenses for annuities can exceed 2 percent. Portions of these premiums are used to cover mortality charges in the event you choose to have your account converted into a life income. Almost no one does, so this is a waste of money. Other expenses include commissions, policy fees, and a variety of other one-time and annual charges.

2. *Potentially higher taxes on withdrawals*. An annuity converts what may have been long-term capital gains, which are taxed at a maximum federal tax rate of 15 percent, to ordinary income, for which tax rates are as high as 35 percent (based on 2011 and 2012 tax law). For example, if you bought a stock index fund, held it for 20 years, and then took your money out, your gains would be taxed at a maximum federal rate of 15 percent. If, on the other hand, you bought a variable annuity and through the annuity invested in a similar stock index fund, when you take your money out 20 years later the gain will be subject to *ordinary* income tax rates. Table 4.6 illustrates in dollar terms the disadvantages of annuities outlined here. Even worse, when you begin withdrawing money from your annuity after age 59 $1/2$, you will be taxed on a last-in-first-out basis unless you annuitize your payments. This means that you will pay ordinary income taxes on *all* distributions until you have withdrawn all of your profits.

3. *Limited investment choices*. Another major disadvantage of annuities is limited investment choices. Many have two dozen or fewer choices. Some have many more, but that's still limiting compared to being able to choose among the entire universe of over 10,000 mutual funds. By way of analogy, let's assume that you and I each have $100 million to buy a baseball team (never mind that this amount wouldn't even buy us a *minor* league team!). There are 20 teams in the league, and I give you first choice. Once you choose your team you are stuck with it for the season. Now it's my turn. But instead of choosing a team, I get to choose individual players! Which option would you rather have?

4. *Potential tax penalties*. The final disadvantage of annuities is that if you had to take your money out before age 59 $1/2$ you would incur a 10 percent penalty in addition to ordinary income taxes. There are cases in which

TABLE 4.6 Comparison of Personal Investment vs. Variable Annuity

Assume: Investor A invests in an S&P 500 index fund.
Investor B also invests in an S&P 500 index fund but uses a variable annuity.

	Investor A without Variable Annuity	Investor B with Variable Annuity
Account Growth for 30 Years:		
After tax contribution	$10,000	$10,000
Growth factor[1]	×16.52	×10.06
Account value in 30 years	$165,200	$100,600
Tax Effect Upon Sale in 30 Years:		
Account value	$165,200	$100,600
Less capital gains tax[2]	−20,124	−0
Less ordinary income tax	−0	−35,219
Net to Investor	$145,076	$65,381
Advantage to investor	$79,695	

[1]The growth factor for both index funds is based on 10% average annual return net of fund manager cost. The growth factor for the index fund that is held personally is reduced by the estimated income tax loads of 0.20% (i.e., tax on annual dividend distributions). The growth factor for variable annuity is reduced by the estimated average annual expenses associated with annuity products (2.0%).
[2]For index fund, reinvested dividends increase the cost basis.
Note: If both investors held their accounts until death, Investor A's heirs would receive a "stepped-up" cost basis and avoid *all* income taxes. Investor B's heirs would eventually be required to pay ordinary income taxes on all gains.

annuities make sense, but they are rare. If someone is trying to sell you one, consult your financial advisor before signing on the dotted line.

For retirees, annuities can provide a guaranteed income stream. You'll want to pay close attention to the credit quality of the insurance company you invest with since you'll be counting on them to make payments to you (and perhaps your spouse) as long as you live. Consider "spreading your risks" by investing with multiple insurance companies.

Life Insurance

Life insurance is a complex product and therefore is often confusing to the buying public. Let's see if we can demystify it a bit. All financial products, including life insurance, are a matter of mathematics. When you buy a cash value life insurance policy, your money (called premiums) goes to the insurance company. A portion of your premium is used to cover the risk of you dying prematurely. This is known as the *mortality charge*. You can think of it as the term insurance charge. Another portion goes to cover the insurance company's overhead, including agents' commissions. The remaining portion is invested by the insurance company for your benefit. The insurance companies have managed to secure some preferential tax treatment. First, the earnings in a cash value policy are tax-deferred until withdrawn. If you do withdraw part of your money, it is taxed on a first-in-first-out (FIFO) basis. This means that you pay no taxes until you have withdrawn all the money you contributed. If you never take your money out and die while the insurance is in force, your investment gains are *never* subject to income taxes. While dying is not our idea of a good investment strategy, we are always happy to avoid taxes.

As an investment, the disadvantages of cash value life insurance center around two issues: potentially high expenses and limited investment choices. Commissions and expenses can easily consume your first year's entire premium. Many contracts take 10 years or longer to break even. Some policies are more competitive than this, but all contain high expenses when compared with direct investments into mutual funds, stocks, or bonds.

As with annuities, your investment options are extremely limited. We should add that cash value life insurance does have an important and appropriate place in estate planning, which we will discuss in Chapter 10. But if you are using it *primarily* as an investment vehicle, you can likely find better alternatives.

To summarize, if you have only a limited amount of money to invest, you will increase the power of your retirement investment program by prioritizing how those dollars are used. First, you want to invest through retirement plans to the maximum amount that the law allows before you invest any money in personal investment accounts. Additionally, you should consider your alternatives carefully before investing in tax-deferred vehicles such as annuities or cash value life insurance.

Some Final Thoughts on Investing

With each passing year our financial markets become more and more complex. Many of our long-held beliefs about what is safe versus what is risky have been shattered. We have witnessed the failure or near failure of some of the largest and oldest financial institutions in America. Formerly esteemed corporate executives have been exposed as nothing more than greedy people with mediocre talent whose focus was on producing quarterly results to impress Wall Street (and line their own pocketbook) at the expense of sound business decisions.

Now, more than ever, designing and monitoring a portfolio that is reponsive to the financial markets we now find ourselves dealing with is more important than ever. If you don't have the time or inclination to do it properly, we recommend that you seek the assistance of a professional. If you would like assistance locating an advisor near you, contact one of us and we'll be happy to assist you. Our contact information is located in Appendix A.

In this chapter we have discussed the importance of investing for long-term growth and choosing the best investment environment for maximizing estate accumulation. In the next chapter, you will learn just how large an estate you will need in order to secure your financial future for as long as you live.

CHAPTER 5

Retire with Dignity

How Much Is Enough?

As you're developing your estate plan, it is vital that you determine how large an estate is necessary to provide for your lifestyle income needs during your lifetime. When the answer to that question indicates a shortfall, you will need to develop a plan for the best way to accomplish this objective. It may involve setting up a retirement plan or other investment program. Some people will find that they have accumulated significantly more assets than they will need to meet all of their financial objectives and retirement income needs. These individuals can begin focusing on wealth transfer strategies during their lifetime instead of waiting until their death. You should assume that until you know whether you have enough assets, you won't be able to implement a truly effective estate plan. In this chapter, we will help you determine the size of the *investment estate* that you will need to accumulate in order to provide for your retirement income needs.

Investment estate: The sum total of all your investments, excluding such items as home, personal property, and so forth.

Your Retirement Requirements

Let's go through a step-by-step process to determine how much additional capital you need to accumulate for a worry-free retirement. Even if you are certain you have enough money for your retirement, you should still go through this process. By calculating your retirement needs, any excess capital can then be used as part of a wealth transfer strategy.

Determining how much capital you will need at retirement is vital to your estate plan. It is an intricate process involving many complex calculations and should be done with the assistance of a professional financial advisor. As a starting point, we will provide two alternative tools you can use to begin to get a feel for the size of the job ahead of you. There are many retirement planning calculators available through the Internet. You will find a user-friendly site at the Resource Center at www.welchgroup.com; then click on "Links"; then click on "Retirement Planning Calculator." For those of you who prefer to do a manual calculation, we have provided an eight-step process to help you determine what your retirement needs are. (Note that readers who have already retired may skip Steps 2 and 6 through 8.)

Step 1. Define Your Assumptions

A word of caution: Many of your assumptions will be little more than educated guesses. Many of these guesses will be wrong. An incorrect assumption can lead to significant errors in the final result. The best solution here is to review your assumptions and expected outcomes often, at least annually. This review and refinement process will lead to much better results.

ASSUMPTION #1: AGE AT WHICH YOU PLAN TO RETIRE

Determining at what age you would like to retire is fairly easy for most people. We find that most people want the *option* of being able to quit many years before the typical retirement age of 65. What they are really searching for is financial *choice* in their life. If their present job becomes too much of a hassle, they want the option of being able, financially speaking, to do something different. The "something different" might be a job that pays a lot less.

ASSUMPTION #2: INCOME NEEDED AT RETIREMENT

Determining how much income is needed at the time of retirement is a more difficult assumption to make. One rule of thumb is to assume that you will need 80 percent of your preretirement income. However, this rule of thumb is not applicable in many individual circumstances. The best way to estimate your future income need is to review current spending patterns and then visualize how expenses will be different at retirement. You will find that many of your current expenses will dramatically decrease or disappear at retirement, while other expenses will increase. For example, the money you spend on children should decrease significantly (does it ever completely go away?). Hopefully, your home mortgage will be fully paid off. Other expenses, such as medical insurance and travel, may be much higher than today. To get a clearer picture, use Worksheet 5.1 to compare your current expenses with estimated expenses at retirement. These retirement expenses should be figured as if you were retiring today. You will adjust the results for inflation later. All expense estimates should be figured on an annual basis. For a more detailed budget, go to the Resource Center at www.welchgroup.com; then click on "Links."

ASSUMPTION #3: PRERETIREMENT RATE OF RETURN

Consider what *average rate of return* you expect to earn on your investments before you retire. For qualified retirement plan accounts, IRAs, tax-deferred annuities, and life insurance policies, the rate you earn will be your *gross* rate of return. For personal investment accounts, you are looking for the *net* rate of return after taxes. As a historical guideline for rate of return, you can expect equity-oriented investments (stocks, real estate) to earn 8 to 10 percent over

WORKSHEET 5.1 Retirement Income Worksheet

	Estimated Current Expenses	Retirement Expenses (Today's $)	Increasing Expense?	
Contributions	$____	$____	Yes	No
Home:				
Mortgage	$____	$____	Yes	No
Insurance	$____	$____	Yes	No
Real estate taxes	$____	$____	Yes	No
Maintenance/repairs	$____	$____	Yes	No
Utilities:				
Electricity/gas/water	$____	$____	Yes	No
Phone (including toll charges)	$____	$____	Yes	No
Cable TV	$____	$____	Yes	No
Security system	$____	$____	Yes	No
Insurance:				
Medical	$____	$____	Yes	No
Personal care	$____	$____	Yes	No
Children:				
Clothing	$____	$____	Yes	No
School tuition/ expenses	$____	$____	Yes	No
Gifts	$____	$____	Yes	No
Other	$____	$____	Yes	No
Debt Payments:				
Autos	$____	$____	Yes	No
Personal loans	$____	$____	Yes	No
Other	$____	$____	Yes	No
Income taxes	$____	$____	Yes	No
Total	$____	$____		

time, while fixed-income-oriented investments (bonds, CDs, money market) to earn 3 to 5 percent over time.

ASSUMPTION #4: POSTRETIREMENT RATE OF RETURN

Many people manage their investments more aggressively prior to retirement. The assumption is that you can afford to be more aggressive when you still have earned income and are continuing to invest new money each month or year, and you are reinvesting all your interest, dividends, and capital gains. Once you retire and start drawing income from your investments, you must take greater care to protect your principal. This scenario is discussed in Chapter 4.

ASSUMPTION #5: ESTIMATED INFLATION RATE

We typically use 2 to 3 percent as the estimated inflation rate. Other advisors sometimes use rates as high as 6 percent. Inflation rates over the last 75 years have averaged 3.1 percent. An independent study has concluded that the way our government calculates the consumer price index (CPI) overstates the rate of inflation by as much as 1 percent. We will leave it to you to decide what inflation rate is appropriate for your case facts.

Step 2. Determine Your Future Income Need

(If you are already retired, you may skip this step.) In Step 1 you estimated what your retirement income needs would be in terms of today's dollars. Now you need to convert that income into future dollars based on the assumed inflation rate (assumption #5). To determine the inflation factor, go to Table 5.1. Across the top of the page, identify the inflation rate you chose in Step 1. Moving down the left margin, identify the number that corresponds with the number of years until you intend to retire. The point where the two numbers intersect is your *inflation multiplier*. For example, if you choose an inflation rate of 3 percent and you have 20 years until retirement, your inflation multiplier is 1.81. Having identified your inflation multiplier, you should now multiply it by your expected retirement income need, which you determined in Step 1. The result is the income you will need the *first* year you retire. Since inflation will continue to erode the purchasing power of your income, we will have to account for continuing inflation in later calculations.

Step 3. Subtract Your Sources of Retirement Income

In Step 2 you determined the total income you would need when you retire. You will need to subtract any income sources you expect to receive at retirement. One source of income will be Social Security. If you have not yet retired, use Table 5.2 to estimate how much Social Security income you will receive.

TABLE 5.1 Inflation Multiplier Chart

Years until Retirement	Estimated Inflation Rate							
	1%	2%	3%	4%	5%	6%	7%	8%
1	1.01	1.02	1.03	1.04	1.05	1.06	1.07	1.08
2	1.02	1.04	1.06	1.08	1.10	1.12	1.14	1.17
3	1.03	1.06	1.09	1.12	1.16	1.19	1.23	1.26
4	1.04	1.08	1.13	1.17	1.22	1.26	1.31	1.36
5	1.05	1.10	1.16	1.22	1.28	1.34	1.40	1.47
6	1.06	1.13	1.19	1.27	1.34	1.42	1.50	1.59
7	1.07	1.15	1.23	1.32	1.41	1.50	1.61	1.71
8	1.08	1.17	1.27	1.37	1.48	1.59	1.72	1.85
9	1.09	1.20	1.30	1.42	1.55	1.69	1.84	2.00
10	1.10	1.22	1.34	1.48	1.63	1.79	1.97	2.16
11	1.12	1.24	1.38	1.54	1.71	1.90	2.10	2.33
12	1.13	1.27	1.43	1.60	1.80	2.01	2.25	2.52
13	1.14	1.29	1.47	1.67	1.89	2.13	2.41	2.72
14	1.15	1.32	1.51	1.73	1.98	2.26	2.58	2.94
15	1.16	1.35	1.56	1.80	2.08	2.40	2.76	3.17
16	1.17	1.37	1.60	1.87	2.18	2.54	2.95	3.43
17	1.18	1.40	1.65	1.95	2.29	2.69	3.16	3.70
18	1.20	1.43	1.70	2.03	2.41	2.85	3.38	4.00
19	1.21	1.46	1.75	2.11	2.53	3.03	3.62	4.32
20	1.22	1.49	1.81	2.19	2.65	3.21	3.87	4.66
21	1.23	1.52	1.86	2.28	2.79	3.40	4.14	5.03
22	1.24	1.55	1.92	2.37	2.93	3.60	4.43	5.44
23	1.26	1.58	1.97	2.46	3.07	3.82	4.74	5.87
24	1.27	1.61	2.03	2.56	3.23	4.05	5.07	6.34
25	1.28	1.64	2.09	2.67	3.39	4.29	5.43	6.85
26	1.30	1.67	2.16	2.77	3.56	4.55	5.81	7.40
27	1.31	1.71	2.22	2.88	3.73	4.82	6.21	7.99
28	1.32	1.74	2.29	3.00	3.92	5.11	6.65	8.63
29	1.33	1.78	2.36	3.12	4.12	5.42	7.11	9.32
30	1.35	1.81	2.43	3.24	4.32	5.74	7.61	10.06

TABLE 5.2 Social Security Benefits Estimate

Assume that worker earnings are at or over maximum Social Security wage base (2010 estimates).		
Age	62	66
Benefit	$21,108	$28,152

Note: These figures are for a worker retiring in 2009. To receive an estimate of your future benefits, contact the Social Security Administration at 1-800-772-1213 or visit www.ssa.gov..

Another possible source of income is your company's pension plan. If your company has one, contact your benefits office or plan trustee and ask for the formula for calculating benefits. Often the formula is based on years of service and average wages during your last few years (often your last five years). While Social Security is indexed for inflation, pension benefits often are not. You will need to take this into account in your final calculations for retirement capital needed. Any other sources of income should be deducted as well. The results of these adjustments will be the income that you need to draw from your investment accounts (including personal investment accounts, IRAs, company 401(k)s, etc.).

For example, let's say that in Step 2 you determined that your annual retirement income needs will be $120,000 at age 65. You estimate that your Social Security benefit for you and your spouse will be $38,000 per year and that your company pension will pay you $29,000 per year. Your results would look as follows:

Retirement income need	$120,000
Social Security benefit	−38,000
Pension benefit	−29,000
Income needed from your investments	$53,000

Tip

Annually, the Social Security Administration (SSA) sends you an estimate of your benefits. If you need an interim report, contact the SSA at 1-800-772-1213 or request it online at www.ssa.gov/mystatement. The income estimate does not include inflation, so you will need to use Table 5.1 to calculate the future benefit. Over the last 10 years, Social Security benefits have increased by approximately 2.3 percent annually.

Step 4. Determine Your Portfolio Withdrawal Rate

As you remember from Chapter 4, the withdrawal rate (also referred to as the withdrawal factor) represents the percentage of dollars that you are withdrawing from your total investment portfolio over a calendar year. You want to ensure that your withdrawal rate is not too high or you will run the risk of depleting your portfolio over time. Based on our experience, an appropriate withdrawal rate scale is as follows:

Conservative: 0.04 (4 percent)

Moderate: 0.05 (5 percent)

Aggressive: 0.06 (6 percent)

For a more complete explanation of the withdrawal rate, review Chapter 4, page 37.

Step 5. Determine Your Investment Account Target

You are now ready to calculate how large an investment account you must accumulate to meet your goals. Take your answer from Step 3 and divide it by the withdrawal rate you chose in Step 4. Your answer indicates how much additional capital you must accumulate for your retirement. If you are already retired, your answer indicates either that you have more investments than you need or that you don't have enough. If you have more than you need, congratulations! You may skip ahead to Chapter 6. If you don't have enough, review Chapter 4 for strategies you can use to improve your results.

Continuing with our previous example, we have determined that the income needed is $53,000. Let's assume that you have decided on a "moderate" withdrawal factor of 0.05 (5 percent). By dividing $53,000 by 0.05, you come up with $1,060,000, which is the amount of capital necessary to produce a lifetime *inflation-adjusted* income of $53,000 per year at your retirement. In our example, each year you will withdraw 5 percent of your account balance (a withdrawal factor of 0.05). Since the account is expected to earn between 6 percent and 8 percent over time (assuming a minimum of 60 percent allocation to stocks), your account balance should be growing *over time*.

Short-term volatility (bear markets) should be expected. The best way to deal with it is to use all portfolio income plus the principal (as needed) from the Safety Net (CDs, bonds, and money market) portion of your portfolio while you wait for the Growth (stocks and stock mutual funds) portion of your portfolio to recover. Once equities rebound, you should then take enough profits to replenish your Safety Net (fixed income) and bring your portfolio back into balance (see Chapter 4, Growth Strategy with a Safety Net®, on pages 33–37).

Step 6. Determine the Future Value of Your Current Investments

(If you have already retired, you may skip Steps 6 through 8.) You know how much money you must accumulate before you retire. Now you will need to determine how far your current investments will go toward meeting your goal. This requires that you estimate the future value of your current investments. You have two choices here. You can assign an average rate of return for all current investments, or you can use a different rate of return for each type of investment. For example, if you have $425,000 in personal mutual funds, $60,000 in certificates of deposit (CDs), $235,000 in your company 401(k) plan, and $22,000 in your whole life insurance policy (see Table 5.3), you can either assume an aggregate rate of return (averaging the rate of return for all your investments) or use a different rate of return for each asset. With assets that are this dissimilar, using different rates of return would be preferable but also would require more work. At this stage, concern yourself not with current and future contributions but only with current balances.

Using Table 5.4, choose the rate of return that you expect to earn on your investments (top row of table). Then, looking down the left-most column of the table, choose the number that represents the number of years until you retire. The point where these two numbers intersect represents your *growth factor*. Multiply this factor by the current value of your investment account(s). Your answer represents the expected value of your investment account(s) the day you retire. Unless you averaged the rate of return for all your investments at once, you will need to repeat this process for each investment. If the earnings rate you have assumed is not represented on this form, you can interpolate your growth factor. For example, if you chose a 9.5 percent earnings rate with 20 years until retirement, your growth factor would be the midpoint between the growth factor for 9 percent (5.60) and 10 percent (6.73). To find the midpoint, add the two numbers together, and then divide the sum (12.33) by 2. The result, 6.165, can be rounded up to 6.17, which is the growth factor for a 9.5 percent earnings rate.

For another example, assume you plan to retire in 20 years and your current investments are those shown in Table 5.3. One of your investments is a $60,000 CD. Since this is a taxable investment, you need to determine your rate of return *after* taxes. We have assumed a 28 percent tax bracket for this example, resulting in a net rate of return of 5 percent. By going to Table 5.4 and finding

TABLE 5.3 Current Investment Assets

$425,000	Personal mutual funds
$60,000	Certificate of deposit (CD)
$235,000	401(k)
$22,000	Cash value whole life policy
$742,000	Total investments

TABLE 5.4 Growth Factor Table

Years until Retirement	Expected Return on Investment										
	5%	6%	7%	8%	9%	10%	11%	12%	13%	14%	15%
1	1.05	1.06	1.07	1.08	1.09	1.10	1.11	1.12	1.13	1.14	1.15
2	1.10	1.12	1.14	1.17	1.19	1.21	1.23	1.25	1.28	1.30	1.32
3	1.16	1.19	1.23	1.26	1.30	1.33	1.37	1.40	1.44	1.48	1.52
4	1.22	1.26	1.31	1.36	1.41	1.46	1.52	1.57	1.63	1.69	1.75
5	1.28	1.34	1.40	1.47	1.54	1.61	1.69	1.76	1.84	1.93	2.01
6	1.34	1.42	1.50	1.59	1.68	1.77	1.87	1.97	2.08	2.19	2.31
7	1.41	1.50	1.61	1.71	1.83	1.95	2.08	2.21	2.35	2.50	2.66
8	1.48	1.59	1.72	1.85	1.99	2.14	2.30	2.48	2.66	2.85	3.06
9	1.55	1.69	1.84	2.00	2.17	2.36	2.56	2.77	3.00	3.25	3.52
10	1.63	1.79	1.97	2.16	2.37	2.59	2.84	3.11	3.39	3.71	4.05
11	1.71	1.90	2.10	2.33	2.58	2.85	3.15	3.48	3.84	4.23	4.65
12	1.80	2.01	2.25	2.52	2.81	3.14	3.50	3.90	4.33	4.82	5.35
13	1.89	2.13	2.41	2.72	3.07	3.45	3.88	4.36	4.90	5.49	6.15
14	1.98	2.26	2.58	2.94	3.34	3.80	4.31˙	4.89	5.53	6.26	7.08
15	2.08	2.40	2.76	3.17	3.64	4.18	4.78	5.47	6.25	7.14	8.14
16	2.18	2.54	2.95	3.43	3.97	4.59	5.31	6.13	7.07	8.14	9.36
17	2.29	2.69	3.16	3.70	4.33	5.05	5.90	6.87	7.99	9.28	10.76
18	2.41	2.85	3.38	4.00	4.72	5.56	6.54	7.69	9.02	10.58	12.38
19	2.53	3.03	3.62	4.32	5.14	6.12	7.26	8.61	10.20	12.06	14.23
20	2.65	3.21	3.87	4.66	5.60	6.73	8.06	9.65	11.52	13.74	16.37
21	2.79	3.40	4.14	5.03	6.11	7.40	8.95	10.80	13.02	15.67	18.82
22	2.93	3.60	4.43	5.44	6.66	8.14	9.93	12.10	14.71	17.86	21.64
23	3.07	3.82	4.74	5.87	7.26	8.95	11.03	13.55	16.63	20.36	24.89
24	3.23	4.05	5.07	6.34	7.91	9.85	12.24	15.18	18.79	23.21	28.63
25	3.39	4.29	5.43	6.85	8.62	10.83	13.59	17.00	21.23	26.46	32.92
26	3.56	4.55	5.81	7.40	9.40	11.92	15.08	19.04	23.99	30.17	37.86
27	3.73	4.82	6.21	7.99	10.25	13.11	16.74	21.32	27.11	34.39	43.54
28	3.92	5.11	6.65	8.63	11.17	14.42	18.58	23.88	30.63	39.20	50.07
29	4.12	5.42	7.11	9.32	12.17	15.86	20.62	26.75	34.62	44.69	57.58
30	4.32	5.74	7.61	10.06	13.27	17.45	22.89	29.96	39.12	50.95	66.21

the intersection of 5 percent and 20 years, you will find that the growth factor is 2.65. Note that if you planned to pay all the taxes on your CD with other funds (i.e., you plan to reinvest your interest), you would use the *before* tax rate of return that corresponds with the growth factor in Table 5.4.

Step 7. Determine Your Retirement Account Surplus or Deficit

This step involves nothing more than simple arithmetic. Subtract your answer in Step 6 (the future value of your current investments) from your answer in Step 5 (your investment account target). If the result is a negative number, congratulations! You will have more money than necessary to meet your retirement income needs (a surplus). If your answer is a positive number, you have a deficit and must continue investing in order to meet your goal. How much will you need to invest? Continue with Steps 8 and 9 to find the answer.

Step 8. Determine Your Monthly Investment Requirements

If your calculations thus far indicate that you will not have accumulated enough money by retirement, you will need to determine how much you need to invest each month in order to meet your goal. If you are currently investing monthly through a 401(k), profit sharing plan, or personal investment plan, you need to determine whether you are investing enough. Be sure to include any employer matching in your calculations.

At this point, it is important to discuss a fundamental investment concept that you must both understand and implement as part of your wealth accumulation plan. The contributions to your investment plan should be based on a *percentage* of your total income, and therefore, the dollar amount invested should increase as your income rises. Many investment programs automatically do this for you. A good example is a 401(k) program. Typically you contribute, through payroll deduction, a certain percentage of your income, say 6 percent. As your income rises, the dollar amount of your contributions also rises. Hopefully, your income will increase at least as fast as inflation does. If you feel this will not be the case, then part of your action plan should be to seek employment where there is more opportunity for you. This may require improving your value through additional education or training.

First, you must decide what is an appropriate *growth rate* on your *contributions*. By what percentage do you think you can increase your contributions annually? This number should be at least equal to the rate you assumed for inflation. If you are on your company's fast track and you expect your income to rise sharply over your career span, you may want to use a higher number. Next, you need to estimate the rate of return you expect to earn on your investments. Remember that different types of investments will earn different returns. You can either choose an aggregate return for all your investments or do a separate calculation for each. Our preference is to use a separate calculation for each investment. Using Table 5.5, find the *contributions growth rate* you have chosen. Across the top of that chart, find the *investment earnings rate* you have assumed for your investment account(s). If it is a taxable investment account, don't forget to adjust your expected earnings rate for taxes! Looking down the left-most column, find the number that corresponds to the number of years until you plan to retire. Finally, find the point where the number of years until retirement and your investment earnings rate intersect. Multiply this factor by your current *annual* investment contributions. The result is the expected value, at retirement, of your future contributions to your investment account(s).

For example, assume that you are currently investing $20,000 per year and that you expect to be able to increase your investment contributions by 4 percent per year. Investments are expected to earn 10 percent, and you plan to retire in 15 years. First, find the portion of Table 5.5 for a contributions growth rate of 4 percent. Next, find the point of intersection between the investment earnings rate and the years until retirement (39.61). Now multiply your investment contributions by this factor:

$$\begin{array}{r} \$20,000 \\ \times\ 39.61 \\ \hline \$792,200 \end{array}$$

Subtract your answer here from your answer in Step 7 (your retirement account deficit). If your answer is still a positive number (i.e., a deficit), you will need to consider your options. Maybe your budget would allow you to increase the amount you are investing now. If not, you could increase the *rate of increases* of future contributions. One excellent way to achieve this is to commit half of all pay raises to your investment program. The other half can be used to improve lifestyle.

Another alternative is to invest more aggressively to increase your potential rate of return. History shows that by increasing the percentage of stocks in your portfolio you increase your *long-term* rate of return. Another alternative is to invest in a stock portfolio that is more aggressive. For example, you could increase your allocation to technology stocks or small-cap stocks. However, doing both—increasing the percentage of stocks in your portfolio and investing more aggressively using tech stocks or small-cap stocks—creates the proverbial double-edged sword. In the short term, you can expect greater losses when bear markets occur. Note that we said *when*, not *if*.

Giving your investments more time to work may easily solve your problem. Are you willing to postpone your retirement date? While working with clients we find that they usually have an ideal retirement age in mind but are perfectly happy to continue working for a few more years if necessary. Finally, you could consider

TABLE 5.5 Growth Rate Calculator

Contribution Growth Rate of 3%

Years	Investment Earnings Rate			
	6%	8%	10%	12%
5	5.97	6.20	6.45	6.70
10	14.90	16.30	17.85	19.58
15	27.95	32.28	37.42	43.51
20	46.70	57.10	70.31	87.11
25	73.27	95.09	124.87	165.63
30	110.54	152.71	214.60	305.92

Contribution Growth Rate of 4%

Years	Investment Earnings Rate			
	6%	8%	10%	12%
5	6.08	6.32	6.56	6.82
10	15.53	16.97	18.56	20.32
15	29.78	34.28	39.61	45.91
20	50.80	61.75	75.61	93.19
25	81.30	104.57	136.15	179.18
30	125.00	170.48	236.77	333.96

Contribution Growth Rate of 5%

Years	Investment Earnings Rate			
	6%	8%	10%	12%
5	6.19	6.43	6.68	6.94
10	16.20	17.67	19.30	21.10
15	31.76	38.44	41.97	48.49
20	55.38	66.92	81.48	99.90
25	90.55	115.40	148.97	194.48
30	142.15	191.36	262.55	366.26

Contribution Growth Rate of 6%

Years	Investment Earnings Rate			
	6%	8%	10%	12%
5	6.31	6.56	6.81	7.07
10	16.90	18.40	20.07	21.92
15	33.91	38.78	44.52	51.28
20	60.51	72.69	88.01	107.32
25	101.22	127.83	163.57	211.80
30	162.55	215.96	292.65	403.61

TABLE 5.5 (*Continued*)

	Contribution Growth Rate of 7%			
	Investment Earnings Rate			
Years	6%	8%	10%	12%
5	6.43	6.68	6.93	7.20
10	17.63	19.18	20.89	22.77
15	36.25	41.31	47.27	54.29
20	66.25	79.13	95.26	115.53
25	113.56	142.10	180.24	231.45
30	186.88	245.04	327.90	446.95

reducing your retirement income goal. Review your estimated expenses from Worksheet 5.1. Are there expense items that could be reduced or eliminated?

It may be difficult for you to make these decisions on your own. Not only are financial advisors skilled in such matters, but they also bring a clarity that is free of emotional bias. To find a financial advisor near you, contact author Stewart Welch III at 205-879-5001 or stewart@welchgroup.com. You now have the tools you need to develop your wealth accumulation plan. Good luck!

In the next chapter, you will learn the pitfalls of dying without a will. You will also establish appropriate goals for your estate plan.

CHAPTER 6

You Don't Have a Will? Big Trouble!

There's no way to get around it. Thinking about death is downright depressing. The emotional burdens of merely considering it can easily overshadow any financial or legal planning. However, not writing your will and failing to do even the most basic estate planning can have disastrous effects on your loved ones and other survivors.

Let's take a closer look at how property is transferred to your heirs if you die without a will. If you die without a will, you are said to die *intestate*. In essence, you have delegated your last wishes to your state legislators. Your unwritten will reads something like this:

I, being of sound mind, do hereby direct that the legislators of my state handle my estate as follows:

The state may appoint my surviving spouse as the administrator of my estate, or in its infinite wisdom, the state may appoint someone completely unknown to my family.

My administrator will be required to post (an expensive) bond to provide "insurance" in case he or she is incompetent as my estate representative.

My surviving spouse is to receive one half of my estate. The other half is to go to my three-year-old daughter.

Since my child is a minor, the state may choose my surviving spouse or someone unknown to my family to act as "conservator" to manage my child's assets. In either case, another (expensive) bond must be purchased annually and the conservator must periodically appear before the court (more fees) to provide an accounting of how my child's assets have been used. I understand that the court can be pretty picky about how money is spent. If the court disagrees with how my conservator has spent money, then my conservator can be held legally liable.

When my daughter reaches the age of majority (age 18 or 19 in most states), she will receive her inheritance outright, and I am going to assume that she is mature enough to handle the money in a manner that would make me proud.

If for some reason my spouse does not survive me (common accident?), I ask the state to decide who would be the best person (or institution) to raise my child. I hope they don't choose my Aunt Thelma!

If my surviving spouse remarries and then has the misfortune to predecease her new husband, it's okay that the assets I left her may go to him and not to my daughter.

I am happy to pay, from the proceeds of my estate, expensive legal, court, and administrative fees.

Finally, I realize that my poor planning may create large estate taxes that could have been avoided if I hadn't been so darn lazy.

Signed,

Your Loving but Procrastinating Husband

We hope you find this will unacceptable. The intestate laws of each state vary widely. To review the intestate laws of your state go to the Resource Center at www.welchgroup.com; then click on "Links"; then click on "Intestate Laws—State by State."

Property Transfers at Death

When you die, your property is going to be transferred to your heirs through one or more of the following distribution channels: probate, direct transfers by title, or living trusts (sometimes called revocable trusts). This is true whether or not you have a will. Each of these transfer methods has both advantages and disadvantages. You need to understand them so that you can intelligently choose the best methods for you. In this chapter, we will cover both probate and direct transfers by title. Transfers through living trusts will be covered in Chapter 9.

Transfers via Probate

Probate is the legal process whereby at your death a probate judge oversees the transfer of your property to your rightful heirs. While the probate process can be complicated and confusing, it can be broken down into nine steps.

Step 1. Locate and Interpret the Will

If you have a valid will, assets titled solely in your own name or assets that name your estate as the beneficiary, such as life insurance, will pass through the probate process. Your will specifies which persons or organizations will receive your property. As mentioned earlier, if you do not have a will, state law will determine who receives your property.

Step 2. Identifying Your Estate Representative

If you do not have a will, the court appoints someone to represent your estate. This person is called an administrator, or in some states a personal representative. This representative is responsible for working with the probate judge and completing the necessary steps to settle your estate and distribute your property to your heirs. In many cases, the court will require your personal representative to post a bond in order to provide some protection for your heirs should he or she be dishonest or incompetent. This bond is paid for out of your assets. Your personal representative is also entitled to compensation for his or her services. Some states have statutory limits on the amount of compensation a personal representative can receive, but most states allow "reasonable" compensation. In all cases, the probate judge must approve the compensation. This is also paid from your assets.

Step 3. Determine Who Your Heirs Are

If you do not have a will, state law will determine your rightful heirs. State laws can vary widely. To find out what your state intestacy laws are, ask one of your local bank trust officers or an attorney or go to the Resource Center at www.welchgroup.com; then click on "Links"; then click on "Intestate Laws—State by State."

Step 4. Locate and Value All Your Property

This is often the most difficult part of the process. If your estate is potentially large enough to be subject to estate taxes, all assets (meaning every item of personal property, real estate, business interest, securities, etc.) must be located, inventoried, and valued. It often requires that appraisals be ordered, which takes time and can be very expensive. Appraisals represent an educated guess of value and therefore are subject to the scrutiny and challenge of the court, heirs, and the Internal Revenue Service.

Step 5. Identify Creditors

Your personal representative must publish legal notices of your death so that potential creditors have an opportunity to file a claim against your estate.

Step 6. Resolve Disputes

Whenever money is involved, it's likely that disputes will arise. These problems can come from disgruntled heirs, creditors, personal representatives, disinherited parties, the Internal Revenue Service, and so on. It's the job of the probate judge to see that whatever problems develop are resolved.

Step 7. Pay All Expenses, Debts, and Taxes

Everyone must be paid before final disbursements are made to heirs. The estate may or may not be large enough to owe estate taxes. If estate taxes are due, cash must be raised to pay them. Often estates are long on assets but short on cash. The law has special provisions for estates made up largely of closely held business interests or farm land that allow the estate taxes to be stretched out, reduced, or eliminated. See Chapter 14 for more details.

Step 8. File All Tax Returns

Your estate representative must file the estate's income tax return, as well as your final income tax return.

Step 9. Distribute Property to Heirs

If you have no will and minor children or incompetent heirs are involved, the courts must appoint conservators and may remain involved for years.

Like most things, the probate process has its advantages and disadvantages.

ADVANTAGES OF THE PROBATE PROCESS

- Probate requires court supervision. It is, after all, a legal process. Your personal representative has a legal and fiduciary responsibility to act on behalf of your legal heirs. The probate judge supervises the process from start to finish. No disbursements are made without ultimate court approval.

- Probate is of limited duration. At the beginning of the probate process, legal notices are published in order to alert your creditors that you have died. This notice effectively sets a time limit, usually six months, after which no creditor can make a claim against your estate.

- Probate allows for postmortem planning. Since your estate is a separate taxpaying entity, your representative has the opportunity to do some post-mortem planning. Through disclaimers and other strategies, taxes can be postponed, reduced, or in some cases eliminated.

DISADVANTAGES OF THE PROBATE PROCESS

- The primary criticism of the probate system is that it is expensive. Depending on the state in which you live, this may or may not be true. Probate costs vary widely from state to state and even from probate judge to probate judge. Many of our states' probate laws officially say that probate costs will be "fair and reasonable." What is fair and reasonable often depends on whether you are the receiver or payer of fees. If you own property in more than one state, you may have to go through probate in those states as well.

- The probate process is slow, often taking six months to several years. While your heirs can receive interim distributions, they are forced to wait for the ultimate distribution of your estate.

- The probate process is public. Anyone can go down to the courthouse and review a copy of your will, what you owned, whom you owed, and to whom you left your money. Not long after Princess Diana's death, copies of her will were being sold for one dollar each! Even if your will is less interesting, you probably don't want it read by anyone other than your heirs and attorney.

Direct Transfers by Title

One way to avoid the probate process is to set up direct transfers through the titling of your property. Property titles can be very tricky, so you must plan carefully to ensure that you achieve the desired results. How you title your property can have a profound impact on estate taxes and, ultimately, on your whole estate plan. Typically couples title all property jointly. While there is no best way to title property for everyone, individual case facts and goals will determine the best way to title property for you. Let's look at the various ways to title property as well as the advantages and disadvantages of each.

The most common ways of holding title are fee simple (also known as sole ownership), joint tenants with right of survivorship, and joint tenants in common. Some states have special laws that govern community property ownership.

Fee Simple Ownership

Under fee simple ownership, you have the title totally in your name: "John Smith." Note that this method of ownership does not avoid probate.

ADVANTAGES OF FEE SIMPLE OWNERSHIP

- Fee simple ownership is easy to establish.
- Fee simple ownership does not require the signatures of other parties.
- Property titled solely in your name allows you the freedom of total control during your lifetime. You can do with this property as you see fit without interference from other people.
- You have total control over whom the property passes to upon your death.
- Fee simple ownership may eliminate the income or capital gains tax treatment of appreciated property. If the property has appreciated significantly, then upon your death it may receive a stepped-up cost basis and the inheriting party will receive the asset at the fair market value as of the date of your death. It should be noted that a few states restrict the transfer of

"fee simple" real estate without spousal consent, especially with respect to a couple's personal residence.

DISADVANTAGES OF FEE SIMPLE OWNERSHIP

- Upon your death, this property will be subject to the expenses and delays of the probate process. If you don't specifically decide who will receive the property, and if you don't execute an instrument (i.e., a will) that will cause the property to go to a specific person or organization, then those decisions would be determined for you by the current state laws.
- If you become incompetent through some form of disability, then the property will likely be referred to a court process to create a control mechanism. In Chapter 7 you will learn how to avoid this potential problem by signing a power of attorney.
- Since the property is held solely in your name, it will be included in your estate and will be subject to potential estate taxes.

Joint Tenants with Right of Survivorship

Property held as joint tenants with right of survivorship (JTWRS) could be titled as follows: "John and Sue Smith, joint owners with right of survivorship." Under this type of ownership, you should not transfer the property or make any dispositions of the property without the written permission of the other joint tenant. If you do, you destroy the joint tenancy survivorship feature and disastrous ownership results can occur. You are, in effect, joined together in all decisions regarding the disposition of this property. Upon death, your interest in the property automatically transfers to the surviving tenant(s).

ADVANTAGES OF JOINT TENANTS WITH RIGHT OF SURVIVORSHIP

While titling by joint tenants with right of survivorship sounds archaic, it is actually the most common form of ownership for married couples and does have some advantages.

- Such property is not subject to probate until the death of the final joint tenant. For example, if you know that at your death you want your wife to have control and ownership of your residence, this method will ensure that it passes to her immediately without going through the probate process.
- This type of ownership is easy to set up. It requires no special paperwork.
- JTWRS is an inexpensive way to hold title.

DISADVANTAGES OF JOINT TENANTS WITH RIGHT OF SURVIVORSHIP

- This type of ownership involves, to some extent, a loss of control over the property during your lifetime. Remember, you and your joint tenant must agree on all decisions regarding the property.

- JTWRS involves a loss of control over whom the property ultimately goes to after your death. The final joint tenant will have the opportunity to decide to whom he or she wishes to leave the property.

- Without extensive post-death planning, this method precludes having the property pass to a credit shelter trust, family trust, or Qtip trust. (These concepts will be discussed in detail later in this book.)

- JTWRS can lead to higher estate taxes if the joint owner is your spouse.

- JTWRS can lead to higher income taxes. Under current law, assets inherited receive a new income tax basis equal to fair value at death. Jointly owned assets receive only a new basis of one-half, although the rules are more generous for community property.

- Eventually property will be subject to probate upon the death of the final joint tenant.

- With this method it is possible that your property may pass to unintended heirs. For example, if your spouse remarries after you die, he or she could change the title to include Joint Tenants with Right of Survivorship with the new spouse. If he or she predeceases that new spouse, the property will automatically pass to the new spouse, not to your children.

- JTWRS can cause unintended estate tax problems. For example, two brothers go in together to buy a lake house. For the sake of simplicity, they decide to title it JTWRS. Upon the death of the first brother, the property automatically passes to the surviving brother. The first brother's share of the property, however, is included in his estate and is subject to the estate tax without having the property available for sale to raise cash to pay those taxes.

- JTWRS leaves property open to the claims of creditors. Take the above example of the brothers who bought the lake house. Let's assume that one of them is sued and receives a judgment. Under the titling of joint tenancy, that property is subject to the claims of creditors. There could be a forced sale of the property, a situation that the brother (who is not a party to the lawsuit) does not have any control over. This same problem could arise if one of the brothers were to get a divorce.

Although JTWRS is one of the most common forms of property ownership in the United States, it is filled with so many pitfalls that anyone owning property under this method of ownership should *carefully* consider all of the ramifications.

Tenants in Common

If you own property as tenants in common, it could be listed as follows: "John Smith and Sue Smith, tenants in common."

The disposition of the property at your death is similar to what happens during your life. You have the absolute right to determine whom your share of the property will go to. If you do not specify who will receive that property in your will, or if you do not have a will, the property will pass according to the laws of the state where you reside.

ADVANTAGES OF TENANTS IN COMMON

- Tenants in common is an easy way to title property and does not require any special paperwork.

- You have absolute control of your share of the property. You can give it away, sell it, and using any method, you can transfer it to someone else. Selling your share of the property does not require the signature or permission of the other tenant(s).

- You are free to dispose of the property as you wish through your will.

DISADVANTAGES OF TENANTS IN COMMON

- You never have control of the entire property, only your portion of, or interest in, that property.

- You could easily end up with other joint tenants who are incompatible with you.

- Your interest will be included in your estate and, therefore, may be subject to estate taxes.

- The property would be subject to probate and the associated costs and time delays.

- As with fee simple property, if you were to become disabled, it would most likely require court intervention in order to handle the control issues, unless you have executed a power of attorney.

- It is difficult to dispose of property owned as tenants in common because a potential buyer is less likely to purchase an undivided interest in real estate. An interested buyer is likely to require a "discount" off the fair market value because of this type of ownership.

Community Property

Nine states have special laws related to what is called community property: Arizona, California, Idaho, Louisiana, Nevada, New Mexico, Texas, Washington, and Wisconsin. In these nine states, the way property is titled is often dictated by state law. The particulars vary by state, so you will need to refer to local professionals for advice if you reside in one of these states (see Appendix A).

All nine states observe some general rules regarding community property. Some property may be classified as *separate property*. For example, separate property could include property that you owned prior to a marriage or property that you inherited. If you want your separate property to remain separate, the title must be kept in your name and must never be changed. *Community property* is any property that was acquired after the date of marriage or any separate property that was sold or retitled. Community property operates much like property that is owned as tenants in common. You can designate whomever you want as a beneficiary to receive your half when you die. As with fee simple titling, your separate property can be disposed of in any manner you wish.

Community property states present special challenges for estate planning. For example, if you and your spouse buy a house together, it is considered community property. If you want your spouse to receive the home when you die, you must specifically state this in your will. Otherwise, the property will transfer according to the laws of the state where you live.

Other Methods of Property Ownership

Less common methods of ownership include life estates, revocable living trusts, and irrevocable trusts.

Life Estates

Life estates provide someone with the right to enjoy the use of certain property for as long as he or she lives. That person is required to maintain the property in good condition and otherwise has no control over the property. At the death of the life owner, the property passes to the beneficiaries of the life estate. This method of transferring and owning property may avoid probate and may provide estate tax benefits as well.

Revocable Living Trusts

As the name implies, with revocable living trusts you retain the right to revoke or dismantle the trust while you are alive and competent. One of the primary advantages of the living trust is that it avoids probate. It is particularly appropriate if you own property in more than one state or your job requires you to move from state to state. With a revocable living trust you avoid the possibility of having to rewrite your will when you move your residence to a new state. During your lifetime, you can serve as the trustee so that control over your assets is relatively trouble free. A disadvantage of this method of ownership is that it requires that you retitle all property in the name of the trust, which can be time-consuming and expensive. (For more about this important method of owning and controlling property, see Chapter 9.)

Irrevocable Trusts

Irrevocable trusts can be established during your lifetime (called inter vivos trusts) or at your death under your will (called testamentary trusts). The beneficiary of an irrevocable trust has no control over the property. That control has been vested in the *trustee*, who is required to follow the instructions written in the trust document. While this may sound restrictive, consider some of the benefits. This type of trust can be used to remove assets from your estate and therefore reduce estate taxes. It can also be used to hold assets for minor children, and in certain states, it can protect assets from creditors. (See Chapters 8 and 10 for more information about the benefits of irrevocable trusts.)

Payment on Death Accounts

Payment on Death (POD) accounts are a special way of owning savings accounts, checking accounts, brokerage accounts, and certificates of deposit. The account holder instructs the financial institution to write on the account a "payable on death" designation. The person(s) named will, by law, receive the account at your death. These accounts, therefore, do not go through probate. This method of titling property is not available in all states.

Beneficiary Designations

Beneficiary designations, while not being a form of title, are another way to avoid the costs, time, and public nature of probate. To accomplish this, you must simply name an individual or organization as the beneficiary of your life insurance, annuity, IRA, or company retirement plan.

Choosing the Best Methods of Ownership

As you can see, each of these methods of owning property has both pluses and minuses and must be carefully reviewed in the context of your overall estate plan. Often, the very best method for owning property is through trust. (Trusts will be discussed fully in Chapters 8, 9, and 10.)

If you still believe that all this estate planning is too complicated, you're not alone. Over 70 percent of adult Americans have no will. However, we believe that one simple case study should convince you of the necessity of carefully choosing how you hold your property and drawing up a will.

Case Study

Ray was a successful salesman, providing for his family with a six-figure income. The family owned a large home and sent their nine-year-old son, William, to a private school. Their lifestyle consumed all their income, so Ray had only a modest savings account. Ray's income was on the rise, so he assumed there would be plenty of opportunity to build up savings and save for retirement later. After all, he was only 42. Then the unthinkable happened. Ray died of a heart attack.

The results of Ray's lack of planning will likely be felt by his heirs for the rest of their lives. His estate consisted primarily of the home, which went to his wife, Sally, by title, and a $1 million life insurance policy. Unfortunately, Ray never bothered to write a will, and he had named his estate the beneficiary of his life insurance policy. Here's where the financial part of the tragedy begins. Because Ray died without a will, his assets were distributed according to state law.

In the state where Ray lived, the law specified that a surviving spouse receive one half of the deceased spouse's estate. The rest was to go to Ray's son, William. Since William was a minor, and since the inheritance was large ($500,000), the court appointed a legal conservator, who was unknown to the family, to watch over his inheritance. The conservator took the position that William's assets could not be used for his support. All support would have to come from Sally. Sally's after-tax income from the $500,000 and Social Security amounted to less than $30,000 per year. The current mortgage payment on their home was $18,000 per year, and William's private school tuition amounted to another $4,000 per year. Sally considered getting a job, but not having been employed in the last 10 years, the job market offered her little opportunity.

The situation left Sally on the verge of a nervous breakdown. There were very few solutions to her dilemma. She ended up selling the home, moving into an apartment, and taking a low-paying job to get extra money in order to keep William in the private school. But this is not the real tragedy here. The real tragedy happened to William. Under state law he was considered an adult when he turned 19. By that time his account had grown to over $800,000, which he received on his 19th birthday! Unfortunately, William knew nothing about managing money and was going through a stage where he had little use for his mother's advice.

Within a couple of years, the money was gone and the relationship between the mother and son was forever damaged. All of this could have been avoided if Ray had just taken the time to develop his estate plan.

Setting Estate Planning Goals

As you begin to develop your estate plan, it is important for you to prioritize your goals and objectives. Once this is accomplished, you can tailor your plan to meet your specific needs. The following list contains a number of common goals. Take some time to review these goals and rate them from 1 to 10, with 1 being the most important and 10 being the least important.

Goals of Your Estate Plan

_____ Providing for your spouse and children.

_____ Protecting assets from creditors.

_____ Making gifts to favorite charities, educational institutions, or religious organizations.

_____ Providing financial help for grandchildren.

_____ Protecting and preserving the family business.

_____ Protecting and preserving real estate holdings.

_____ Minimizing estate and income taxes.

_____ Minimizing administrative expenses and delays in settling your estate.

_____ Providing specific bequests for relatives or unrelated persons.

_____ Dividing assets fairly.

_____ Maintaining the privacy of your financial affairs.

You will want to refer to this checklist when you begin to implement your estate plan. It is particularly important to discuss your goals and objectives with the financial advisor you choose to help you with your planning. Take your goals along with you when you meet with your financial planner or the attorney who is advising you on your will.

In this chapter, you have learned the significance of writing a will and determining how your assets will be divided upon your death. Planning is necessary not only to ensure that your loved ones are left with property or investments to support them, but also to limit the amount of estate taxes that they will owe on your assets. In the next chapter, you will learn more about how to use a will to accomplish your estate planning goals.

CHAPTER 7

Where There's a *Will,* There's *Your* Way!

In the last chapter, you learned about the many potential pitfalls of dying without a will or of relying on property titles to transfer your property for you. A logical solution is a properly drafted Last Will and Testament (referred to hereafter as a "will"). In this chapter, we will discuss the basic structure of a will along with advice on making key decisions concerning guardians, trustees, executors, and trusts.

What Is a Will?

A will is a legal declaration giving instructions as to what person(s) or organization(s) is to receive your property after your death. This declaration names the executor or personal representative who will be responsible for settling your estate, the trustee(s) responsible for managing any trusts you have created, and the guardian(s) who will care for your minor children.

Types of Wills

The concept of wills dates back to British law in the mid 1500s. Before that time, when a commoner died, part of his property automatically reverted to royalty. The Parliament passed a law establishing the *Statute of Wills*, which allowed these commoners to leave all of their property to whomever they chose under certain rules and guidelines.

Today, there are many types of wills. While it may be helpful for you to know that many varieties exist, you should definitely avoid some of them.

Oral, or Nuncupative, Will

Although most states require that wills be in writing, a few states *do* allow oral wills. Oral wills are usually associated with deathbed situations when the testator (the person dying), in front of witnesses, states his or her final wishes. Typically at least three witnesses are required to be present during the testator's statement and the testator must die within a certain period of time. You should avoid this approach to estate planning, because not only are these wills easily contested but usually they are not well thought out.

Holographic Will

A holographic will is one that someone makes in his or her own handwriting and that is sometimes referred to as a homemade will. Only about 15 to 20 states allow holographic wills. Some states allow holographic wills only when the testator is a member of the armed services and is stationed outside the United States. You remember the old war movies in which an infantryman was about to go into a fierce battle and at the last minute hand scrolls a will leaving everything to his beloved mother or sweetheart. While this solution is better than the oral will, you should still avoid it.

Joint Will

A joint will is one document, usually between a husband and wife, in which it is declared that all property passes to the surviving spouse upon the death of the first spouse. The document further indicates where the property must go upon the death of the remaining spouse. While at first glance this might appear to be a simple and less expensive solution than each spouse having a separate will, it is not. Many states have taken the position that this is in reality a contract between the two parties. This could cause you to lose the benefit of the unlimited marital deduction, which could cause immediate taxation on a portion of your estate at the first spouse's death. Since avoiding this potential problem is tricky, your legal fees are likely to be *higher* than if you had separate wills prepared. The better solution is to have a separate will for both you and your spouse.

Simple Will

Between spouses this is sometimes referred to as an "I love you" will because it essentially says that you intend to leave everything to your surviving spouse. Obviously, simple wills are often not simple and are also used by unmarried people. The point of this type of will is for someone to indicate where his or her property will go when he or she dies. What is implied in the simple will is that your property distributions will be outright distributions and that your estate isn't large or complex enough to require tax and other financial planning. We have often found that, unfortunately, while the client believes this to be the case, more complex planning is in fact necessary.

Testamentary Trust Will

This type of will directs that a *portion* of your property, *all* of your property, or a portion of your property *under certain circumstances* go to a trust that has been established under your will. There may be many reasons for this type of planning, including reducing taxes, providing professional management for heirs, protecting your estate from creditors, and maintaining control over the final disposition of your property.

Advantages and Disadvantages of Wills

The bottom line is that almost everyone needs to have a will. While there are many advantages of having a will, there are also several disadvantages.

Advantages of Having a Will

- A will allows you to specifically direct who is going to receive your property at your death. If your will has been correctly drafted and signed, you can be confident that your wishes will be carried out. If you want specifically to prevent someone from receiving your property at your death, you can do so through your will (except that most states do not allow you to totally exclude your spouse).
- Your will can be used as a strategy for reducing estate taxes by employing the unlimited marital deduction, the credit shelter trust, and the charitable bequest, as well as an array of other strategies.
- Your will can establish a trust to manage assets for your adult or minor children. Since minor children cannot receive assets in their name, your will allows you to decide who will manage your children's assets, how those assets will be managed, and for how long the assets will be managed.
- Your will is the only way you can nominate who will be responsible for the care of your minor children.
- Your will can reduce certain costs of settling your estate. For example, you can direct that your executor or personal representative will serve without the need to post a bond.
- Through your will, you can leave money or property to your favorite charity, educational institution, or religious organization.

Disadvantages of Having a Will

- Property passing by way of your will must go through probate. As you read in Chapter 6, probate in some states can be both expensive and time-consuming.

- Wills are public documents. It is a requirement that your will be filed with the court when you die. You may feel that it is important that your financial affairs not be available for public inspection. There are actually Internet sites that display the wills of famous people (try www.welchgroup.com and click on Resource Center; then click on "Links"; then "Wills of Famous People"). If you find yourself wanting to put this book down and visit this Internet site, then you know exactly why some people want their financial affairs kept private. Remember, the onlookers may be more than curious. Some have ill intentions in mind.

- A will that is properly written and signed in one state will likely be valid in all states. However, how your will is *interpreted* can vary widely from state to state, possibly resulting in your wishes not being carried out to your satisfaction. You should focus on this situation if your job causes you to move periodically from one state to another or if you own property in more than one state. Say, for example, that you wrote a will while you lived in Georgia, but you have since moved to Louisiana and have not written a new will. You die while living in Louisiana. Will Georgia law or Louisiana law prevail? The result in such a situation could be a major disaster for your loved ones.

- Your will cannot provide for your care in the event that you become incapacitated or incompetent. This issue must be addressed through documents other than your will, such as a power of attorney or a revocable living trust. Your will may not control all your property. We have often seen instances in which people are confident that their affairs are in good order based on their wills, but then they discover that much of their property will pass outside of their will because of joint tenancy titles and beneficiary designations.

- Wills can be contested. It's not surprising that money can bring out the worst in people. This is particularly the case when someone dies and disgruntled heirs or others feel they had a right to some portion of the assets of the deceased. Often it doesn't matter whether there are valid grounds for the contest or not. Many times the rightful heirs would rather settle than risk an expensive and lengthy court battle.

We wish we could say that all your estate planning problems could be solved by rewriting your will. Unfortunately, while a properly drafted and executed will is an important part of your estate plan, many other issues must also be considered.

Many of the disadvantages of wills can be resolved by using a revocable living trust, which will be discussed in detail in Chapter 9. However, for now, let's discuss the essential elements of a well-crafted will. If you already have a will, use the following section as a way to review your will.

Intelligent Decisions Concerning Your Will's Basic Provisions

While there is no perfect formula for drafting a will, certain common provisions should be considered carefully.

Opening Declaration

Your opening declaration should make it clear that this document represents your Last Will and Testament and that it revokes all prior wills. Here's an example:

> I, James Dean, a resident of Hollywood, California, being of sound mind and disposing memory, do hereby make, publish, and declare this instrument as and for my Last Will and Testament and hereby expressly revoke any and all Wills, codicils, and other testamentary dispositions heretofore made by me.

Item 1. Payment of Debts and Funeral Expenses

This section allows your executor or personal representative to immediately proceed with paying off debts and funeral expenses.

> As soon as practical, I direct that my funeral expenses and all my enforceable, secured, or unsecured debts be paid in full, or according to the terms of any instrument evidencing such indebtedness, as my executor deems advisable.

This sounds simple and straightforward on the surface, but be careful. The above language excludes the payment of any *un*enforceable debt. Without such language, creditors from a prior bankruptcy may try to enforce a legally discharged debt from your estate. The language *"paid in full, or according to the language of any instrument"* gives your executor the option of keeping in place such debt arrangements as residential mortgages.

Item 2. Personal Items

Sometimes referred to as the "specific legacy" clause, this section is where you direct who will receive items of a personal nature, such as jewelry, furniture, clothing, automobiles, cash, and so on.

> I give all my tangible personal property and insurance thereon to my beloved wife, Beatrice Dean, if she survives me. Otherwise, I give said property in equal shares to my children who survive me and to the descendants, per stirpes, of any of my children who do not survive me.

"Insurance" in this section does not refer to life insurance. It refers to insurance proceeds that might be received owing to the destruction of property such as by fire or accident. For example, if your death was caused by a boating accident, your heirs would receive the property insurance proceeds, not the destroyed boat.

This is the most personal section of your will. If you have personal items that you want to go to certain people (called "general bequests"), include them in this section. For example, if you want your stamp collection to go to your son, you would indicate so by saying something like this:

> I hereby bequeath my stamp collection to go to my son, James Dean Jr.

You should note that unless you state otherwise, any debt owed on bequeathed property as well as the expense of moving it must be born by the legatee (the person receiving the gift). If you would like to leave a specific amount of money to individuals or charities, you would do so by saying something like this: *"I devise the sum of twenty-five thousand dollars to my sister, Jean S. Daily."* After paying your debts and distributing your personal property, the next $25,000 will go to your sister, *before* any other money is distributed to any other heirs (including your spouse).

Item 3. Residence(s)

If you are married, you will likely want your home to go to your spouse. This section is included assuming that you own your home in your name solely or under joint tenants in common. (See Chapter 6 for more details concerning how to title property.) Often, homes are owned between spouses as joint tenants with right of survivorship. If this is the case, your home will pass by title, not by your will.

> I devise to my wife, Beatrice Dean, if she survives me, all of my right, title, and interest in and to any residences which I own at the time of my death, subject to any mortgages or encumbrances thereon at the time of my death.

Note that in this case, the spouse was left the home, *including* the mortgage, which means the spouse is required to satisfy the mortgage by either continuing payments or paying it off. If your preference would be for the mortgage to be satisfied from proceeds of your estate, then your will would read *"free of mortgages or encumbrances."*

Item 4. Division of Residuary Estate

Residuary means "everything that is left." Everything that you have not already given away in your will is included in this section.

> I give all the rest, residue, and remainder of my estate to my wife, Beatrice Dean, if she survives me. If she does not survive me, my residue shall be divided equally between my children who survive me and to the descendants, per stirpes, of any of my children who predecease me.

Here you should give serious thought to what you would like to do with the balance of your estate. If you are married, do you want it to go outright to your spouse or would it be better to have it go into a trust for his or her benefit? Is your spouse capable of financial management or is management best left to a qualified trustee? You calculated your potential estate taxes in Chapter 3. Should a trust be used to reduce potential estate taxes? (How to best utilize trusts under your will will be covered in Chapter 8.) If you have minor children, you will need to make provisions here or in another section of your will to provide for trusts, trustees, and so on.

Item 5. Payment of Taxes

This section outlines how your estate and inheritance taxes will be paid. First, you should estimate the total amount of taxes that you are likely to owe (see Chapter 3). Then, you need to determine how they are to are to be paid. You have several options, including the following:

- *Statutory appointment.* In this case, each beneficiary would pay the taxes that his or her bequest generates. The language might read something like this: *"each beneficiary shall bear a pro rata portion of the estate and inheritance taxes due."*

- *Off the top.* This section would read something like this: *"all estate and inheritance taxes will be paid prior to any distributions from my estate to my heirs."* This has the effect of paying taxes before the residuary estate is distributed and before any *general bequest* is satisfied.

- *From your residuary estate.* Here you might say something like this: *"all estate and inheritance taxes will be paid from my residuary estate."* This means that those persons or organizations receiving general bequests from your personal property will do so free of any taxes. Your residuary beneficiary will bear the burden of taxes for your entire estate. Unlike the off-the-top method, this option could result in your residuary beneficiaries bearing a disproportionate share of the taxes if one group of beneficiaries is exempt from taxes while another group is not. Be careful to calculate what those taxes are likely to be, and be sure that there will be enough cash available to pay them. This can be a particular problem if the residuary estate consists primarily of property that is not liquid, such as real estate.

- *Paid from a general bequest.* Here you would say something like this: *"all estate and inheritance taxes to be paid from the general bequest to the American Cancer Foundation."* If a general bequest was a large portion of your estate, you might want to have your taxes paid from that bequest to make certain that other persons indicated in your will receive a share of your estate.

Item 6. In Terrorem Clause

If you specifically intend to exclude someone who would normally be included in your will, you would do so in this section. In almost all states, you cannot completely disinherit your spouse. This is not the case with children or other family members. Let's assume that you wish to disinherit your son David. If your will simply stated that your estate is to be equally divided among your children Dolly Dean, Debbie Dean, and James Dean Jr., David could contest the will, claiming he was left out as an oversight. This issue is resolved by specifically stating that he is to receive nothing from your estate: *"It is my full intention that my son David Dean receive no share or portion of my estate."* Some attorneys will take a different approach by specifying that the disinherited person is to receive $1. This indicates that you did not forget them, and that you did not think much of them. However, there may be a drawback to this practice. In one case a child received $1 from his parents' estate, but no one knew where the child was currently living. The executor had to spend a large amount of money tracking down the son so he could receive his $1!

Item 7. Minors Trusts

If you have minor children, this section will establish and outline how assets payable to them will be handled. You have two appropriate choices here:

- Have the assets paid to a custodial account. Here you might say something like this: *"should any part of my estate become payable to any person(s) under the age of twenty-one, then my executor shall pay such share to my spouse or my child's guardian as custodian under the Uniform Transfer to Minors Acts."* In our opinion, unless you expect it to be a very small amount of money, this approach is not advisable. Under the Uniform Transfer to Minors Act, your child would receive his or her inheritance at the age of majority for your state of residence (age 18 or 19 in most states). Most 19-year-olds are not prepared to handle money at such an early age. The following alternative is preferable.

- Have the assets paid to a trust. Here you would say: *"should any part of my estate become payable to any person(s) under the age of twenty-one, then my executor shall pay such share to a trust for the benefit of said person(s)."* You would then go on to outline the specific terms of the trust.

If you have children, even children who are no longer minors, this is one of the most important sections of your will and deserves considerable thought. First, imagine the worst possible scenario, that both you and your spouse die in a common accident. If you are like most people, if there is no surviving spouse, all assets are left to your children. The size of the estate is likely to be large, because in addition to your assets there may be life insurance proceeds payable on both you and your spouse. Your goal should be to make sure your children's needs are met without overwhelming them with money and possibly destroying their ambition and work ethic by providing them with too much money too soon. Remember, neither you nor your spouse will be there to impart your values to your children. You will be counting on your trust documents, your trustees, and your guardians (for minors) to do this for you.

It is our opinion that holding assets in trust until midadulthood is not such a bad thing. We typically recommend holding children's assets in trust until they turn 30 or 35, at which time we will disburse one-third of the trust assets. Final disbursements from the trust usually come five years later. The reasoning behind this strategy is simple. If you give a 21-year-old child a large sum, say $500,000, he or she has two choices: to spend it or to invest it. If the money is spent, it would likely be spent on something you would not approve of. If your child invests it, owing to a lack of investment experience, your child could well lose it. In most cases it is better to hold the assets in trust until your children are likely to have gained the maturity necessary to handle large sums of money.

Until that time, the trustee provides for the children's needs with income and, if needed, principal of the trust. This trust can be as flexible or as restrictive as you desire. For example, clients often include provisions allowing the trustee to make disbursements for the down payment on a home or to start a business. Because of the importance of education, clients almost always include provisions for covering all costs of advanced education, including college, graduate school, medical school, or law school. Certainly you will want your trustee to have the right to invade principal to cover the costs of any health issues.

Children who receive too much money too soon often develop a poor system of values. A trustee can never provide the caring guidance of a parent, but a well-drafted trust agreement can provide a guide for carrying out your wishes for your children.

Item 8. Executors

The position of executor is usually one of relatively limited duration, usually lasting six to twelve months but can last several years. Your executor is charged with the responsibility of settling your estate and distributing your assets to those people or organizations indicated in your will. The language in your document might read something like this: "*I hereby appoint my wife, Beatrice Dean, to serve as executor under this, my Last Will and Testament. In the event that she shall fail to qualify, die, or resign, then I appoint my brother, Robert Dean, as executor hereunder, or if he shall fail to qualify. . . .*"

One major decision you need to make is whether you should nominate a family member, a close friend, or a professional such as an attorney or a bank as your executor. Our preference is normally to choose a family member or friend. Such a person will often serve for no fee or a nominal fee and would retain an attorney or bank trust officer to do most of the work. If you nominate a professional or financial institution, there will be little control over fees that will be charged. We were involved in a case in which the estate representative (a bank) estimated total professional fees to be $450,000! This was a $10 million estate, but it was not a complicated one. To allow for the unexpected, you should list a succession of people to serve as your executor should your first choice be unable to serve because of his or her death, incapacity, or lack of desire. It is also a good idea to ask these people whether they are willing to serve *before* you make your will. If you are married, your spouse is normally a good choice as first executor. Be sure to include language indicating that your executor will serve without being required to post a bond: *"No executor hereunder shall be required to give bond or to file an inventory or accounting in any court."*

Item 9. Trustees

Choosing your trustee(s) will be among the most important decisions you will make with regard to your estate plan. These are the people charged with the responsibility for carrying out your wishes regarding management of your investments and other assets. They will often serve in this capacity for years or even decades. Ideally, for this role you would want to designate someone who has financial experience. A family member or trusted friend is often a good choice. Remember, the trustee has the option to hire professional investment managers to do the work. He or she could even hire a bank trust department to perform most of the duties normally associated with being a trustee. The advantage of using a family member as trustee is that he or she is in a position to negotiate fees and change investment managers as appropriate. This person will best understand the needs of your family members who are beneficiaries of your trust.

When deciding on trustee candidates, consider their age. One or both of your parents may have the wisdom you seek in a trustee, but they may not be around for the full term of the trust. Make sure that at least one or more of your trustees is young enough to survive the term of the trust. As with executors, you need to list a succession of trustees in your will. We usually ask clients to list at least three people. You can have people serve alone or as cotrustees.

Because trusts often last for years, we recommend that, after you have selected all the people you can think of as appropriate trustees, you nominate a corporate trustee. *Always* give someone the right to replace your corporate trustee with another corporate trustee. Typically we give this right to the majority of the beneficiaries. The language to remove a corporate trustee may read something like this: *"Any corporate trustee may be removed by a majority of the adult income beneficiaries and the guardians of any minor beneficiaries . . . to be replaced by a qualified trust company."* We had a case in which a young lady whose parents died, leaving her money in trust with a local bank, tried numerous times to contact her trust officer, but he would not return her calls. She sat in our office with tears of frustration as we reviewed her trust document. Her trust contained a clause that allowed her to move the account to another corporate trustee. We picked up the phone and left a message that if she did not receive a phone call from her trust officer in the next 10 minutes, we intended to move the account to another local bank. We got the call, and now she is regularly invited to meetings with her trust officer at the bank's executive dining room! The power to move your account creates a lot of incentive for a corporate trustee to provide good service.

WHEN AN INDIVIDUAL SERVES AS YOUR TRUSTEE

If you plan to have an individual (versus a professional or corporate representative) serve as your trustee, be sure to ask whether the person is willing to do so. In our experience, most people are flattered and will most likely agree to serve. However, being a trustee is a big responsibility and can be very demanding. Before someone agrees to serve as the trustee for your family, ask that person to read the following section of this book.

YOUR ROLE AS A TRUSTEE

It's an honor to have a friend or family member ask you to be a trustee. It means that that person holds you in high regard. Your first inclination may be to accept. However, before you do, you should consider the magnitude of the responsibilities involved. The following is a list of duties associated with being a trustee. Note that this list is not all-inclusive.

- *Read and understand the trust document.* As a trustee, you are a fiduciary and therefore liable for your actions. Ignorance is never an accepted excuse for mismanagement. Be sure to read the trust document *before* you agree to act as a trustee. If there are items that you do not understand, ask for clarification in writing.

- *Meet with the beneficiaries periodically.* You will need to spend time with the beneficiaries to understand their needs. Some beneficiaries can be quite difficult, and you must be emotionally prepared to deal with confrontational situations.

- *Keep detailed records under the assumption you will have to go to court and prove everything you have done.* You do this because, in fact, you may indeed have to go to court and prove everything you've done.

- *Manage the money.* You should first develop a written investment policy statement (IPS) based on the investment powers outlined in the trust document. Then the IPS would be used as the framework for ongoing investment management. For a downloadable IPS, go to the Resource Center at www.welchgroup.com; then click on "Links"; then "IPS — Download."

- *Carry out the trust policy.* In addition to investment management, trust documents typically call for the trustee to make many decisions requiring sound judgment. For example, the trust may allow the trustee to disperse money to a beneficiary "to maintain his or her accustomed lifestyle." You have to decide what is appropriate in a given situation. Do you buy the BMW the beneficiary wants, or is a Ford more reasonable?

- *Keep the beneficiaries and the grantor, if living, informed.* People hate surprises. The best solution is to maintain ongoing communication.

- *File the trust income tax return.* A trust is considered a separate tax entity and therefore a separate income tax return must be filed for it every year.

If you are asked to act as trustee by a friend or family member, you may find that you are being asked to serve without compensation. In some cases this is appropriate, but you should consider this carefully. It is possible that your role as trustee will last for many years, and it may take a great deal of time and work to do the job well. Decide whether you are willing to do this work for free.

If all of this sounds a bit overwhelming, realize that, as the trustee, you can hire professionals to do much of the work required. For example, you can hire a CPA to file the tax returns or a professional money manager to invest the assets. An attorney can assist you with interpretation of the trust agreement. Make sure the trust document allows you to hire and compensate other professionals. And remember that, even though you have hired a professional, you continue to remain responsible for everything related to the trust.

Acting as a trustee can be a very rewarding experience. It gives you the opportunity to be involved in a positive way in the lives of people you care about. At the same time, it is a tremendous responsibility and one that you should consider carefully before you accept.

Item 10. Trustee Powers

Under this section you will list the trustee's powers. This is usually several pages of boilerplate language provided by your attorney giving the trustee very broad powers regarding how your money can be invested and managed. You should read through this material to be sure that you agree with all the terms. You may find that it has been years since your attorney has read it!

This section will also outline how trust assets will be distributed for your adult and minor beneficiaries. Typical trust language provides that the beneficiary's primary benefit from the trust will be the income (interest and dividends) generated by the trust assets. Access to the "principal" of trust assets is either forbidden or available only under certain restricted circumstances. This language creates a classical conflict for the beneficiary, particularly in cases of second marriages.

By way of explanation, let's look at an example. A husband and wife each have children from a previous marriage. The husband wants to make sure that if he predeceases his wife, she will be financially secure for her lifetime. However, if he leaves his $3,000,000 estate to her outright, he's concerned that his children may end up receiving nothing from his estate. He decides to leave his estate to his wife in trust for her lifetime, with the remainder going to his children upon her death. The trust dictates that she will receive *all of the trust income* at least quarterly.

When the husband dies, the trustee must resolve the apparently opposing objectives of the surviving spouse and the deceased husband's children. The wife would like to maximize her income and requests that 100 percent of the assets be invested in bonds and other debt instruments. The current yield on such investments is approximately 5 percent, so she figures her income will be about $150,000 per year. The children want maximum growth and would like to see 100 percent of the assets invested in a diversified portfolio of stocks. Who said beneficiaries are reasonable people! If this were done, the income available for the spouse would be significantly reduced. The trustee is in an awkward position, because either possibility is likely to leave one party unhappy.

This same conflict arises even when a second marriage is not involved. You, too, will likely want your surviving spouse to have access to maximum income, and you will want to maximize estate growth for your children at your surviving spouse's death. The solution is to set up a *total return trust*. The concept is simple. In our earlier example, the husband's will would establish a trust that provides the wife with payments equal to a fixed percentage of the total value of the trust assets. These payments are not directly tied to the income that the trust investments generate. Rather, they represent a distribution based on the *total value* of the trust. This approach allows the trustee to invest the trust assets more aggressively and would satisfy the remainder beneficiaries while providing the wife with the income stream she needs. Because the market can (and does) fluctuate dramatically, it may make sense to tie the annual distributions to the trust account balance based on the average balance over several years. Another approach would be to have the trustee pay the wife a *fixed income* that would periodically be adjusted for inflation. In our example, the trust document could specify that the trustee would pay the wife $120,000 per year, which would be adjusted periodically for inflation.

The question of what is a proper payout rate will inevitably come up. The studies that we have reviewed indicate that 4 percent to 5 percent is a reasonable rate, assuming that a 40 percent to 60 percent allocation to stocks is used. For a more detailed review of how to implement this strategy, review the section on the Growth Strategy with a Safety Net® presented in Chapter 4.

Item 11. Guardians

If you have minor children, there can be no more important decision than who will care for your children in the event that you and your spouse die prematurely. Language in your will might read as follows: "*If my spouse predeceases me and I leave minor children, I appoint my sister, Jean S. Daily, as the guardian of the persons and property of said minor children. If she does not qualify to serve or for any reason fails to serve, then I appoint my brother, Robert Dean. The appointed guardian shall have custody of my minor children and shall serve without bond.*" We encourage you to think of people who have *values* similar to yours. In the case of guardians, you will definitely want to ask if persons you are considering would be willing to serve in this way, and you will want your will to list at least two successor guardians. Someone who agrees to take your children into his or her home should you die today may not be in a position to do so just a few short years from now.

In many cases, people have the guardian also serve as custodian of the children's assets. We believe these should be separate decisions. The person who is the best choice to raise your children may not be the best choice to handle their money. If you decide that these positions should be handled by different people, it is advisable to try to choose guardians and trustees who would likely work well together. You should consider giving the trustee broad discretion regarding use of children's assets for their benefit. For example, if you have three minor children, you may want the trustee to have the ability to provide the guardian funds to add on to their home or to help pay the costs of family vacations.

Item 12. Simultaneous Death Clause

If you and a devisee (i.e., spouse) are killed in a common accident, this section provides instruction as to who is presumed to have died first for the purpose of settling your estate and for the purpose of estate tax planning. The language can be fairly broad: "*If my spouse does not survive me by a period of six (6) months, then my spouse shall be deemed to have predeceased me for the purpose of this Will.*" Your spouse's will would contain similar language. Although this may appear to create a contradiction, it simply allows each separate estate to be carried out as each person had planned.

Item 13. Perpetuities Clause

The notion of leaving a trust that will perpetuate for many generations of your family is intriguing, but it is not permitted under the laws of many states. This clause prevents the adverse tax consequences from happening by distributing trust assets just prior to the time the law would be violated. Typical language might read as follows: "*Notwithstanding anything to the contrary, if any future event shall postpone the vesting of any interest created by this Will beyond the period permitted by law, then at the expiration of such period, the property in each such trust shall immediately be distributed to the primary income beneficiary or beneficiaries of that trust."*

Item 14. Spendthrift Provision

Some beneficiaries don't want their money in trust; they want it *now*. What's to prevent them from using their trust as collateral for a loan? The spendthrift provision, of course! It might read something like this: *"To the extent permitted by law, the interest of any beneficiary in principal or income of any trust under this Will shall not be subject to assignment, alienation, pledge, attachment, or to the claims of creditors of such beneficiary."*

Executing Your Will

After having read through many pages of legalese, you may think that executing your will refers to taking out your gun and filling the document full of holes! Nonetheless, executing your will refers to the formal legal procedure of signing your will. The signing ceremony should be witnessed by two or three witnesses, depending on your state laws. These witnesses should not be potential beneficiaries in your will. You will be required to state aloud something to this effect: "I declare that this is my Last Will and Testament. I have read it, and I understand it." The witnesses must then watch you sign it. Then they also must sign it. To avoid having to track down the witnesses when you die, you should add a *self-proving affidavit*. This is an attached page that you and your witnesses again sign, which is then notarized.

To avoid confusion, you should sign only one original of your will. You should have several unsigned or signed copies available for easy reference, and you should give one to your attorney and keep one in a readily accessible location for yourself. Today, some people are videotaping the will-signing ceremony. Not only does this allow you to provide additional "proof" of the signing of your will, but it also allows you to personalize it with comments to family members. Videotaping your will-signing ceremony should be done with care and caution. It may be easier to contest a videotaped will signing, and you will want to follow appropriate signing procedures to ensure the validity of your will.

Where to Store Your Will

It should be obvious that your will needs to be stored in a safe place. Many people choose to store their wills in a bank safe deposit box. Before you do so, you will need to do a little homework. Many states require that a person's safe deposit box be "sealed" upon that person's death. Because this can cause long delays in the probate process, in such a case a safe deposit box should not be used for this purpose. Ask your banker and double-check with your estate planning attorney. If this is not a problem in your state, be sure your personal representative and several family members know where your safe deposit box is located *and* where you keep the key.

Our second choice for your original will would be a secure location at your office or at your attorney's office. Be sure to quiz your attorney about his or her procedures for storing clients' wills. You'll find that some use fireproof safes and detailed filing records, whereas others do little more than put them in a desk drawer. Avoid the latter. If you lose your will or if it is destroyed, be sure to have it replaced as soon as possible. You can take one of your copies to your attorney to be redrafted. With today's technology, your attorney will likely maintain a copy on his or her word processor, or he or she may be able to scan it into a computer.

Other Important Documents

Power of Attorney

A *power of attorney* is a vital document that *every* adult should have. This document allows you to appoint another person as your "attorney-in-fact," which gives that person the authority to act on your behalf in legal matters should you not have the capacity to do so. A power of attorney can be drafted in several forms. The *springing power of attorney* becomes effective only under certain conditions, usually owing to your incapacity. One significant disadvantage of the springing power of attorney is that, when someone attempts to use it on your behalf, that person may be required to prove that you are actually incompetent. This can create both inconvenience and significant delays. With a *general power of attorney*, you give your attorney-in-fact the authority to act on your behalf *at any time*. However, if you become incapacitated, this document is null and void. To solve this problem, you can draft a *general and durable power of attorney*, which allows your attorney-in-fact to continue acting on your behalf in the event of your incapacity. Finally, there is the *limited power of attorney*, which allows someone to act on your behalf only under very specific circumstances, such as giving your attorney-in-fact the authority to sign a specific legal agreement while you are out of the country.

First, you need to decide which power of attorney is most appropriate for your circumstances. Then you need to decide whom you would appoint as your attorney-in-fact. If you are married, a natural choice might be your spouse. But you should also have at least one successor attorney-in-fact. Note that if you die, any and all power of attorney documents you have executed become null and void. You should also redraft this document every four to five years. Many institutions such as banks are reluctant to accept a power of attorney document that is older than that. These are powerful legal instruments, and care should be taken to keep up with who has possession of such documents.

Living Wills, Advanced Medical Directives, and Health Care Powers

Living wills, advanced medical directives, and *health care powers* (also referred to as a *durable power of attorney for health care* or *health care proxy*) are documents that indicate to others the level of care you desire should you become severely incapacitated. Many states have passed living will legislation that allows you to sign a document requesting that your life not be maintained on life support systems. With medical technology as advanced as it is, someone who is brain-dead can be kept alive for a long time. Some physicians and hospitals are reluctant to take a patient off life support without that person's express permission. As you might imagine, it's difficult to give your approval while you are in a coma. The result can easily be that all of your life savings and assets are used to keep you alive. If this is not your intention, then consider signing a living will.

The living will covers only life support system issues. To give directions regarding quality-of-life issues, you will need a health care power. With a health care power, you appoint someone to make medical decisions on your behalf if you are unable to do so. These kinds of decisions are broad in scope and could include such directives as discontinuing feeding tubes or refusing operations.

Once you have signed these documents, be sure to let the appropriate people know that you have done so and where these documents are kept. As with your power of attorney, these documents should be resigned every four to five years to indicate that they still represent your wishes.

To download your state's living will fill-in-the blank form, go to the Resource Center at www.welchgroup.com; click on "Links"; then click on "Living Wills—State by State."

Letter of Instruction

Although it is not a legal document, a *letter of instruction* is an important part of your estate plan. Its purpose is to make life easier for the loved ones you leave behind. Important elements of your letter of instruction include the following:

- *Instructions and contact list.* The list of people to contact typically includes your professional advisors, such as your attorney or financial advisor, but it could also include lifelong friends and relatives you wish to be contacted. Use Worksheet 7.1 as an attachment to the letter to help you list your professional advisors and others you wish to be contacted.

- *Location of important documents.* Sadly, family members often have to search, sometimes in vain, for important papers and documents requested by various entities and government agencies soon after the death of a family member. By completing this checklist now, you can save your family untold hours of searching and anxiety. It will assist them in locating papers and items you probably had no idea they needed. You may need to contact some

WORKSHEET 7.1 Letter of Instruction, Attachment A: Persons to Be Notified at Your Death

Provide the following details for each person to be notified at your death.

Relationship codes: Use these to identify each person. Include *all* codes that apply. For example, if the same individual provides the client with legal, tax, and accounting advice, then enter 3,4, *and* 5.

1 Friend	6 Banking advisor
2 Relative	7 Investment advisor
3 Legal advisor	8 Insurance advisor
4 Tax advisor	9 Financial advisor
5 Accounting advisor	10 Other

For relationship codes 7 and 8, use the following letter codes to provide more detail about the type of advice offered. For example, if the same insurance agent provides you with life and health coverage, then enter I and J as the insurance codes for the advisor.

Investment Codes		Insurance Codes	
A Stocks	E Options	I Life	L Property & Casualty
B Bonds	F Real Estate	J Health	M All Coverages
C Mutual Funds	G General	K Disability	
D Commodities	H Other		

Name	Firm	Address	Telephone	Relationship Codes
1.				
2.				
3.				
4.				
5.				
6.				
8.				
9.				
10.				
11.				
12.				
13.				
14.				
15.				
16.				
17.				
18.				
19.				
20.				

government offices to locate some items, and you may need to make lists of other assets. Include a list that gives the location of all your important documents, papers, insurance policies, and the like. Go ahead—make the lives of your loved ones easier. They'll say a special prayer for you. To assist you in completing this task, use Worksheet 7.2.

- *Funeral instructions.* Although the idea of planning your own funeral may be distasteful, it will save your family time, money, and heartache. Funerals can be quite expensive, and your grieving family may not be in the best frame of mind to make appropriate decisions. By taking the time to convey your wishes now, you will provide your loved ones with invaluable help at what is often a stressful time in their lives. Use Worksheet 7.3 to assist you with this matter.

- *Personal messages.* The letter of instruction is a perfect place to leave messages of a personal nature to your family members.

Working with Your Attorney

When it comes to estate planning, attorneys are worth their weight in gold. Speaking of gold, attorneys can be expensive! What they have to sell is their time and expertise. The more organized you are *before* you meet with them, the smaller your bill will be. In fact, being prepared can save you a *lot* of money. To prepare for your first meeting you should prepare or bring the following:

- Copies and original(s) of your current wills.

- A complete list of your assets and liabilities. You should have developed this list in Chapter 3. Use Worksheet 3.3. Do not rely on your memory regarding whose name your property is in. You should confirm this by checking the actual titles.

- All of your life insurance policies. For group life insurance, bring the certificate if available. Be sure to confirm the beneficiary and owner of each policy.

- For your real estate, bring your deed(s). In some cases the deeds need to be transferred to another person, such as your spouse, in order to equalize your estates and reduce taxes.

- Copies of all notes and mortgages that you owe or that are owed to you.

- Copies of any trust agreements in which you are a grantor or beneficiary or in which you have a power of appointment.

- Employee benefits summary, including retirement plans, employee death benefits, stock purchase plans, deferred compensation agreements, and incentive stock options.

- Information regarding any business interest you have.

WORKSHEET 7.2 Letter of Instruction, Attachment B: Essential Document Locator

Date_____

We will list four possible locations. Each asset should be (or should be placed) in one of these areas. Some areas have more than one location. For example, if your will is at your home in your safe, you would circle "B" and write "1." Be sure to note each location of an item if there is more than one.

Locations

A. Safe deposit box located at_____Bank, box#_____

B. Residence: (1) Safe   (2) File Cabinet   (3) Desk

   (4) Other:

C. Business office: (1) Safe   (2) File Cabinet   (3) Desk

   (4) Other:

D. Personal handbook, which is located_____

E. With attorney: Name_____Phone_____

F. Other:

G. I do not have one of these.

Bank Records							
List of all savings/checking accounts	A	B__	C__	D	E	F	G
Bank statements	A	B__	C__	D	E	F	G
Cancelled checks	A	B__	C__	D	E	F	G
Checkbooks	A	B__	C__	D	E	F	G
Certificates of deposit	A	B__	C__	D	E	F	G
Savings passbooks	A	B__	C__	D	E	F	G
Insurance Policies							
Property and casualty	A	B__	C__	D	E	F	G
Health	A	B__	C__	D	E	F	G
Life, individual	A	B__	C__	D	E	F	G
Life, group	A	B__	C__	D	E	F	G
Other insurances	A	B__	C__	D	E	F	G
Other death benefits	A	B__	C__	D	E	F	G
Investments							
Bonds and list of bonds owned	A	B__	C__	D	E	F	G
Brokerage account records	A	B__	C__	D	E	F	G
Mutual fund records	A	B__	C__	D	E	F	G
Partnership agreements	A	B__	C__	D	E	F	G
List of partnerships	A	B__	C__	D	E	F	G
Record of securities	A	B__	C__	D	E	F	G
Stock certificates	A	B__	C__	D	E	F	G
Stock option plans	A	B__	C__	D	E	F	G
T-bills	A	B__	C__	D	E	F	G
Children's Assets							
Savings accounts	A	B__	C__	D	E	F	G
Brokerage accounts	A	B__	C__	D	E	F	G
Mutual fund records	A	B__	C__	D	E	F	G
Prepaid college records	A	B__	C__	D	E	F	G
Trust/custodial account records	A	B__	C__	D	E	F	G

WORKSHEET 7.2 (*Continued*)

Real Estate

Titles and deeds	A	B__	C__	D	E	F	G
Title Insurance policies	A	B__	C__	D	E	F	G
Mortgages and notes	A	B__	C__	D	E	F	G
Termite bond	A	B__	C__	D	E	F	G
Rental property records	A	B__	C__	D	E	F	G

Retirement plans

Annuity contracts	A	B__	C__	D	E	F	G
Corporate plans	A	B__	C__	D	E	F	G
IRA documents	A	B__	C__	D	E	F	G
401 (k) plans	A	B__	C__	D	E	F	G
Pension/profit sharing plans	A	B__	C__	D	E	F	G
Other:	A	B__	C__	D	E	F	G
Beneficiary designations	A	B__	C__	D	E	F	G

Other important records

Wills	A	B__	C__	D	E	F	G
Trust documents	A	B__	C__	D	E	F	G
Auto ownership records	A	B__	C__	D	E	F	G
Other vehicle ownership records	A	B__	C__	D	E	F	G
Safe combinations	A	B__	C__	D	E	F	G
Safety deposit box key	A	B__	C__	D	E	F	G
Passports	A	B__	C__	D	E	F	G
Birth certificates	A	B__	C__	D	E	F	G
Adoption papers	A	B__	C__	D	E	F	G
Marriage certificate	A	B__	C__	D	E	F	G
Divorce/Separation papers	A	B__	C__	D	E	F	G
Military discharge papers	A	B__	C__	D	E	F	G
Tax returns	A	B__	C__	D	E	F	G
Names/addresses of family/friends	A	B__	C__	D	E	F	G
List of professional/fraternal orgs	A	B__	C__	D	E	F	G
List of credit cards w/addr/tel.nos.	A	B__	C__	D	E	F	G
Other:	A	B__	C__	D	E	F	G

- Copy of your most recent federal and state income tax returns.
- Location and list of general contents of your safe deposit box.
- Lists of advisors with whom you currently work (see Worksheet 7.1).

Next you will want to compile the personal information that your attorney will need about you and your family members:

- For you, your children, and anyone who is a potential beneficiary under your will, list full name, date of birth, and Social Security number. You should let your attorney know whether any of your children are adopted.
- List any prior marriages and any children by a prior marriage. Include any support payments for which you are obligated or of which you are the recipient.

WORKSHEET 7.3 Letter of Instruction, Attachment C: Last Wishes and Memorial Planning

Funeral home desired (name, address, phone):

_____

_____

Have funeral arrangements been prearranged?

Yes   No   With whom? _____

Name, number, and location of cemetery plot (if one is owned):

_____

_____

Do you wish to be cremated?

Yes   No

Notify: _____   Phone: _____

Are you donating your body or any organs to medical science?   Yes   No

Institution to be notified: _____

_____

Instructions concerning the funeral service (open/closed casket, songs, type of burial):

_____

_____

_____

_____

Donations in your memory should be sent to what organizations?

_____

_____

_____

Clergy to officiate:

Name: _____   Phone: _____

Casket bearers:

Name: _____   Phone: _____

Name: _____   Phone: _____

Name: _____   Phone: _____

Name: _____   Phone: _____

Name: _____   Phone: _____

Name: _____   Phone: _____

- Describe any health issues regarding you or your family members. For example, if your child is physically or mentally challenged, the attorney will want to discuss possible special trust arrangements, called a Special Needs Trust, to care for that child should you die prematurely.

- Provide any appropriate information regarding your parents. Do you expect to ever be required to provide financial support? What do you expect to inherit from them?

The balance of the information your attorney will need relates to the key provisions you want to include in your will. This is the section over which most people waste a lot of their attorney's time (and their money!) belaboring who gets the money and who gets the kids. Impress your attorney by resolving these issues ahead of time. If your attorney brings up an issue you cannot resolve immediately, make a note and move on to the next issue. Resolve the issue at home, and then give your attorney a call or send an email. Remember, attorneys often charge $150 to $900 per hour!

We have discussed many of the key will provisions earlier in this chapter, so you should already have had a chance to give them some thought. Here's a rundown:

- *Personal property.* Whom do you want your items of personal property to go to? If you are married, most often the personal property is left outright to your spouse.

- *General bequests.* You can leave specific personal items, money, or real property to someone through a general bequest.

- *Disinheritances.* If there is someone you intend to disinherit, be sure to let your attorney know.

- *Your residence(s).* The home often passes by title. Remember joint tenants with right of survivorship? If you own your home, you need to decide whom you want to leave it to. If you are married, your spouse may be the obvious choice.

- *Residue.* Residue refers to what's left after giving away your personal property and home. Whom do you want the residue to go to? Do you want that person to receive it outright, or do you feel that he or she should receive it in trust?

- *Executors or personal representatives.* The personal representative is the person responsible for settling your estate. In addition to choosing a personal representative, you will also need at least one and preferably two successors.

- *Trustees.* The trustee(s) will manage your assets for your beneficiaries. Again, you should have one or two successors, and the final choice should be a corporate trustee. You should include language that allows the beneficiaries of your trust to replace a corporate trustee with another corporate trustee. This provides a procedure for your beneficiaries to find a trustee with whom they are compatible.

- *Guardians.* For minor children, you will need to name guardians for their care. This can be one of the most difficult decisions that couples make. Be sure to name as many successor guardians as you think appropriate (the more, the better). Remember, the guardian who will raise your children does not have to be the same person who will manage your assets for the benefit of your children. And in many cases, it's best that the guardian not be the trustee. You should decide this before you meet with your attorney.

- *Trusts.* Your attorney will discuss with you the advisability of setting up trusts. If you do plan to have a trust for your children, you should decide how you want the trust income to be distributed, whether you want to empower your trustee with the right to make principal distributions, and under what circumstances and at what age(s) you want the trust dissolved.

- *Charitable donations.* Do you want to leave any of your estate to charities, religious organizations, or educational institutions? If so, let your attorney know so that he or she can suggest the most advantageous strategies (see Chapter 12).

Before you begin working with an attorney, you should discuss fees. Most attorneys charge an hourly rate, although some prefer a set fee arrangement. Those who charge hourly should be able to give you a reasonable estimate of what your fee will be. Avoid attorneys who do not produce itemized bills. Such attorneys are likely to be disorganized, and when they have to remember how much time they have on your case, you could end up being overcharged. Once the attorney gives you an estimate of your fee, require him or her to notify you immediately if it appears that your actual fee will exceed the estimate. You should request fee estimates in writing.

When to Review Your Estate Plan

Life has a way of changing rapidly, causing yesterday's well-devised estate plan to become outdated. When any of the following events occur in your life, you should review your plan immediately.

- *Marriages.* If you marry, you will need to change your will, among other things. The marriage of your children might also cause you to consider changes.

- *Births.* If you have a child, you should review your will and other documents. Most wills provide that all children are automatically included whether or not they are specifically named in the will. For sentimental reasons, many parents want each child listed by name. Some situations—such as a child with special needs—may call for unique attention. Also, the birth of a grandchild may cause you to make additional provisions in your plan. You may want to make a general bequest to pay for a prefunded college education plan.

- *Divorces.* If you get divorced, you will need to rewrite your will. Virtually all states nullify an ex-spouse's rights under a will. But there are many other considerations, including removal of your ex-spouse as executor and trustee, as well as removing your ex-spouse as the beneficiary of your life insurance, retirement plans, and other employee benefit plans.

- *Inheritances.* If you or a family member inherits a large sum of money, you may want to change your plan.

- *Deaths.* If a spouse or child dies, you need to review and consider changing your plan. You will need to do likewise if someone designated as executor, guardian, or trustee dies.

- *Career changes.* A simple change of career may necessitate changes to your plan. For example, your new job may offer substantially more or less life insurance. If you have business interests that change significantly, your plan should again be reviewed.

- *Moves out of state.* As we have discussed before, the laws of different states can vary widely, resulting in undesirable interpretations of your will.

- *Changes to the tax law.* Congress seems compelled to make significant changes in the law every couple of years. This often results not in better laws but busier lawyers, accountants, and financial advisors. For example, in 1913, the income tax law was a total of 14 pages. Today, the law has expanded to more than 10,000 pages including more than 16,000 changes in code subsections over the past 28 years! Is it any wonder that taxpayers are confused and frustrated?

- *Changes in estate values.* If the value of your estate rises or falls significantly, you should review your estate plan. It is a good idea to update your estate net worth statement every year (see Chapter 3).

These are just some of the major events that should prompt you to review your estate plan. Even if you feel your facts have not changed at all, you should review your estate plan every three to five years at the very least. If you do decide that changes are appropriate, then you have two choices. For relatively minor changes, you can have your attorney draw a codicil to your existing will. A codicil is, in effect, an amendment to a specific section or item in your will. The codicil must be witnessed using the same procedure as your will was. Your other alternative is to rewrite your entire will. Although this may seem to be an unnecessary complication, many attorneys prefer this method because it reduces the chance of overlooking conflicting language and instructions in your will. You can imagine the potential for trouble if over the years you add several codicils. Often your attorney will maintain a copy of your will in his or her word processor so that the cost of redoing it is not significantly different from drawing a codicil. If you do rewrite your will, be sure to destroy your old original(s) and all copies.

Tip

If you have adult children, be sure that they have executed appropriate wills. If an adult child dies without a will, the surviving parent(s) will often be drawn into the complications of the situation because of inheriting property under intestate laws or simply by virtue of needing to help straighten the mess out. They should also have a durable power of attorney (for incapacity) and consider a living will or advance directive for health care.

In this chapter you have learned how important it is to understand the impact of your decisions about the disposal of your property and assets upon your death. We have discussed the need for carefully planning how you want to own property and to whom you want to leave it. You should also remember that writing a will is not a once-in-a-lifetime event. Rather, you should review your will every three to five years or more frequently if major life events have occurred.

In the next chapter you will learn about the various types of trusts that can be used to protect your property and help you leave it in the most practical ways from an estate and tax viewpoint.

CHAPTER 8

Using Trusts in Your Estate Plan

In Chapter 7, we reviewed the key elements that should be considered in all wills. At what point should you consider more complex estate planning? Additional planning is appropriate if you feel it is desirable to maintain some control over your property after you die. In this situation, establishing one or more trusts under your will may be advisable. Also, if you are married and the total of your and your spouse's estates (including life insurance death benefits) exceeds the *applicable exclusion amount*, you need to consider a more complex will. As you recall from the last chapter, two important tax strategies may be available to you.

The first strategy, available only if you are married to a U.S. citizen, is called the *unlimited marital deduction* (or, simply, the marital deduction). Under federal tax laws, you may give an unlimited amount of assets to your spouse without incurring gift or estate taxes. These gifts can be made during your lifetime or at your death. This means that Bill Gates, reportedly one of the richest people in the world, could give or leave his entire fortune to his wife and she would not owe a dime of federal estate taxes. However, when she dies, taxes would be due. We discuss strategies associated with the marital deduction later in this chapter.

The second strategy relates to the *applicable exclusion amount*. This section of the law allows you to give a certain amount of your assets to someone other than your spouse, either during your lifetime or at your death, free of federal gift or estate taxes. This "other" amount can be a trust called the *credit shelter trust*.

The Credit Shelter Trust Will

The purpose of the credit shelter trust will is to take advantage of the *applicable exclusion amount* and thus reduce the estate taxes that will be due when you and your spouse both have died. Your credit shelter trust will can be set up for the specific purpose of benefiting your spouse and/or anyone else you desire. For example, for 2011 and 2012 you could avoid federal estate taxes on up to $5,000,000 by placing that amount in your credit shelter trust as directed by your will. (See Chapter 3, Table 3.1). Both you and your spouse can *each* use this exclusion, so if you plan well, the two of you could have combined estates of up to $10,000,000 in 2011 and owe no federal estate taxes. The applicable *gift tax* exclusion amount is $5,000,000. Oddly, the 2010 tax law is scheduled to sunset in 2013 and revert back to pre-Tax Relief Act–2001 tax law for estate ($1,000,000) and gift ($1,000,000) taxes unless legislation is enacted prior to that time, which is what we anticipate. As a result, this is partially a use-it-or-lose-it proposition, so it's important to plan appropriately. A case study that shows both an ineffective plan and an effective plan is presented in the following section.

Case Study

It is the year 2011. Frank and Sally are married and have one child, Jan. Their combined estates equal $10,000,000. They remember from an estate-planning seminar they attended that joint property is an unwise way to own assets in the context of a large estate (with the uncertain future of portability provisions in the law), and that they should equalize their assets as much as possible. They have divided their assets so that they each own $5,000,000 in their separate names. They currently have simple wills in which they leave all their assets to each other upon their death. Their current tax situation is as follows:

Possibly Ineffective Estate Plan
Frank Has a Simple Will and Dies Leaving an Estate
of $5,000,000 Outright to Sally[1]

Frank's gross estate	$5,000,000
Less unlimited marital deduction	−$5,000,000
Taxable estate	$0
Estate tax at Frank's death	$0
Assets passing to Sally	$5,000,000

Sally's Gross Estate:

Sally's separate estate	$5,000,000
Received from Frank's estate	+$5,000,000
	$10,000,000

[1] Results may change dramatically post-2012 depending on several legislative factors.

Tentative Tax Calculation at Sally's Death

Federal tax on $10,000,000 (per Table 3.2)	$3,480,800
Less unified credit (per Table 3.3)	−$1,730,800
Estate tax at Sally's death	$1,750,000
Net estate available for heirs	$8,250,000

If Frank and Sally both die in a year that has portability as an option, and if all the requirements for portability are met at both Frank's death and Sally's subsequent death, the estate tax due at Sally's death can be avoided if the proper steps are taken at Frank's death to invoke portability. If either Frank or Sally die in a year in which portability is not available (currently after December 31, 2012), or if all the requirements for portability are not otherwise met, taxes would be due. Although $8,250,000 is a large sum of money, consider using a credit shelter trust will to provide certainty for a more tax efficient outcome, as follows.

Effective Estate Plan

Frank Has a Credit Shelter Trust Will and Dies in 2011
with an Estate of $5,000,000[1]

Frank's gross estate	$5,000,000
Assets passing directly to Sally	−$0
Assets passing to credit shelter trust	−$5,000,000
Taxable estate	$5,000,000
Estate tax	$1,730,800
Less unified credit	−$1,730,800
Net tax at Frank's death	$0
Sally's own separate estate	$5,000,000
Frank's assets passing directly to Sally	$0
Sally's gross estate	$5,000,000
Less unlimited marital deduction	−$0
Sally's taxable estate	$5,000,000
Tentative tax calculation on Sally's death	$1,730,800
Less unified credit	−$1,730,800
Estate tax at Sally's death	$0
Net estate available to heirs	$10,000,000

[1]Results may change dramatically post-2012 depending on several legislative factors.

By utilizing a credit shelter trust will, we were able to eliminate Frank and Sally's federal estate taxes and preserve the maximum amount of assets for their daughter Jan saving some $1,750,000. For a graphic description of the simple will versus the credit shelter trust will, see Figures 8.1 and 8.2. The results of these examples may differ dramatically in 2013 when the applicable exclusion amount is reduced to $1,000,000. Even without a Credit Shelter Trust the tax savings may be achieved by use of portability added in the 2010 Tax Relief Act for 2011 and 2012. Portability would require filing with the IRS an Estate Tax Return. In addition, this portability benefit could be lost if the surviving

Phase I: Frank Dies in 2011[1]

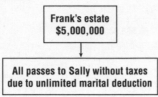

Phase II: Sally Inherits, Then Dies Later in 2011

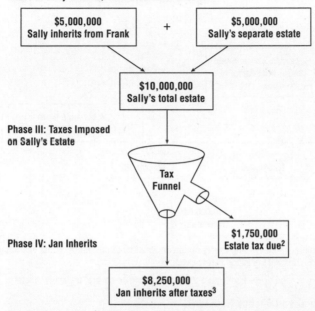

Phase III: Taxes Imposed on Sally's Estate

Phase IV: Jan Inherits

[1]Results may change dramatically post-2012 depending on several legislative factors.
[2]If 'portability' is invoked at Frank's earlier death and the requirements for portability are met at Sally's subsequent death, then there would be no tax.
[3]Jan could inherit $10,000,000 if the portability feature of the 2010 Tax Relief Act has been fully implemented.

FIGURE 8.1 Simple Will

spouse remarried. Rarely are the facts this straightforward, however. Usually, you must shift assets from one spouse to another. Some assets are easy to move, and other assets may be impossible to move. However, if done correctly, you can achieve dramatic tax savings. You can also meet other goals including providing professional management of assets and protecting your assets from the potential future creditors of your surviving spouse. Note that the credit shelter trust will often is structured to provide your surviving spouse with all the income from the trust as well as the principal for certain specific reasons. Legally, these reasons are referred to as *ascertainable standards* and include distributions for health, maintenance, education, and support. This definition is sufficiently broad to cover most reasonable requests for additional money. In

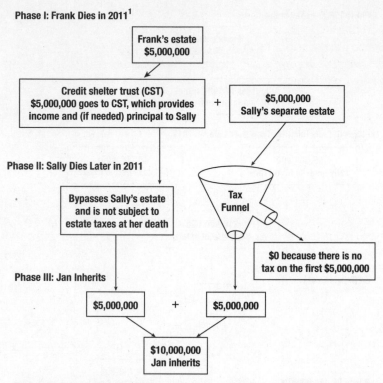

FIGURE 8.2 Credit Shelter Trust Will

addition, the law permits what is referred to as the "five and five power." If you choose to include this language in your trust it would permit your spouse to take a distribution from the trust each year equal to five percent of its total value or $5,000, whichever is *greater*. Your surviving spouse can also serve as the trustee or cotrustee of the trust.

In working with clients, we sometimes recommend a provision that we call the *remarriage provision*. Some clients are primarily concerned with their surviving spouse's income needs only as long as he or she remains unmarried. If the surviving spouse remarries, the clients would prefer that the assets from their credit shelter trust benefit their children or some other beneficiary. To resolve this issue, a provision is included that states that if the surviving spouse remarries, his or her benefits under the credit shelter trust shall cease. Several years ago, we observed an interesting twist involving this remarriage provision. In this particular case, the surviving spouse remarried, thus forfeiting her interest in her deceased husband's credit shelter trust. Her second marriage failed within two months. Instead of getting a divorce, she got an annulment, which in effect revived her status as a surviving spouse, as well as her interest in the credit shelter trust.

Another provision to consider as part of your credit shelter trust will is the *income sprinkling provision*. This provision allows the trustee to pay trust income to trust beneficiaries *other* than the surviving spouse, typically the children. Often, the assets left to the surviving spouse outside of the credit shelter trust, when added to the surviving spouse's own assets, are expected to be more than sufficient for his or her lifestyle needs. In these cases, if you *require* the credit shelter trust to pay the surviving spouse all of the trust income, you will effectively increase the estate taxes paid by the surviving spouse's estate and reduce the inheritance received by your heirs. This is because your surviving spouse, not needing the trust income, will stack it up in his or her estate, and it will only be taxed later. Not only is the income taxed, but the *growth* on the income is taxed as well. This sprinkling provision can be an effective tool that allows your trustee to distribute income to your family members who have the greatest needs. Note that if this sprinkling provision is used, your spouse can be a cotrustee but cannot be a sole trustee.

Disclaimers

A *disclaimer* is the refusal to accept property that has been given to you either by gift or through someone's will. It may sound strange that anyone would refuse an inheritance, but there can be very good reasons for doing so. The most typical reason is to avoid or at least postpone estate taxes. Let's say that you are single and in your will you leave all your estate to your sister if she survives you, otherwise you leave everything to her children. When you die, your sister is elderly and has a large estate of her own. She has no need for your money, so if she does receive it, it will be added to her estate and taxed at her death. Instead, she disclaims it. In the eyes of the law it is as if she has predeceased you, which means that under the terms of your will, it passes to her children. It will be a long time before they are likely to have to pay estate taxes on your money. Note that disclaimers are not all-or-nothing. Your sister could have disclaimed only a portion of your estate. She could even have disclaimed specific items of your estate. A disclaimer is often used in conjunction with a credit shelter trust and is called a *disclaimer credit shelter trust will* (or simply a disclaimer trust will). Essentially, a disclaimer credit shelter trust will is a simple will that allows the surviving heir(s) the option to convert to a trust-type will in order to reduce future estate taxes.

We revisit our first example with Frank, Sally, and Jan. Suppose that when Frank and Sally first wrote their wills, they had a much smaller estate. They were, however, optimistic about their financial future, and they wanted their will to reflect that optimism. To accommodate them, their attorney prepared their will with disclaimers in mind. Frank's will was set up so that if Sally disclaimed any portion, that portion would go into a credit shelter trust that was set up

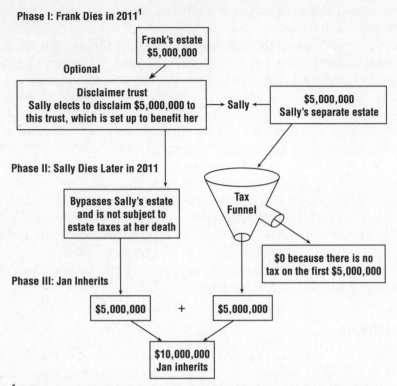

Phase I: Frank Dies in 2011[1]

Frank's estate
$5,000,000

Optional

Disclaimer trust
Sally elects to disclaim $5,000,000 to
this trust, which is set up to benefit her

Sally

$5,000,000
Sally's separate estate

Phase II: Sally Dies Later in 2011

Bypasses Sally's estate
and is not subject to
estate taxes at her death

Tax
Funnel

$0 because there is no
tax on the first $5,000,000

Phase III: Jan Inherits

$5,000,000   + $5,000,000

$10,000,000
Jan inherits

[1]Results may change dramatically post-2012 depending on several legislative factors.

FIGURE 8.3 Simple Will with Disclaimer Credit Shelter Trust Option

to provide Sally with income (and principal for certain reasons). Sally now has the *option* of sending money to the disclaimer credit shelter trust or receiving the money outright. This strategy allows her to do postmortem planning, which is very helpful since the future of portability is unknown after 2012. If it is tax beneficial to do so, she disclaims the appropriate amount of money to a trust that is set up to benefit her. Graphically, the disclaimer credit shelter trust will is depicted in Figure 8.3.

Certain criteria must be met for the disclaimed property to bypass the disclaiming heir's estate for estate tax purposes. First, the disclaimer must be irrevocable and unqualified. Second, it must be in writing. Third, you must not have accepted any interest in or received any benefit from the disclaimed property. Fourth, you must disclaim the property within nine months from the time you were eligible to receive it. Finally, you must have no say as to whom the disclaimed property goes.

Marital Trusts

Marital trusts will generally fall into one of three types: the *general power of appointment trust*, the *qualified terminable interest property* (QTIP) *trust*, and the *qualified domestic trust* (QDOT). The purpose of each is to allow you to exercise some control over how your assets will be handled after your death. Which trust you choose will depend on the *degree* of control you wish to exercise.

General Power of Appointment Trust

There may be situations in which it is not desirable to leave assets outright to your spouse. For example, if your spouse has little experience in managing money, you may want to remove that burden from him or her by establishing a trust run by a professional money manager. The *general power of appointment trust* allows you to place certain controls on the assets that you leave to your spouse while continuing to qualify those assets for the unlimited marital deduction. For this trust to qualify for the unlimited marital deduction and therefore not be taxed at your death, your spouse must receive *all* the income from the trust at least annually. Also, as the name implies, your spouse must be given a *general power of appointment* that allows him or her to determine which person(s) or organization(s) receives the trust property at his or her death. Other than these two requirements, the trust can be very flexible or very restrictive. You can give your spouse the power to terminate the trust, although most trusts of this type are irrevocable. You can give the trustee the power to distribute principal at his or her discretion. This makes certain that there will be access to trust principal for appropriate needs. At the opposite end of the spectrum, you can structure the trust so that your spouse receives only the income during his or her lifetime. As with the credit shelter trust and disclaimer trust, you can appoint your spouse as the trustee, the cotrustee, or you can have someone else serve as trustee. Often the general power of appointment trust is used in conjunction with the credit shelter trust and graphically looks as depicted in Figure 8.4.

Notice that the use of the marital trust does not affect estate taxes. At your spouse's death, all the assets in the marital trust plus any of your spouse's separate property will be included in his or her estate for federal estate tax purposes. A disadvantage of the general power of appointment trust is that it is your spouse, not you, who determines who will eventually receive your property. If you would like to place more restrictions on the assets you leave your spouse, consider the benefits of the Qualified Terminable Interest Property Trust (QTIP) trust.

The Qualified Terminable Interest Property Trust

Under a QTIP trust, *you* decide who will ultimately receive your property at your spouse's death. This determination is specifically indicated in your will. As with the general power of appointment trust, to qualify for the marital deduction, your spouse must receive *all* the income from the trust at least annually. People often use QTIP trusts in cases of second marriages. Consider this example: Thomas and Rebecca recently married. They both have children

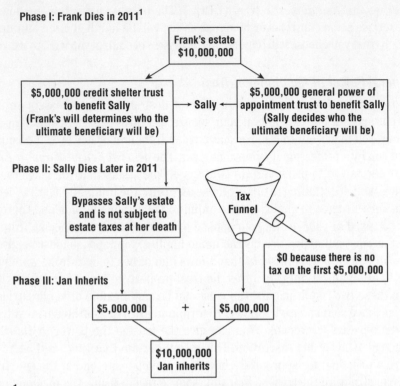

Phase I: Frank Dies in 2011[1]

Frank's estate
$10,000,000

$5,000,000 credit shelter trust to benefit Sally (Frank's will determines who the ultimate beneficiary will be) → Sally ← $5,000,000 general power of appointment trust to benefit Sally (Sally decides who the ultimate beneficiary will be)

Phase II: Sally Dies Later in 2011

Bypasses Sally's estate and is not subject to estate taxes at her death

Tax Funnel

$0 because there is no tax on the first $5,000,000

Phase III: Jan Inherits

$5,000,000   + $5,000,000

$10,000,000 Jan inherits

[1]Results may change dramatically post-2012 depending on several legislative factors.

FIGURE 8.4 Two-Trust Will Utilizing a General Power of Appointment Trust and a Credit Shelter Trust

from prior marriages and both have brought assets into the marriage. Thomas' total estate is $6,500,000, and Rebecca's assets total $800,000. Their goals are twofold. When the first of them dies, they would like their assets to be available as a source of income for the surviving spouse during that spouse's lifetime. At that spouse's death, they want to make certain that their assets go to their children. Their attorney recommends a QTIP trust. Under the provisions of the QTIP trust, if Thomas dies first, his assets would go into the trust and pay Rebecca all the income as long as she lives. Because Rebecca is receiving all the income, Thomas' property passing into the trust qualifies for the unlimited marital deduction and thereby avoids taxation at his death. The trust does *not* give Rebecca a general power of appointment and states that at her death the trust assets go to his children. Rebecca's will is a mirror of Thomas' will. As a result of this planning, both of their goals have been met. The surviving spouse has the income from the deceased spouse's estate, and the deceased spouse is certain that his or her estate eventually passes to his or her children.

The QTIP trust is an important planning technique. Think of what might happen without the QTIP trust. Thomas dies and leaves all of his assets to

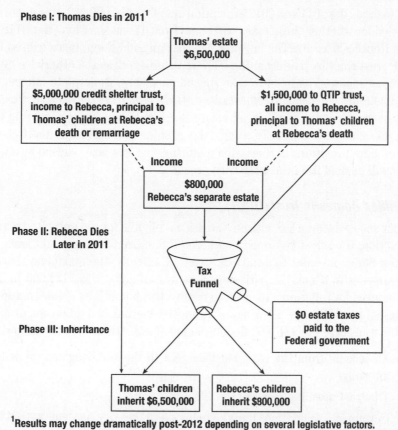

Phase I: Thomas Dies in 2011[1]

Thomas' estate
$6,500,000

$5,000,000 credit shelter trust, income to Rebecca, principal to Thomas' children at Rebecca's death or remarriage

$1,500,000 to QTIP trust, all income to Rebecca, principal to Thomas' children at Rebecca's death

Income   Income

$800,000
Rebecca's separate estate

Phase II: Rebecca Dies
Later in 2011

Tax
Funnel

Phase III: Inheritance

$0 estate taxes
paid to the
Federal government

Thomas' children
inherit $6,500,000

Rebecca's children
inherit $800,000

[1]Results may change dramatically post-2012 depending on several legislative factors.

FIGURE 8.5 Two-Trust Will Utilizing a QTIP Trust and a Credit Shelter Trust

Rebecca with the presumption that she will take care of his children. Rebecca remarries and over time loses touch with Thomas' children. Her will already leaves all of her property to *her* children. When Rebecca dies, Thomas' children receive nothing. Alternatively, if Thomas dies without a will, the laws of intestacy in his state of residence direct that one-half of his property passes to Rebecca and the other half passes to his children. Rebecca later leaves her portion to her children. As with the marital trust, the QTIP trust is often used in conjunction with the credit shelter trust. Graphically, this planning strategy is depicted in Figure 8.5.

Figure 8.5 shows that at Rebecca's death in 2011, the assets from the QTIP trust ($1,500,000), which will go to Thomas' children, *plus* Rebecca's own separate assets ($800,000), which will go to her children, are added together for estate tax purposes. The result is that Rebecca's estate owes no federal estate taxes. However, if Thomas and Rebecca's combined estates exceed $10,000,000, some estate taxes are due at the death of the last to die. Note that a completely different result would occur in 2013 if Congress failed to enact new legislation that extends the 2011 and 2012 exemption amount of $5,000,000. It is important to consider whether these taxes will come from Thomas' assets (the QTIP) or from Rebecca's assets. The law provides that any additional taxes caused by a QTIP trust shall be paid from the QTIP trust unless directed otherwise by the surviving spouse. You need to take special care here. Boilerplate language in many wills provides that *all estate taxes are to be paid from the residuary estate*. This oversight could result in all estate taxes of Rebecca's estate being paid from her children's share. To resolve this problem, both Thomas and Rebecca should have provisions in their wills requiring that any taxes caused by a QTIP trust will be paid from the QTIP trust assets.

Qualified Domestic Trust (QDOT)

If your spouse is not a U.S. citizen, you are not eligible for the unlimited marital deduction. (Congress reasoned that a non-U.S. citizen spouse might leave the United States in order to avoid U.S. taxes.) Currently, the maximum that you can transfer to a non-U.S. citizen spouse free of gift tax is $134,000 in 2011 (as indexed for inflation). In order to resolve this potentially unfair treatment, Congress passed a law allowing an unlimited marital deduction for property that is transferred to a QDOT. Requirements of a QDOT include the following:

- All income from the trust must be paid to the surviving spouse at least annually.
- The trust must be irrevocable.
- Certain IRS regulations must be included in the trust agreement that have the effect of ensuring that trust assets will not escape U.S. taxes.
- Generally, at least one of your trustees must be either a U.S. citizen or a U.S. corporation *at all times*. Be sure that your trust document has language that assures this result.

Certain foreign countries do not recognize either trusts or noncitizen trustees that, in effect, would prohibit you from establishing a QDOT. To address this problem, Congress has provided for the Treasury Department to make exceptions under certain conditions. If this is the case for you, consult with an attorney that specializes in such matters.

Spendthrift Trust

A *spendthrift trust*, originally intended as a way to protect people who tend to squander their money, is appropriate under numerous circumstances. Essentially, this trust provides the trustee with very strict guidelines as to how much and under what conditions money can be distributed to your beneficiary(s). The language in the trust forbids using the trust assets or the trust income as collateral or pledge for any type of loan. If a lender accepts any interest in the trust as a pledge, that pledge is not valid even if the loan is provable. The trustee can simply refuse to disperse funds to the creditor, and the creditor will have no recourse against the trust or trustee. Spendthrift trusts are normally set up for the lifetime of the beneficiary(s). Another circumstance where a spendthrift trust can prove useful is where a beneficiary, due to his or her profession, is a likely candidate for a lawsuit. The classic examples would include the doctor or commercial building contractor. Say your daughter is a physician and is concerned about being subject to a large malpractice judgment. Instead of giving your daughter her inheritance outright, you give it to her by way of a spendthrift trust. By doing so, those assets will be protected from creditors. However, in most states, it is not possible for you to receive this creditor protection by placing your *own* assets in a spendthrift trust. A spendthrift trust is also appropriate if you have a beneficiary who is incompetent.

Standby Trust

If you were to become incompetent because of an accident or sickness, who would handle your financial affairs on your behalf? Would you want them to have specific instructions? If you don't know the answer to the first question, and/or you answer "yes" to the second question, then you might want to consider a *standby trust* (sometimes referred to as an *unfunded revocable trust* or *living trust*). This trust will state who your trustee will be and outline instructions for how trust assets are to be handled. The trust would remain unfunded until there is a triggering event, such as your incompetency. Your standby trust will be used in conjunction with a durable power of attorney that has specific language allowing your assets to be transferred to your trust under the conditions that you specify.

Other Trusts

With the exception of the standby trust just discussed, all the trusts that we have reviewed in this chapter have been *testamentary trusts*. That is, they are trusts that you created under your will. *Inter vivos trusts* are trusts that you create during your lifetime and can also be an important part of your estate planning arsenal. They include the revocable living trust, the irrevocable insurance trust, the 2503(c) trust—which is sometimes referred to as the qualified minors trust—and various charitable trusts. In Chapter 9, we discuss the details of the revocable living trust. Charitable trusts are covered in Chapter 12. The irrevocable insurance trusts are covered in Chapter 10, and the 2503(c) trust is discussed in Chapter 11.

Understanding the Living Trust

As its name implies, a living trust is one that you establish during your lifetime. The trust *can* be irrevocable, but the term usually refers to a revocable trust. Living trusts are sometimes touted as the worry-free estate planning vehicle. This is typically not the case; however, the living trust can be an excellent estate planning device in the right circumstances.

In the typical living trust, you set up the trust and make yourself the trustee. You then retitle your property in the name of the trust. Once this is completed, you manage your property as you always have, with one or two key exceptions. One of the key ingredients in the living trust is that you will name a successor trustee in the event of your death or incompetence. This explains why people often think of the living trust as a substitute for a will. This is only partially true. As you will find out, there are both significant advantages and disadvantages of the living trust. By examining them fully, you will be in a better position to determine if a living trust is appropriate for you.

Advantages of Living Trusts

- The most often-cited reason for setting up a living trust is to avoid the probate process. As we discussed in Chapter 6, probate in some states can be an expensive and time-consuming process. Any property that you transfer to your living trust will avoid the probate process altogether. This means you avoid some expenses and lengthy delays as they relates to the property owned by the living trust. Some opponents of living trusts suggest that these advantages are overstated because probate is not expensive in many states. However, even without costs, the issue of time delays can be significant. Even the simplest of estates may take at least six months to settle.

- Because property placed in a living trust is not subject to probate, your records are not made public. If you prefer to keep your financial matters out of the public eye, a living trust is an excellent tool.

- As we have mentioned, at your death, there are minimal time delays incurred in transferring assets to heirs. The assets are already in your trust, and the only thing that changes is your trustee. The trustee is someone whom you have selected.

- Should you become incompetent due to an accident or illness, your living trust can provide for a quick transfer of management of your assets. In these circumstances, without a living trust or at least a durable power of attorney, the courts would appoint a conservator to manage your property for your benefit. This takes time and can be expensive.

- A living trust is simple to establish. Any attorney versed in estate planning should be able to set up one. There are even do-it-yourself books that take you step-by-step through the process. However, we highly recommend that you have a lawyer establish your living trust because of the many complex issues and provisions involved.

- It is easy to make changes to your living trust. Trusts, unlike wills, generally do not require much administrative formality in either the initial setup or amendments. You simply decide what changes you want to make, write them down, and have two witnesses attest to your signature on the amendments. Again, it is best to do so with the assistance of an attorney to make sure the amendment is valid. Some states may require a Notary Public.

- Another advantage to trusts is that they can be very difficult for anyone to contest. On the other hand, we have already discussed how easily a will can be contested. In addition, the Uniform Trust Code gives certain beneficiaries rights to contest a trust administration, just as they would be able to contest an estate administration. You should consult your state's laws to determine if the Uniform Trust Code has been adopted.

- There is some benefit to consolidating your assets under one management system. This is especially important if you choose to have someone other than yourself act as trustee. With a living trust, you have the opportunity to observe the trustee in action.

- Living trusts have low maintenance costs. A living trust is treated much the same as outright ownership of property for income tax purposes. If you are your own trustee, there are not any additional taxes, tax returns, or other costs associated with your living trust. Also, using a living trust does not restrict any of your potential estate tax savings strategies. Every technique for reducing taxes that we discuss in this book can be used in conjunction with a living trust.

- If you die and you own real or tangible personal property in more than one state, chances are your will would have to be probated in each of those states. A living trust is a perfect solution for this situation. Remember, the property in your living trust is not subject to probate at all. If your job causes you to move from state to state, your living trust removes the necessity of having to draw a new will every time you change your state of residence (however, state trust laws should be reviewed).

Disadvantages of Living Trusts

- Opponents of the living trust often cite the cost of drafting the document and the cost of transferring property into the trust as the main reasons to avoid them. You actually need to draft two documents: (1) the living trust and (2) a will. The purpose of the will is to direct any assets that you failed to place in your living trust to your trust at your death. In addition to the expense of drawing two documents, you also incur the expenses of transferring the title to your property into your trust. For example, you would need to transfer the deed to your home, which would include some filing fees and possibly attorneys' fees. Your mortgage company may also charge a transfer fee if a mortgage is involved. Possible filing fees also apply to car titles, bank accounts, investment accounts, and so on. Although it is true that the initial cost of setting up your living trust is likely higher than the costs of preparing a will, over the long run the costs are likely to be similar. For example, if you utilize a will for your planning instead of the living trust, your executor would still incur the expense of transferring your property to your heirs. In one sense it may be cheaper to pay the cost while you are living. This is because you are in control, can negotiate fees, and can do much of the work yourself. As a separate matter, if someone other than you is the trustee of your living trust, some states may require that trustee to file an annual income tax return.

- A legitimate disadvantage of the living trust is that some time and effort must be made to move your property into your trust. You must locate all your property deeds and titles and write letters to your banks, brokerage firms, and employee benefits office in order to move all your property into your trust. In addition, every time you purchase property or open a new bank account, you must remember to make your trust the owner. Obviously, if you plan to use the living trust as your basic estate planning device, you can't procrastinate, or you may forget to move some property into the trust.

Remember, at some point someone must do this work. If you don't do it, you are leaving it to someone else to do it for you.

- Some states have homestead laws that provide for a reduction of property taxes on your home. If your living trust, not you, owns your home, depending on your state's laws, you may lose the homestead exemption, which will cause an increase in your property taxes. If you are married, one possible solution to this problem is to title your home as "joint tenants with right of survivorship." However, this form of titling property may increase estate taxes.

- Current law provides that the first $250,000 ($500,000 for married couples) of profit from the sale of your home is not subject to federal capital gains taxes. Having your living trust own your home will not affect this valuable benefit.

- If you get a divorce, your living trust will not automatically remove your ex-spouse as a potential beneficiary unless the trust contains provisions to do so. To remove your spouse, you must amend your trust. In the case of wills, divorce does automatically remove your ex-spouse as a potential beneficiary.

How a Living Trust Operates

Trust laws vary from state to state so you should seek the counsel of an experienced trusts and estates attorney. To set up your living trust, you must go through much of the same process as you would to draw up a will as described in Chapter 7. You have to make decisions concerning trustees, guardians, and when income and principal are to be distributed and under what conditions. These issues relate to what you want to happen to your property after your death. Furthermore, you need to decide how you want your trust to operate during your lifetime. Some of the more important living decisions are included in the following sections.

Choosing the Trustee

Are you going to be your own trustee during your lifetime, or are you going to appoint someone else? Most people make themselves the trustee of their trust. As your own trustee, you are able to operate your trust in much the same manner as you do now without a trust. The key difference is that you would have to sign your name as "John Smith, *trustee.*" Some people prefer to leave the administrative details of handling their finances to someone else, often a professional trustee such as a bank trust officer. Taking this route, you choose a trustee and pay him or her an ongoing fee, and the trustee does as much administrative work as you request. This may include such tasks as depositing a monthly check in your checking account, paying your bills, doing your tax returns, and investing your money. A professional trustee can simplify your life, but as you might imagine, he or she can be quite expensive. One major advantage of hiring a professional trustee during your lifetime is that you get to see how competent he or she is. If the trustee does not perform satisfactorily, you are free to seek out someone else before you die.

Revocable versus Irrevocable

Do you want your trust to be revocable or irrevocable? Most people set their trust up as a revocable trust, which provides for maximum flexibility. With a revocable trust, you can make changes anytime, move property into and out of your trust as you desire, or abandon the trust altogether. Reasons for using an irrevocable trust include providing a level of protection against creditors or creating tax benefits by removing assets (and the growth of those assets) from your estate. The creditor protection benefits are very state law specific, and in most cases under the irrevocable trust, the trust maker must give up all control.

Funded versus Unfunded

With your living trust, you have the option of fully funding your trust, partially funding your trust, or leaving your trust unfunded until you die or become incompetent. Some people even leave their trusts unfunded until just before they die. The idea here is that unless your death comes suddenly, you will have time to transfer your property when you actually become ill. However, if the primary goal is to avoid probate, we believe that the best method is to fully fund your trust at the time that it is established. This may be more trouble initially, but it will provide you with greater control and certainty of desired results.

One Trust or Two?

If you are married, should you use one trust for both you and your spouse? In most cases, you and your spouse should each have a separate trust. This is particularly true if you have reasons to keep property separated, as may be the case with a second marriage. Remember, the act of placing your property into your living trust does not eliminate the need for estate tax reduction strategies, nor does it prohibit you from directing that your property goes to a certain person(s). In addition, it does not insulate the property from the claims of a soon to be ex-spouse.

Incompetence Provision

One of the key benefits of the living trust is that it can provide instructions for your care should you become incompetent due to sickness or accident. You should include trust language that indicates the level of care you desire and who your successor trustee will be in the event you become incompetent. In addition, it is advisable to include a separate durable power of attorney that gives someone you trust the power to transfer into your trust property you own that is not titled in your trust. In your trust agreement, you can be as explicit as you wish concerning the type and level of care you desire during your disability. For example, you could specify that you wanted hospice care versus a nursing home. Or you could designate which nursing home(s) would be acceptable. In most cases a durable power of attorney would not be this specific.

Wills

A living trust can be a substitute for a will *if* you transfer *all* your property into your trust. In our experience, people are rarely successful in transferring 100 percent of their property into their trust. First of all, certain property, such as jewelry, clothes, furniture, stamp collections, guns, and other personal property, is almost impossible to title at all. Secondly, you have what is called "the forget and procrastination factor." As you acquire new property, you must title each asset in the name of your trust. This requires some extra effort, and you just might not do it. To resolve this potential problem, you need to have a will in addition to your living trust. This will is often described as a "pour-over" will because it instructs your personal representative to pour any of your remaining assets over into your trust. This is not a complex will and should not add much additional expense to the cost of setting up your living trust. If you have children who are minors, you list choice(s) for guardian(s) here.

Transferring Property into Your Living Trust

The greatest challenge in setting up your living trust is likely to be transferring the title to your property to the name of your trust. This task is actually more time-consuming than it is difficult. However, under certain circumstances, retitling property in the name of your trust can cause problems. In some states you are required to file your trust agreement with the court or probate records if you transfer the title to real estate into a trust. Some transfer agents require a copy of your trust agreement in order to transfer title of your securities. Your bank may require a copy of your trust if you put your safe box in the name of your trust. This is to make sure that you, as the trustee, have the authority to transact these transfers. You could simply supply these people or institutions with a copy of your trust document, but one of the main features of your living trust is that it keeps your financial affairs private. Passing your trust document all over town hardly meets this objective. There are two effective solutions to this problem. The first is called an *affidavit of trust* or *certificate of trust*, which is a notarized statement indicating the name of the trust, the names of the trustees, the trust powers, and pertinent provisions of the trust including revocability, successor trustees, and signature page. The affidavit of trust provides proof that your trust is legitimate and that you have the authority as trustee to transact business on behalf of your trust.

The second solution to this problem is called a *nominee partnership*. Some institutions are more comfortable dealing with partnerships rather than trusts. A nominee partnership *controls* rather than owns property. The partners of the nominee partnership are usually the same as the trustees of your trust. The idea of a nominee partnership may sound strange, but businesses and financial institutions have used this method for decades.

Transferring property into your living trust need not be an expensive process. Let your attorney know that you would like to do as much of the legwork as possible. Together, you can then divide the work according to who can best complete each job. Your attorney will also be able to alert you to any potential tax or other problems. Much of the work assigned to you can then be completed with the aid of your other advisors such as your banker, investment advisor, insurance agent, and employee benefits specialist.

Your attorney, however, should review all of the final transfers. You want to make certain that one professional accepts overall responsibility for the implementation of your plan. If mistakes are made, this person can be held accountable. More important, this person can help prevent mistakes. This responsibility should be spelled out in your engagement letter with your attorney so that there is no misunderstanding as to the scope of his or her responsibility. Use the following sample engagement letter for hiring your attorney:

Dear (your attorney's name),

I enjoyed meeting with you today and look forward to working with you on establishing and funding my living trust. As per our conversation, you will be responsible for transferring titles to the following property into my trust:

I will be responsible for transferring title and beneficiaries of all my other property. Once completed, I am asking that you review all property transfers to ensure that they have been properly completed.

You have indicated that you expect to have ____ hours in completing this project and that you expect your total fee to be $ ____ to $ ____. Please notify me immediately if it appears that your time or fees will exceed these estimates.

Further, you have indicated that you expect to complete the drafting of my trust agreement and the property transfers that you are responsible for by *date*. Time is of the essence, so I appreciate your attention to this matter.

Sincerely,

Your name

You need to become organized before you meet with your attorney. Complete the following checklist and bring it along with the evidence of title for all your assets. (For example, bring the deed to your home and your car title with you.)

You and Your Family

——— Your full name
——— Date of birth
——— Social Security number
——— Spouse's full name
——— Spouse's Social Security number
——— Spouse's date of birth
——— Each child's full name
——— Each child's date of birth
——— Each child's Social Security number

Your Trustee

——— Trustee's name
——— Cotrustee's name (if any)
——— First successor trustee
——— Second successor trustee
——— Third successor trustee

Your Property and How It Is Currently Titled

——— Residence
——— Other real estate
——— Any mortgages
——— All bank accounts
——— Brokerage accounts
——— Individual stock certificates
——— Individual bonds
——— Vehicles, boats, campers, etc.
——— Other—list untitled assets

Your Beneficiaries

——— Life insurance
——— Disability income insurance
——— IRAs
——— Retirement plans
——— Annuities

This list is not intended to be all-inclusive, but the list you take to your attorney should be. You should also be prepared to make decisions on all of the issues we discussed in Chapter 7. These issues include how income is to be distributed to your heirs and under what conditions the trust principal is to be distributed. This preparation will save your attorney time and thereby reduce your legal fees.

Types of Property Likely to Be Transferred

Real Estate

Ownership in real estate is evidenced by a deed. To change the ownership, you need to have a new deed prepared and filed with the court. You will want to enlist the aid of your attorney in this process. Most real estate mortgages have a so-called due-on-sale clause that requires you to pay off your mortgage in full if the property is sold or transferred out of your name. Because you are transferring your property from yourself to yourself via your trust, this due-on-sale provision should not apply. However, contact your mortgage company ahead of time to determine if it requires any special procedures for the transfer. If the property you are transferring is your residence, and your county has homestead laws, you should also contact your county clerk's office and determine if any special procedures are required in order to maintain your homestead exemption.

Bank Accounts and Bank Money Market Accounts

Changing title of your bank accounts should be a relatively straightforward matter that you can handle yourself. Simply contact your bank and ask about the procedure. In most cases the bank requires little more than a copy of your affidavit of trust.

Brokerage Accounts

In order to transfer the title of your brokerage accounts, you may need to close out your current account and open a new one in the name of your trust. Your broker can do this for you based on a letter of instruction and your affidavit of trust. Once your new account is opened, your broker then journals the securities from your current account to your new account. This procedure does not trigger an income tax event.

Individual Stock Certificates and Individual Bonds

If you hold stock certificates or bonds that have not been left in your brokerage account, there are two ways to transfer the titles to your trust. Most brokers will assist you for no fee. In other cases, they will charge a small fee for each certificate or bond. Alternatively, you can deal directly with the issuer of the certificate or bond, which is more challenging and may be more expensive than getting your broker's help.

Life and Disability Insurance

Your insurance agent can be a big help to you here. With a letter of instruction, she or he does much, if not all, of the work for you. Ask the agent to complete your ownership and beneficiary forms for you rather than sending blank forms for you to fill out. These forms can be confusing to those who have never completed them. You should not be charged for this service. Note that in many cases it is advisable to have your life insurance owned by an irrevocable trust rather than your living trust. This subject is discussed in the next chapter.

Vehicles, Motorcycles, and Boats

The laws for transferring title to vehicles, motorcycles, and boats vary widely from state to state, so consult with your attorney and possibly local and state agencies for advice. For this type of property, you typically receive a certificate of title that indicates that you are the owner. This certificate often has a section that allows you to transfer the title to someone else. An alternative is to dispose of this property through the pour-over provision in your will.

Individualized Retirement Accounts and Other Retirement Accounts

You should be especially careful in dealing with your IRAs and retirement accounts. First, the law does not allow you to transfer ownership of retirement accounts, and changing your beneficiary to your trust could create adverse income and estate tax consequences. Also, qualified retirement plans such as 401(k) plans, profit-sharing plans, and defined contribution plans do not allow you to remove your spouse as the beneficiary unless he or she signs a release giving his or her permission. You definitely should consult with your attorney or financial advisor regarding these changes.

Annuities

As with retirement accounts, annuities must be handled with care. If you are married and your spouse is the beneficiary, there is no immediate income tax due upon your death. If someone other than your spouse is your beneficiary, then that individual may have to pay income tax on the gain within five years of your death. One possible solution is to make your spouse the primary beneficiary and your living trust the contingent beneficiary. Be sure and discuss this with your professional advisor.

Property Having No Title

Much of your personal property will not have evidence of title. Property that falls into this category includes jewelry, furniture, furs, coin stamp and art collections, and clothes. This property can be handled in one of four ways:

- You can use your pour-over will to sweep all untitled property into your trust. The disadvantage here is that this property goes through probate. But because your will leaves the property to your trust, the ultimate distribution of this property remains private.

- Your trust can state that all other property is deemed to be owned by your trust. This may solve the problem, but it could be contested.

- Through your trust agreement or through your will, you could make a specific bequest of certain untitled property.

- You can prepare an assignment document which purports to transfer all of your untitled personal property to the trust during your lifetime. To promote formality, you can have the document executed by one or more witnesses. Like option number two, this may solve the problem, but it could be contested.

Jointly Held Property

Another area that deserves special attention is transferring property that you own jointly with someone else. Negative gift, income tax, and estate tax consequences can occur if the transfer is handled improperly. This is especially true if you own property with someone other than your spouse. Consult your attorney before proceeding.

Living Trust Myths

Some myths concerning living trusts continue to prevail today. Although a living trust can solve many of your estate planning problems, it does not solve them all. The following list contains the most prevalent myths along with the realities.

Myth 1: A Living Trust Protects My Assets from Creditors

A living trust provides no protection from creditors. Part of the reason is that the trust is revocable. If it were irrevocable, some creditor protection might be available depending on your state's laws, but of course, you would lose control over your property.

Myth 2: A Living Trust Saves Taxes

The act of creating a living trust does nothing to reduce your tax burden. However, all of the estate tax saving strategies available to you under traditional will planning are also available to you with your living trust. By including appropriate language in your trust, you can reduce estate taxes.

Myth 3: If I Have a Living Trust, I Do Not Need a Will

As we mentioned earlier in this chapter, you will still need to have a will drawn in addition to your living trust. Its purpose is to direct any property not already owned by your living trust to your living trust and to name guardians for any minor children. You won't need a complex or expensive will, but it *is* necessary.

Myth 4: All My Property Will Ultimately Be Directed to My Living Trust

Some people believe because their living trust is set up to handle all their property, eventually all their property will end up in their trust. Nothing could be further from the truth. Property held as *joint tenants with right of survivorship* will pass according to the title no matter what your trust says. The same is true for beneficiary designations of life insurance, retirement plans, and annuities. You must play an active role in seeing that your property ends up in your trust.

Myth 5: When I Die, My Living Trust Will Prevent Delays Typically Associated with Probate

It is true that the time delays at your death are likely to be much less than that of probate, but some delays will take place. Your trustee must still complete many of the administrative duties of an executor, including the preparation and filing of your estate tax return, payment of debts, creditor notices, and so on. The process is more difficult in some states than others, so check with your attorney. If time delays are likely to be a problem in your state, make certain that your spouse will have sufficient assets to meet living expenses until trust assets are released.

Myth 6: A Living Trust Eliminates the Cost of Probate

Again, this is only partially true. Many of the tasks normally performed by an executor must now be completed by your trustee. Depending on your state of residence and choice of trustee, the cost savings can be significant or minimal. A living trust *does* put you in a better position to control costs at your death.

It is your responsibility to develop the complete list of your assets. You should use your checklist to make sure that all property has been properly handled. Be sure to have your attorney review *all* of the property transfers and beneficiary changes. You should have your attorney acknowledge in writing that he or she has reviewed each transfer and that it has been properly completed. Be sure to keep a record of all this correspondence. If there is ever a problem, you or your family members will be able to return to your attorney and have him or her correct the problem.

Transacting Business with Your Trust

Once you have set up your trust and transferred your property into it, you will have to transact your business in a slightly new way. If you buy property, be sure to buy it in the name of your trust. Your purchases will be made in your name as trustee. This may take a little getting used to, but you will become accustomed to it. One exception is your checking account. It is not necessary that the name of your trust be listed on your checks or that you sign your checks as trustee. When you decide to sell property you will do so as trustee. Be sure to keep a copy of your affidavit of trust or nominee partnership papers close at hand. In most cases you will not need them, but if you do, having them handy will save time and frustration.

A living trust is an excellent tool for the right person. Although the living trust can have many advantages over traditional will planning (depending on your goals), we believe that you should consider setting up a living trust if any of the following are true:

- You have substantial assets and are concerned about keeping your financial affairs private or just want to save your family the complexity of your state's probate process.

- You want a well-defined mechanism in place to take care of you in the event you become incapacitated—something more specific than a durable power of attorney.

- You own property in multiple states and want to avoid multiple probate proceedings.

- Your job causes you to move from state to state, you don't want to incur the expense of having to draw a new will every time you move. Although this may still be necessary because of different *state* estate tax laws.

CHAPTER 10

Using Insurance in Your Estate Plan

The average family spends some 10 percent to 15 percent of its disposable income on insurance premiums. You would never consider owning a home without property and casualty insurance that would replace it should it burn to the ground. Most people feel the same way about health insurance. The potential costs of medical care are just too expensive to try to self-insure. In this chapter we will focus on two types of insurance that play an important role in protecting your estate plan—life insurance and long-term care insurance. Another vital type of insurance, liability insurance, will be covered in Chapter 15.

Life Insurance

Life insurance serves three important purposes in your estate plan. If you have not accumulated enough financial assets to provide financial independence for yourself and your family, life insurance provides a means of replacing income should the family income earner die prematurely. Secondly, if you have accumulated enough assets to be financially independent, then life insurance can be used as a source of cash to pay estate taxes. Finally, life insurance can be used to leverage the size of your estate. We will cover each of these issues in this chapter as well as discuss the various types of life insurance policies, under what circumstances each is appropriate, and the amounts of life insurance you will need.

TABLE 10.1 $1,000,000 Term Life Insurance for Male, Age 50

10-year level term	$1,100 annually
15-year level term	$1,560 annually
20-year level term	$2,000 annually

Note: Premiums are guaranteed not to rise and policies are guaranteed convertible to cash value ("permanent") policies without proof of insurability.

Life Insurance Basics

Before we discuss the best use of life insurance in your estate plan, let's first review the basics of how life insurance works and the various types of policies offered.

Life insurance is one of the most confusing financial products sold today. While life insurance policies come in many shapes and sizes, all life insurance falls into one of two categories: term insurance or cash value insurance. *Term insurance* is pure insurance. You pay a premium that covers you for a certain period of time. If you die during that period of time, your beneficiary collects the face amount of the policy. If you do not die, you do not get any money back, and you must renew the insurance by paying an additional premium if you want the coverage to continue. *Cash value insurance* is nothing more than term insurance with a savings feature. In addition to the term premium, called mortality reserves, you give the insurance company extra money which it invests for you. Later, that savings can be accessed through loans or, in some cases, withdrawals. At the time of your death, your beneficiary receives the term insurance plus the savings account.

To help you decipher your life insurance options, here's a more detailed look at the various term and cash value policies.

Term Insurance

Term insurance plans are typically sold as either annual renewable term insurance or level term insurance. With *annual renewable term insurance*, your premium increases each year because as you get older, you are statistically more likely to die. With *level term insurance*, the insurance company levelizes the premium for a stated period of time, typically 10, 15, or 20 years. The longer the term period, the higher your premiums will be. Look at Table 10.1 for comparable premiums. Most policies allow you to convert to a cash value policy without having to pass a medical exam, but you should check with your insurance carrier for details.

Cash Value Insurance

As with term insurance, there are also various types of cash value insurance. Several of the more popular products include:

- *Whole life.* This product represents the traditional cash value type of insurance. With whole life insurance, you commit to a fixed premium that includes the term insurance charge plus the savings feature. The insurance company takes the savings portion of your premium and invests it for you as part of their general assets. These general assets include real estate, commercial mortgages, bonds, and to a limited extent, stocks. You receive a guaranteed rate of return—usually 3 percent—and, in many cases, annual dividends that are declared by the board of directors.

- *Universal life.* Universal Life insurance became popular in the 1980s when interest rates were very high. With this type of policy, your savings are invested in interest-sensitive investments such as certificates of deposit, commercial paper, and bonds. You are notified periodically of the interest your savings is earning. Unlike whole life policies, however, you pay flexible, rather than fixed premiums. You must pay an amount that covers the term insurance premiums, but the insurance company allows you to vary the amount you contribute toward the savings program.

- *Variable life.* As mutual funds became increasingly popular, the insurance companies developed a life insurance product that uses mutual funds. With variable life you must pay your term insurance charge, but you can then direct your savings into various mutual funds offered by the insurance company. The company typically offers a range of choices such as stock funds, bond funds, money market funds, and guaranteed interest rate contracts, which are similar to certificates of deposit. You make the decision which funds to invest in, and you are allowed to switch among the investment choices.

- *Survivorship life.* This product was developed specifically for the estate planning marketplace. Survivorship life covers two lives, but it does not pay a death benefit until the *second* person dies. Assuming that the two people are a husband and wife, the policy death benefit becomes available at just the time when it is needed to pay the estate taxes. Statistically, the odds of the insurance company having to pay a claim early are very low. As a result, the mortality charges for these policies are very low.

Using Life Insurance to Replace Income

Life Insurance for Income Earners

One of the primary reasons to purchase life insurance is to provide a source of income for your family should you die prematurely. Obviously, this assumes that your family is dependent on you for financial support. If you don't have someone dependent upon you for his or her financial support, you do not need life insurance as an income replacement device. Many people misunderstand this concept and end up buying life insurance they do not need. Here are some specific situations:

- You are single without children. Most single people have no dependents and, therefore, no need for life insurance.

- You are married without children. If both you and your spouse work, in all likelihood neither is financially dependent upon the other. Again, no life insurance is necessary. If one spouse is unemployed, you may need some life insurance to provide a bridge of income until the other person can acquire the training necessary to get a good job. You may also need life insurance to cover a portion of joint debts such as a mortgage that are being paid from both incomes.

- You are married with children. Because you have dependents, you should consider your life insurance needs carefully. You should buy enough insurance to maintain a similar lifestyle for your surviving family.

- Insurance on children. Unless your child is a movie star, it is unlikely that you or anyone else is dependent on him or her for financial support. Life insurance on children is a luxury, not a necessity. Many agents suggest that you buy insurance on your children to "protect their insurability," meaning that you buy it for them now while they are healthy (insurable) and don't take the chance that their health status will change before they need life insurance to protect their own family. The policies the agents offer have an option that gives your child the guaranteed right to buy more insurance at standard rates throughout their early adult years. This is not a bad idea if you have the extra money for annual premiums. Just remember that it is not likely that your child will become uninsurable, so if these resources are needed elsewhere, this is insurance you can afford to pass up.

How Much Life Insurance Do You Need?

Ask 10 professionals how much life insurance is advisable and you are likely to get 10 different answers. First, if you are married and have no children, you only need enough life insurance to pay off any joint debts. If, on the other hand, you have children, your need for life insurance increases substantially. Use the following three-step process to determine your life insurance needs:

Step 1

If you are the sole income provider, multiply your gross annual income by .80. (*Note:* If both you and your spouse work, combine both incomes and multiply by .80.) This results in reducing your income by 20 percent. The reason you do this is because there would be one less spender in the household (you!).

Step 2

Divide your answer in Step 1 by the rate of return you would reasonably expect to earn on the life insurance proceeds once they are invested. Your answer here indicates how much money you will need in order to continue the necessary income stream to your surviving family.

Step 3

Subtract any savings or investments you already have from your answer in Step 2. This is the amount of life insurance you should own.

Case Study 1

Edward and Jean Anderson have two children. Edward earns $250,000 a year and Jean stays home to raise the children. The couple assumes that they could earn 7.5 percent on investments; they have $225,000 in personal investments and $475,000 in their retirement plans.

Step 1

Edward's Income	$250,000
One-Less-Spender Factor	×.80
Adjusted Income Need	$200,000

Step 2

Adjusted Income Need	$200,000
Divided by Expected Rate of Return (7.5 percent)	÷.075
	$2,666,666

This amount of money invested at 7.5 percent will provide the needed $200,000 per year for Jean and the children.

Step 3

Capital Needed	$2,666,666
Minus Current Savings and Investments	−$700,000
Edward's Life Insurance Need	$1,966,666

Case Study 2

If both Edward and Jean work, the example changes. Assume their total income is $265,000, but Edward's earnings are $90,000 and Jean's earnings are $175,000. To see how much life insurance Edward needs, complete the following calculation.

Step 1

Multiply the family income of $265,000 by .80. This equals $212,000. Again, the survivor's income need is reduced because Edward is no longer a spender. Because Jean plans to continue working, subtract her income also

WORKSHEET 10.1 Life Insurance Needs Worksheet

Step 1	
Your annual family income	$
Discount factor	×.80
Total income needed by surviving family	$
Subtract surviving spouse's annual income	−
Surviving family income need from outside sources	$

Step 2	
Divide by your estimated rate of return on invested assets	÷
Total amount of money needed to provide for survivors	$

Step 3	
Subtract your current savings and investments	−
Equals total life insurance needed	$

($212,000 − $175,000 = $37,000). This $37,000 represents the income that needs to be replaced upon Edward's death.

Step 2

Divide $37,000 by their expected rate of return (7.5 percent). $37,000 ÷ .075 = $493,333.

Step 3

Subtract their current investments ($700,000) from $493,333. This equals −$206,666. Because your result is negative, there is no life insurance needed on Edward's life.

Note: Because the family also depends on Jean's income, you now need to complete this exercise for her to find how much life insurance Jean needs! (Hint: The answer in Jean's case is $926,666 of life insurance is needed).

Now calculate *your* insurance needs using Worksheet 10.1.

The answer you get after completing this three-step process should only be used as a rule of thumb. You should personalize the solution to your particular situation. For example, you may want to increase the amount of insurance to help cover the costs of funding college expenses for your children. Or, you may want additional insurance that would be used to pay off some of your debts. If your goal is to provide a *lifetime* income for your dependents, additional insurance will be needed to offset the ravages of inflation. If you would like a more detailed online analysis go to the Resource Center at www.welchgroup.com; then click on "links"; then click on "Life Insurance Needs Estimator," or you can have your life insurance agent assist you.

You may be eligible for Social Security benefits; there is a Social Security Survivors Benefit to help surviving spouses with minor children. Each person receives an annual statement from the Social Security Administration about three months before their birthday. The statement is a record of your earnings and has your estimated benefits paid to you and your family in the event of retirement, disability or death. If you have misplaced your statement then you can access your benefits information online at www.ssa.gov or request a statement by phone at 1-800-772-1213. We recommend that you view these benefits as extra money and not as part of your calculation for life insurance needs. Remember, these benefits end when your youngest child reaches age 16.

What Type of Life Insurance Is Best for You?

If your primary purpose is to provide your family with a source of income should you die prematurely, then level term insurance is your best bet. This assumes that you have a wealth accumulation plan in place as outlined in Chapter 5. In working with our clients, we normally recommend either 15-year or 20-year level term policies. This is because we have implemented a wealth accumulation plan that is expected to achieve total financial independence by the end of that period. For example, let's say that you determined in Chapter 5 that you need to accumulate $3,000,000 of investment capital to be financially independent. Once you have accumulated that sum, you no longer need life insurance as a source of income protection for your family. It is possible that you might need permanent (cash value) life insurance for *other* reasons, such as estate liquidity. Remember, because you can convert term insurance to permanent insurance without having to pass a new physical exam, you have left your options open.

Insurance on a Homemaker

If you have young children, replacing the services of a homemaker can be quite expensive. Ask yourself this question: If my homemaker spouse were to die, could I afford to pay someone to perform those services out of my current income? You may be lucky enough to have a family member who could step in and provide child care services. In this case, no life insurance would be necessary. On the other hand, if you decide life insurance on a homemaker is necessary, a $150,000 to $500,000 term policy should provide adequate coverage. By buying a 10- to 15-year level term insurance policy, you will provide coverage until the children are old enough to assist with their own care.

Insurance on Adult Children

If you have adult children who have started their own families, you might consider buying insurance on their lives to provide protection for their families. We are sure you can remember how tight cash flow was when you first started your family. This is a situation where you have the cash and they have the need.

From a selfish point of view, if you had a breadwinner son-in-law die without enough life insurance, you might feel compelled to step in with financial support for your daughter and grandchildren. Believe us, paying the premiums on a large term life policy for your son-in-law is a lot more palatable than financially supporting a second family! The latter could have a serious negative impact on your own estate and retirement plan.

How to Get the Best Deal on Term Life Insurance

Fortunately for the consumer, term insurance is a very competitive product. In terms of planning and budgeting, 10-, 15-, or 20-year level term is advised. That way, you have a predictable premium for a fixed period of time. To access competitive quotes on-line go to the Resource Center at www.welchgroup.com; then click on "Links"; then click on "Life Insurance Quotes."

To get the best deal, first decide how much life insurance you need and what kind of term insurance best fits your circumstances. For example, if you decide that you need $750,000 of 15-year level term life insurance, first, go online to get a quote. Then, if you have a local agent, ask him or her for a quote. A simple comparison will ensure that you get the best deal. Personally, we prefer to work with a local agent because you will receive a more personal level of service.

Insurance Warnings!

Not all insurance is good insurance, and not all insurance companies are good companies. A few warnings are in order here.

Financial Strength

Make sure the company you use is financially strong. Accept only a company that is rated AA or better by one of the three major rating services: AM Best Co., Standard & Poor's, or Moody's. Request this information at the same time you request your premium quotes.

Mortgage Life Insurance

If you borrowed money to buy your home, you undoubtedly have received offers to buy mortgage life insurance. This particular type of policy is a decreasing term insurance policy that provides enough insurance to pay off your mortgage if you die before your mortgage is paid off. While you may want to have enough life insurance to pay off your mortgage if you die, these policies represent poor values. Consider the following comparison. A client had a $200,000 15-year mortgage. Through his mortgage company, he received an offer for mortgage life insurance costing about $141.40 per month. However, a 15-year *level* term life insurance policy for $200,000 costs only $36 per month. That amounts to savings of almost 400 percent! Mortgage life insurance is a deal you can afford to pass up.

Credit Life Insurance

Credit life is similar to mortgage life except that it is used to pay off non–real estate loans such as car, appliance, and furniture loans. Here is a typical scenario. You're about to finalize the loan when the banker asks, "You do want this car loan to be paid off if you die, don't you?" You then sign a credit life insurance application without reviewing the cost. Premiums for credit life can be up to 10 times higher than normal policies. It will probably not surprise you to find out that your banker often receives incentive compensation for selling these policies.

Using Life Insurance for Estate Liquidity

If you have accumulated enough assets to be financially independent, then your estate may be sizeable enough to face estate taxes. If this is the case, you need to determine where your heirs will get the cash to pay your estate taxes. The following are three extreme case examples. In all three cases, the estate equals $15,000,000, yet the planning strategies are different.

Case Study 1

Edward and Cindy Johnson have a total estate valued at $15,000,000. They have implemented all the typical estate reduction strategies including a credit shelter trust. Their financial advisor estimates that they still have an estate tax liability of approximately $1,750,000. They are trying to decide if they should buy life insurance to cover their tax liability. A review of their assets indicates that they own $12,000,000 in real estate and business interests and $3,000,000 in stocks and bonds. One solution to their tax problem would be for their executor to sell $1,750,000 of stocks and bonds to pay the taxes and distribute the remaining estate to the Johnson family heirs. If the Johnsons are comfortable with this solution, it would not be necessary to purchase life insurance.

Case Study 2

Our second case scenario changes the asset mix a bit. In this case, the Adams' estate consists of $10,000,000 of illiquid real estate and business interests plus $5,000,000 in stocks and bonds. However, in their case, the stocks and bonds are all in various retirement plans. If the executor were to take $1,750,000 from the retirement plan to pay the taxes, he would immediately trigger *income taxes* on the money. To pay the added income tax, the executor would need to sell more securities from the retirement plan thus triggering even more income tax. For the Adams', a solution would be to use life insurance to provide cash to pay the taxes so that the retirement plan assets can continue to be deferred as long as possible while avoiding a forced sale of illiquid assets.

Case Study 3

In our final scenario, we will consider the estate of John and Beth Walker. The bulk of the Walkers' estate is made up of illiquid real estate. A forced sale of their real estate to pay estate taxes would likely result in fire sale prices. Clearly, the best choice here would be life insurance.

How Much Is Enough?

In Case Study 2, the Adams family had an estate tax problem of $1,500,000 with no liquid assets available to pay the tax. How much life insurance do they need to solve their problem? The obvious answer—$1,500,000—is wrong! Edward and Cindy Adams are both alive today and the odds of at least one of them remaining alive for years to come is very good. This being the case, their estate is likely to continue to grow as will their tax problem. At first glance, it appeared that there was a simple solution, but, in fact, this situation needs to be carefully evaluated. You must review your overall estate planning strategy and perform some estate growth projections. These projections will give you a much better sense of how much insurance you will ultimately need. For example, assume in this case that the Adamses have established a family limited partnership (see Chapter 13) and placed all their real estate in it. They have a large number of children and grandchildren. Based on discounted annual gifts to all family members, they project that over the next 10 years they can give away enough partnership interests to reduce their estate tax liability to zero. They have solved their long-term problem and, therefore, should consider term life insurance to solve their short-term need. If they did not have a large number of children or were unwilling to make family gifts, then their future life insurance need could easily exceed $3,000,000 and would likely require the purchase of permanent or cash value life insurance such as Survivorship Life Insurance. Again, you must take the time to run realistic projections.

What Type of Life Insurance Is Best for Estate Liquidity?

Once you've decided that life insurance is the best solution to providing for part or all of the cash needed for your estate taxes, consider these three choices:

1. Use term life insurance. If you plan to institute an aggressive program of estate reduction strategies such as those outlined in this book with the intention of reducing your estate below the taxable limits, then term life insurance may be your least expensive choice. For example, say that you plan to use a combination of strategies such as rolling Grantor Retained Annuity Trusts (GRATS), gifts, and grantor trusts and expect that you will reduce your estate below the taxable amount within ten years; you could buy a 10-year level term policy to serve as a stop-gap until your goal was realized.

2. Use survivorship life insurance. This type of life insurance is tailor-made for paying estate taxes. It is also often referred to as *second-to-die insurance*. As described,earlier in this chapter, this insurance is written on two lives, usually a husband and wife, and pays off when the second insured dies. This coincides with the time estate taxes are due. Survivorship life is a cash value policy, not a term life policy. This permanent-type policy is helpful because it remains in force as long as you or your spouse is living. This would not be the case with term life insurance. Survivorship life is available as whole life, universal life, or variable life. The whole life version will contain more guarantees, but it will also have the highest premium. If you are somewhat adventuresome, you might want to consider the variable life version. Regardless of your choice, you don't want to buy this type of insurance mail order. You should consult a qualified agent who is knowledgeable about this product and estate planning. We recommend that you only consider an agent who has at least 5 years of experience in the field and who has obtained the Chartered Life Underwriter (CLU) designation or Chartered Financial Consultant (ChFC) designation. A good place to find one is by contacting the president of the nearest Estate Planning Council. You can get the name and number of the local chapter president nearest you by calling the National Association of Estate Planners and Councils at (866) 226-2224 or online at www.naepc.org.

3. Use cash value life insurance. In cases where survivorship life is not available because either there is no spouse or one spouse in not insurable, you could use any of the other types of cash value policies on the life of the insurable party. This would include whole life, universal life, or variable life. All the other rules apply, including having a trust own the policy or having the children own the policy with the parent making gifts that the children can use to pay the premiums.

As with all life insurance, you want to make certain that you are dealing with a financially strong company. Choose a company that is rated AA or higher by the major rating services.

In the case of our friends the Adamses, let's assume that they determined that they needed $1,750,000 of life insurance to pay their (potential) estate taxes. They find an agent, take the necessary physical exams, pay the premium, and they are set, right? Unfortunately, they may well have created a major problem for their heirs and unwittingly made their estate tax problem worse. Because their life insurance policy is now also part of their estate, the insurance death proceeds will be subject to the estate tax. To resolve this problem they need to consider the *irrevocable life insurance trust*.

The Irrevocable Life Insurance Trust

The primary reason for establishing an irrevocable life insurance trust is to remove the life insurance from your estate so that it will not be subject to estate taxes. Here's how these trusts work:

Step 1

You have your attorney draw up the trust. It will usually have the same or similar provisions as your credit shelter trust (Chapter 8). Typically, it provides that the income goes to your spouse along with access to principal for certain reasons. At your spouse's death, the trust either continues for the benefit of your children, or the trust terminates and trust principal is distributed to them outright.

Step 2

Once the trust is established, you make a gift to the trust in the amount of the premium of your life insurance policy or policies. It is important to review the gift tax consequences, if any, with your tax advisor.

Step 3

The trustee sends all beneficiaries a written notice that they have a right to withdraw the money that you have just contributed to the trust. This notice is technically referred to as a *Crummey notice* (the name comes from a 1968 court case *Crummey vs. Commissioner*, which Mr. Crummey won). This notice will give your beneficiaries a time period in which to request a distribution. The time period is typically 30 days. If the beneficiaries don't request a distribution within the time period, their ability to take a distribution expires. Because it is your intent that the money be used for payment of life insurance premiums, your assumption is that no beneficiary will request a distribution. When we work with our clients, we normally request that each beneficiary acknowledge notice of the right to take a distribution. This provides proof for the Internal Revenue Service that the letters were actually sent and received. The effect of giving the beneficiaries the right to withdraw money now creates a gift of a *present interest* to the trust and, thus, qualifies your premium contributions for your annual gift tax exclusion.

Step 4

Once all beneficiaries have declined their right to take a distribution, or the time period for exercising that right has expired, the trustee pays the life insurance premium.

Step 5

When you die the trust is funded via the death benefit proceeds and the trustee uses the money to provide financial support for your beneficiaries or to provide liquidity to pay estate taxes. The death benefits are not part of your estate and, therefore, no estate taxes are due.

In order to consolidate the number of trusts a family has, we will sometimes recommend that the credit shelter trust pour over into the irrevocable insurance trust at the death of the grantor.

Irrevocable life insurance trusts are an excellent strategy for reducing estate taxes. Let's look at an example of this strategy in action.

Case Study

Edward and Barbara Millhouse are married and have four children. In addition to their $9,000,000 net worth, Edward owns a $2,500,000 term life insurance policy on his life payable to Barbara. For illustration purposes, we will assume that Edward dies first and that all of the assets are in his name. They have basic wills that utilize the credit shelter trust. Without an irrevocable life insurance trust, the Millhouses' estate tax situation would appear as depicted in Figure 10.1.

If, on the other hand, Edward established an irrevocable life insurance trust that was the owner and beneficiary of his life insurance policy, the estate taxes would have been zero. Take a look at Figure 10.2 to see how this works.

Getting Your Life Insurance into Your Trust

If you move existing life insurance policies into your trust and die during the first three years of that transfer, the insurance proceeds will be included in your estate. This is exactly what you are trying to avoid. The only way to solve this problem is to live the three years or use *new* insurance. When using new insurance, you must first establish your irrevocable life insurance trust, then have the trustee apply for the life insurance policy on your life. Your trustee will be both the owner and beneficiary of the policy. By following this procedure, you will have never had an *incident of ownership* in the policy. The result is that the insurance proceeds will never be included in your estate, as long as you follow the Crummey procedures outlined earlier in this chapter.

Disadvantages of the Irrevocable Life Insurance Trust

- *Irrevocable*. Once the trust is established, it cannot be changed. A decision you made a few short years ago may be inappropriate for your current circumstances. If you have funded your trust with term life insurance, you can simply write a new trust and buy new term insurance to put in it. If you are not insurable, or if you used cash value life insurance, you may be stuck

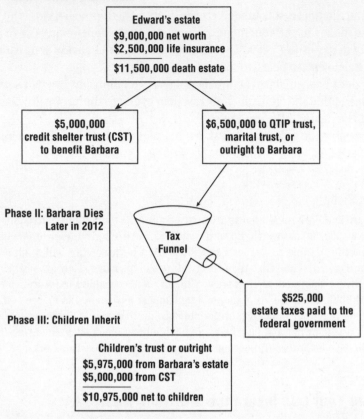

FIGURE 10.1 Millhouse Estate Plan without Irrevocable Life Insurance Trust

with your original trust. Because the trust is irrevocable, you will want to give thoughtful consideration to all the provisions and have your attorney provide as much flexibility as possible.

- *Gift tax problems.* You have to follow the rules when you make gifts to your trust so that you don't create gift tax problems. The number of beneficiaries of your trust will determine how much money you can contribute without creating gift taxes. Your attorney or financial advisor can assist you with this decision.

- *Crummey procedures.* In order to be certain that your gifts are considered gifts of a present interest, you must strictly follow the notification rules. Failure to follow these rules could have adverse tax consequences. Implementation is not particularly time consuming, but you and your trustee must be consistent in your follow-through.

- *Separate entity.* Your trust is a separate tax-paying entity. If it has income, it must file a tax return and pay taxes. Your trustee must also apply for and

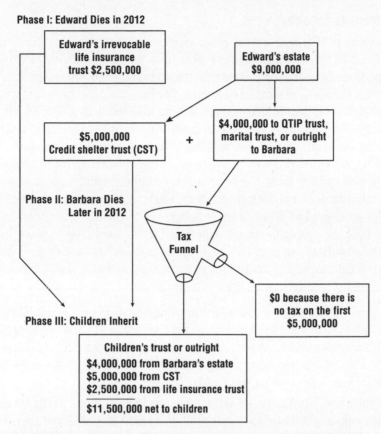

FIGURE 10.2 Millhouse Estate Plan with Irrevocable Life Insurance Trust

receive a tax identification number. If your trust does have income, but the income is passed through to your beneficiaries, then that income is taxed to the beneficiaries not the trust.

- *Expense*. Depending on your attorney's fees and the complexity of your trust, your fee could range from a few hundred dollars to a few thousand dollars. However, this expense can be quite small compared to the potential estate tax savings.

Using Life Insurance to Leverage Your Estate

Thus far, we have touted the estate tax savings benefits of the irrevocable life insurance trust, but you can also use this type of trust to leverage the *size* of your estate. The purpose is not to cover your estate taxes but rather to create a much larger estate for your heirs. This type of irrevocable trust is often referred to as a *dynasty trust*. The procedures for setting up your dynasty trust are the same as we have discussed for the irrevocable life insurance trust.

How Much Is Enough?

The amount of life insurance to place in your dynasty trust is typically determined one of three ways. The first method is for you to decide how large a premium commitment you are comfortable making. Then you would have your life insurance agent determine how much life insurance the premium will buy. For example, you decide that you are willing to commit to a $20,000 per year premium. You then have your life insurance agent determine how much life insurance that $20,000 premium will buy with a competitive company.

The second method is for you to predetermine the amount of insurance you want in your dynasty trust. Say you have three children and want to make sure they each receive a $1,000,000 inheritance. You would have your insurance agent shop for a competitive $3,000,000 life policy.

The final method of figuring out how much life insurance to place in your dynasty trust is to make gifts based on the maximum you can give without incurring gift taxes. The maximum you can contribute to your trust without paying gift taxes is defined by two constraints:

1. Annually, the maximum you can contribute is based on the Annual Gift Tax Exclusion. For 2011 the maximum tax-free gift is $13,000 per beneficiary. If you are married and you and your spouse join in the gift, you can give up to $26,000 per beneficiary. These dollar limits may increase in the future based on the consumer price index (CPI).
2. Under the 2010 Tax Relief Act, for gifts made in 2011 and 2012 that exceed the annual gift limits, the tax-free gift limit is $5,000,000 If you are married, both you and your spouse can each gift $5,000,000 for a total of $10,000,000.

The combination of your annual gift tax exclusion and lifetime applicable exclusion amount (for gifts made during your lifetime) leaves plenty of room for large premiums and correspondingly large amounts of life insurance.

Types of Insurance

What type of insurance is best for your dynasty trust?

TERM INSURANCE

If your spouse would need the income from the insurance proceeds at your death, and you want to minimize your initial premiums, then term life insurance should be considered. Using term insurance for a dynasty trust is a short-term solution only, because if you live to anything close to life expectancy, term insurance will become too expensive. Make sure that the term insurance that you *do* buy is convertible to permanent cash value life insurance without further evidence of insurability. Later, when you can afford to pay the higher premiums of a cash value policy, you will be guaranteed the right to do so. Avoid any term life plans that are not convertible during their last few years.

CASH VALUE INSURANCE

If your spouse would need the income from the insurance proceeds at your death and you can afford the premiums, then you should consider purchasing a cash value life insurance policy such as whole life, universal life, or variable life.

SURVIVORSHIP LIFE INSURANCE

If your assets outside of your dynasty trust are sufficient to provide adequate financial support for your surviving spouse and family, then you can maximize the leverage by using a survivorship life insurance policy. This is because premiums for survivorship life are about one-third that of traditional cash-value life insurance policies.

Comparative premiums and cash values for each type of policy for a male age 50 are shown in Table 10.2.

About Your Cash Values

You probably have noticed the significant amount of cash value buildup in the policies illustrated in Table 10.2. Because this is an irrevocable trust, do you give up the access to all that cash? What if you have an emergency and really need your cash value? The answer lies in a technically drafted clause called a *limited power of appointment*. This clause in your trust allows the holder of the power to make trust distributions at anytime to you (the grantor) or others (presumably children) designated in the trust. Typically, your spouse would be the holder of this trust power. Note that the power holder couldn't be forced to make distributions. Distributions must be at his or her sole discretion. This provision allows you some access to your cash values during your lifetime. As an added bonus, in most situations these cash values would be insulated from your creditors and potential lawsuits.

The Joint Dynasty Trust

Your dynasty trust can include life insurance policies on the lives of people other than yourself. Most typically, the "other" is your spouse. If neither of you needs the life insurance proceeds at the death of the other, placing your policies into your dynasty trust can be an excellent strategy. The result is the transfer of a large asset (the life insurance death benefits) to future generations of heirs free of income and estate taxes.

Dynasty Planning without a Trust

Although a trust is often used in dynasty planning, it is not a requirement. Nontrust dynasty planning is most often used in conjunction with annual gifts to children. The typical situation looks something like this: You decide that you want to make annual gifts to your adult children, but you are concerned that they

TABLE 10.2 $1,000,000 Life Insurance Premium Comparison for Male, Age 50

Year	Cumulative Premium	Cash Value[1]	Death Benefit
20-Year Level Term: $2,000 annual premium			
1	$2,000	$0	$1,000,000
5	$10,000	$0	$1,000,000
10	$20,000	$0	$1,000,000
20	$40,000	$0	$1,000,000
Whole Life: $23,540 annual premium			
1	$11,270	$0	$1,000,000
5	$56,350	$9,835	$1,000,000
10	$112,700	$83,684	$1,000,000
20	$225,400	$235,964	$1,000,000
Universal Life: $18,750 annual premium			
1	$18,750	$0	$1,000,000
5	$93,750	$50,063	$1,000,000
10	$187,500	$175,291	$1,000,000
20	$375,000	$493,216	$1,000,000
Variable Life: $19,000 annual premium			
1	$19,000	$0	$1,000,000
5	$95,000	$58,199	$1,000,000
10	$190,000	$191,201	$1,000,000
20	$380,000	$563,323	$1,000,000
Survivorship Life:[2] $4,550 annual premium			
1	$4,550	$0	$1,000,000
5	$22,250	$0	$1,000,000
10	$45,500	$15,241	$1,000,000
20	$91,000	$115,551	$1,000,000

[1] Cash values are for surrender values.
[2] Survivorship life for a male age 50 and female age 50.
Note: Premiums and cash values are based on current mortality costs and current dividends/interest and are not guaranteed. For variable life policy, an 8% gross rate of return is assumed.

might squander the money. An excellent solution is to have them apply for and own a life insurance policy on your life. You then gift them an amount of money each year equal to the life insurance premiums. At your death, they receive the death proceeds both income and estate tax-free. You could accomplish the same result using life policies that you already own, but existing insurance would be included in your estate if you died during the first three years from the date of transfer. Remember, if you want to maximize the leverage of premiums paid, the best type policy for this purpose is the survivorship life insurance policy.

One Final Benefit of Dynasty Planning

By establishing a dynasty trust or plan, you have, in effect, provided a substantial inheritance for your children or other heirs. This allows you the freedom to spend all your other assets so as to maximize your retirement lifestyle. Too often, we find retired people are denying themselves the style of retirement they deserve so that they can leave an inheritance for their children. Dynasty planning allows you to die broke without guilt.

Long-Term Care Insurance

Long-term care (LTC) insurance is a complex issue with few perfect answers. What is right for one person may be inappropriate for another. The optimal way to handle it is to meet with your financial advisor or someone who specializes in elder care issues. The cost of nursing home care varies widely from approximately $50,000 to more than $200,000 per year and will likely triple over the next 20 years. When purchasing a policy, consider these guidelines:

- Long-term care insurance is most suitable for people with assets between $200,000 and $3,000,000 (excluding your home). If your assets are less than $200,000, LTC premiums may be unaffordable, especially if you're over age 65. Furthermore, you would soon become eligible for Medicaid. With assets greater than $3 million, you can probably afford to pay for services out of your assets. If you are age 50 today, the cost of a comprehensive LTC policy ranges from about $1,000 to $1,500 per year for a $150-per-day benefit. After age 55, premiums increase about 50 percent every five years so that by the time you are age 70, this same coverage would cost you $5,000 or more per year.

- Shop for coverage. Coverage provisions vary widely from policy to policy and company to company. You should be able to tailor a policy to your specific needs and desires. If you own an older policy, have your agent compare it to a new one. Some companies will allow you to upgrade or exchange your coverage. To compare coverages of several major LTC insurance writers, go to www.welchgroup.com; click on Resource Center; then click on "Links"; then "Compare LTC Policies."

- If you are married, you should purchase coverage on both you and your spouse. You don't want to be in a position where the spouse without coverage goes into a nursing home and depletes family assets that may be needed by the healthy spouse to cover his or her living expenses and subsequent long-term care needs.

- The younger you are, the more important it is to buy an inflation rider. Consider a 5 percent *compound* inflation rider if you are under age 60. If you are over age 60, consider a 5 percent *simple* inflation rider. Beyond age 75, it may be wiser to spend your premium dollars on additional daily benefit rather than an inflation rider.

- Today, approximately 80 percent of long-term care is received in the home rather than in a nursing care facility, and more than 22 million Americans are providing unpaid care for a parent. The value of these unpaid services exceeds $20,000 per year per caregiver. If home care is important to you, be sure your policy includes a rider that covers this benefit.

- Most policies provide a waiver of premium benefit that waives further premium payments once you begin receiving benefits. Some policies waive the premiums only during nursing home stay, not home health care. Because 80 percent of the care is in the home, be sure your policy waives premiums for home health care as well.

- The probability of staying in a nursing home for more than five years is less than 10 percent. Therefore, the best buy in long-term care insurance is a policy with a five-year *benefit period*. Lifetime coverage is available, but it is much more expensive.

- If you can afford to self-insure the first 90 days of a nursing home stay, you will reduce your premiums 5 percent to 10 percent or more. Be sure to choose a contract that requires you to satisfy your elimination period only once. Because you may go through several phases of need and recovery, you want to avoid having to satisfy the elimination period several times.

- The daily cost of nursing home care varies widely depending on where you live. Also, depending on your source of income and assets, it may only be necessary to insure a portion of the daily cost of care. Consult with your advisor regarding the costs in your area. He or she can advise of the appropriate amount of *daily benefit* you should purchase.

- How the insurance companies determine and calculate how benefits are paid can vary widely. The more liberal policies (called an *indemnity model*) pay full benefits *directly to you* without regard to actual expenses incurred, once you qualify. For example, if you purchased a $100-per-day daily benefit but the actual services you received from a home healthcare provider costs only $40 per day, your insurance company would send you a check for $100 per day. More restrictive policies (called *reimbursement model*) provide reimbursement of actual expenses incurred, paid either directly to you or to your healthcare provider. This latter method requires you to be responsible for record keeping. Generally, the indemnity type policy is preferred. This puts you in a better position to negotiate and control costs as well as the quality of your care.

- Over the past few years, some innovative policies have been created that combine long-term care with other insurance products. With these policies, if the benefits you receive do not exceed the premiums you paid, your beneficiary will receive a portion or all of the difference in the form of annuity payments or a survivorship benefit. The merit of these deals varies widely, so be sure to consult with your financial advisor.

- As with all insurance products, you will want to make certain that you choose an insurance company that is financially sound. Select a company that is rated AA or better by one of the major rating companies such as Standard & Poor, Moody, or Best. Also, dozens of companies sell LTC policies. Some of the major players are: Mass Mutual, Prudential, Mutual of Omaha, Genworth, John Hancock and Northwestern.

Estate Planning Benefits of Long-Term Care Insurance

If you have an estate of over $3,000,000, you can probably afford to self-insure against potential long-term care costs, but that may not be your best estate planning strategy. We have found that one of the biggest reasons people are not willing to give away assets during their lifetime is because of fear of needing those assets if they suffer a catastrophic illness. By purchasing a high-quality LTC policy, you are free to transfer your reserve assets, knowing that the risk of paying for a catastrophic illness has now been shifted to your insurance company. Remember, by giving the assets away now, you also give away the future *growth* of those assets, thus further reducing the estate taxes paid by your heirs.

As you can see, both life insurance and long-term care insurance can be powerful tools in developing your strategic estate plan. Many of the ideas discussed in this chapter revolve around gifting money for paying life insurance premiums. Reducing your estate through gifting programs is a basic, yet important estate planning strategy. In our next chapter, we will cover this issue in more detail.

CHAPTER 11

Smart Strategies for Gifting Assets to Family Members

One of the most straightforward ways to reduce estate taxes is to give away your assets. However, many people are reluctant to do this, fearing that they might need those assets at some future date. The best way to overcome these fears is to understand how much in assets you'll need in the future. To do this, complete the analysis in Chapter 5. Knowing that you have substantially more assets than you need for your retirement years should make you more confident about giving away assets. In this chapter, we examine the most popular strategies for gifting assets to family members.

The Annual Gift Tax Exclusion

You may think that giving away your assets shouldn't include interference from the government. After all, it is your property, and you should be able to do with it as you please. There was a time in our history when this was the case. The result was deathbed gifts of all one's property in order to avoid estate taxes. After all, we as Americans are quite ingenious at learning how to avoid taxes. But newer laws have changed the nature of the game, and you must follow the new rules if you're going to successfully minimize your taxes. The rules for annual gifting are as follows:

- In any calendar year you are allowed to give away up to $13,000 per person to as many people as you desire without triggering any gift taxes. The gifts can be in cash or property. This $13,000 annual exclusion is indexed for inflation.
- If you are married, you may give away up to $26,000 per year to as many people as you desire. This assumes that your spouse consents to make

TABLE 11.1 Applicable Exclusion Amount Increases (2005–2011)

Year	Exclusion Amount (Death)	Exclusion Amount (Gift)
2005	$1,500,000	$1,000,000
2006	$2,000,000	$1,000,000
2007	$2,000,000	$1,000,000
2008	$2,000,000	$1,000,000
2009	$1,000,000	$1,000,000
2010	$1,000,000	$1,000,000
2011 & 2012	$5,000,000	$5,000,000
2013[1]	$1,000,000	$1,000,000

[1] Assumes Congress does not extends the 2011 and 2012 exclusion amount.

the gifts with you. This is called a "split gift." Again, this amount will be adjusted for inflation annually.

- Your gift must be a gift of a present interest versus a gift of a future interest. For example, assume that you deeded your 25-year-old son a piece of land, but the deed said he would not receive title until his thirtieth birthday. This would be considered a gift of a *future* interest and would not be eligible for the annual gift tax exclusion.

- Gifts to spouses who are U.S. citizens are unlimited.

- If your gift results in a gift tax, you, not the receiver of the gift, are responsible for paying the tax. The gift tax return (Form 709) and the taxes on gifts in excess of the annual gift tax exclusion can be handled in one of two ways. You can pay the tax on the gift on or before the time your income tax return is due (April 15 of the following tax year or later if you file an extension), or you can use a portion of your applicable exclusion amount for any federal gift tax due. If you remember from previous discussions in this book, the federal tax law allows you to give to whomever you wish, either during your lifetime or at your death, an amount equal to the lifetime applicable exclusion amount free of federal estate taxes (see Table 11.1).

Unintended Gifts

It is possible to make a gift to someone without realizing what you have done. The result can create unintended tax consequences. Some typical examples are as follows:

- You add your child's name to your savings or checking account. This is considered a gift the moment your child makes a withdrawal. If the withdrawal exceeds the allowed annual gift tax exclusion, it will be considered a taxable gift.

- You want to be certain that a particular person receives a specific piece of real estate at your death. Your solution is to add their name to the deed. When the deed is executed, you have just made a gift for gift tax purposes.

- You decide to buy a security, such as a stock, bond, or limited partnership interest, in both your name and someone else's name. As soon as you designate the joint owner, a gift is deemed to have occurred.

  Under each of the preceding examples in which you created a joint ownership arrangement, at your death the entire value of the property is included in your estate. This is because you provided all of the financial consideration. If this is not your intended result, you can attempt to resolve the problem by making qualified gifts and filing a gift tax return.

- If you guarantee a loan for someone else, the guarantee could be deemed a gift for gift tax purposes. Assume that your child wants to start a business with start-up costs of $95,000. Your child has no money or collateral with which to obtain a loan from the bank. You agree to guarantee the loan at the bank. Based on the 1984 Supreme Court case *Dickman v. United States,* the Internal Revenue Service concluded that the act of guaranteeing a loan created a gift. The amount of the gift was to be based on the difference between the value of the loan the child could have received on his or her own versus the deal they received with your help. You can imagine the difficulty of arriving at an appropriate figure for gift tax purposes. Since this ruling, the Internal Revenue Service has indicated that no gift is imputed unless there is an actual default on the loan that requires you to satisfy the debt for the benefit of your child. If this occurs, you are deemed to have made a gift for the full unpaid balance of the loan less any repayments to you by your child.

Providing loan guarantees can also create negative estate tax results. When you die, your loan guarantee becomes an obligation of your estate. As such, it might not qualify for the marital deduction and could disqualify a QTIP election. The Internal Revenue Service has issued both favorable and unfavorable private letter rulings on this subject. If you're involved in this type of situation, proceed with caution and get assistance from a competent legal advisor.

Filing a Gift Tax Return

Gifts that you make to someone for less than $13,000 do not require the filing of a federal gift tax return. If you and your spouse jointly make a gift, you are required to file a federal gift tax return (Form 709). This is true even if the combined gift is less than $26,000, and no gift tax is due. All gifts of a future interest, and gifts of a present interest greater than $13,000, require the filing of a federal gift tax return. If your state of residence has a gift tax, you may also have to file a state gift tax return.

The Lifetime Applicable Exclusion Amount

In addition to the annual exclusion, you are also allowed a lifetime applicable exclusion amount. This lifetime applicable exclusion amount represents the amount of money or property that you can give to someone other than your spouse free of gift or estate taxes. If these gifts are not made during your lifetime, they can be used at the time of your death. In 2011 and 2012, the amount of these tax-free lifetime gifts is limited to $5,000,000.

Although most people wait to use their lifetime applicable exclusion amount at death, it can be advantageous to use it while you're alive. If you own an asset that you expect to appreciate rapidly, you can remove the asset plus the *appreciation* of that asset from your future estate by giving it away before your death. For example, suppose you own 100 acres of farmland that is presently valued at $400,000 on the outskirts of town. Your town is growing rapidly, and the growth is all headed in your direction. If the growth continues, you speculate that your land value could increase tenfold or more. You decide to use part of your lifetime applicable exclusion amount and gift the property to your children via a trust. It turns out that your estimates were low and the land ends up being valued at $10,000,000. By giving the property to your children, you save the estate taxes on $9.6 million of appreciation.

Outright Gifts

Based on an evaluation of your estate, you determine that you have excess assets and can therefore afford to begin a gifting program for your children. Now that you have made this decision, what is the best way to maximize the power of your gifts? The answer is to evaluate the different assets that you own that are available to give away. The following sections present a review of the pros and cons of several different possibilities.

Outright Gifts of Cash

Perhaps the easiest gift to make is cash. You simply write a check to your child or other donee. The recipient receives the money and does with it as he or she pleases. The disadvantage is that your child may spend the money unwisely. We have seen many cases where children become dependent on annual gifts from their parents. Another disadvantage is that the money you give could become subject to either a divorce proceeding or a creditor's claim.

Outright Gifts of Appreciating Property

The value of giving away property that is expected to appreciate rapidly is that you are also giving away the *future growth*. Suppose you give your child $13,000 worth of stock in a start-up company that you expect to appreciate significantly. As it turns out, you were correct, and the stock appreciates on average 15 percent per year over the next 25 years. By making a gift of $13,000 in the present, you have removed an asset that would have grown (compounding appreciation) to $427,946 in the future.

Outright Gifts of Appreciated Property

Some people choose to give away assets that have already appreciated substantially. If you expect the asset to continue to appreciate rapidly in the future, then you will receive some of the same benefits mentioned previously. Gifting appreciated property can have its disadvantages. Some of your gifts of appreciated property are subject to divorce proceedings and creditor claims. Also, if you hold appreciated property until you die, your heirs receive a stepped-up cost basis. Your heir could then sell the property and pay no capital gains or income taxes.

Roth IRAs

It may seem strange to discuss Roth IRAs in the section on giving assets to your children, but one of the true power plays is to give your children the money to make a Roth IRA contribution. Assume that your 19-year-old daughter works summers to earn extra spending money. Her total earnings are $6,500. You give her $5,000 so she can make a contribution to a Roth IRA. Her contribution to the Roth IRA is not deductible, but because of her low tax bracket this is unimportant. The true value of the Roth IRA is *tax-free* growth. The earnings will never be taxed if she adheres to the following rules:

- If she waits until after she turns age $59\frac{1}{2}$, withdrawals are tax-free.
- If she were to become disabled, withdrawals would be tax-free.
- If she uses the money for a qualified purpose, there is no tax on withdrawals. A qualified purpose includes withdrawals of up to $10,000 in acquisition costs for her first home.
- Another qualified purpose is withdrawals for tuition payments of qualified higher education expenses for herself, her spouse, or her children.
- Generally, no tax-free withdrawals are allowed during the five taxable year period beginning with the first taxable year for which the contribution was made.

Although a $5,000 contribution may not seem significant, the results can be quite dramatic. Let's assume that your daughter invests in a stock mutual fund that earns on average 10.5 percent, and she does not touch it until she is age 75. Your small one-time gift of $5,000 has turned into $1,340,000! This is the type of gift you will want to make each year. As an added bonus, because it is a retirement account, she is less likely to squander the money.

When the Donee Is a Minor

If you have decided to begin making gifts to your children, but they are minors, you will need to make special preparations. Although the law allows minors to receive property in their name, no state allows them to sign legally binding contracts, so future dealings involving their property can be difficult. Practical ways to manage minor children's property include using custodial accounts or minor's trusts. In the following sections, we examine each approach.

Custodial Accounts

Most often, assets are transferred to minors under either the Uniform Gifts to Minors Act (UGMA) or the Uniform Transfers to Minors Act (UTMA), depending on which act your state has adopted. The forerunner of these was the UGMA, which allowed an adult (the custodian) to act on the behalf of a minor concerning the minor's property. Under this act, the custodian can invest the child's money in bank accounts, securities, annuities, and life insurance. The UTMA expanded the types of investments to include real estate and tangible personal property.

ADVANTAGES

- Custodial accounts are easy to set up and make it easy to transfer property. To set up a custodial account all you need to do is open the account by listing the name of the child and custodian as follows: "Richard B. Franklin (the name of the custodian) as Custodian f/b/o (for the benefit of) Sara J. Franklin (the name of the child) under the (your state) Uniform Gifts (or Transfers) to Minors Act." Transferring title to existing property is equally as easy.

- To set up a custodial account, no additional documents or agreements are required, so the costs are minimal.

- Custodians are not required to post any bonds and are not required to provide any reporting to the courts.

- The custodian is allowed broad powers to transact business on behalf of the minor child.

- The gifted assets and the future appreciation of the assets may be removed from your estate.

- The assets can be used for the health, education, maintenance, and support of your child (with certain restrictions).
- Transfers to custodial accounts are treated as gifts of present interests and therefore qualify for the annual gift tax exclusion.

DISADVANTAGES

- The gifts are irrevocable. Once you have made a gift, you cannot change your mind later and take the property back.
- Your child will get legal control of the property no later than his or her twenty-first birthday. The UGMA requires transfer of the property at the age of majority for your state of residence, usually age 18 or 19. Under the UTMA, some states allow the transferor to select when the child receives the property outright between the ages of 18 and 21. Other states set the age of legal transfer at age 21. If you have a choice in your state, we prefer the UTMA with age 21 as the legal age of transfer. The obvious concern is that children between ages 18 and 21 may not be mature enough to handle money without parental supervision.
- The assets you have gifted your child may become part of your estate for estate tax purposes. Few states allow minors to draw a will. If a minor child dies, the laws of intestacy of your state of residence determine to whom the child's estate will go. In virtually every state, a minor child's property reverts to the parents. The only way to avoid this pitfall is to establish a trust. Also, if you act as both the transferor and custodian, and you die before your child reaches the age of majority (as defined under the UGMA or UTMA), the property you gave your child will be included in your estate for estate tax purposes. One solution to this problem is to have your spouse act as the custodian. However, this too can be an issue in some states if your spouse is legally obligated to support your minor child and state law does not preclude the use of custodial funds for this purpose. Consult competent legal advice before proceeding. A better strategy would be to choose another family member or friend to act as the custodian. By so doing, you have effectively resolved this problem.
- Your child can sue the custodian. This may sound far-fetched, but it does happen. Once your child reaches the age of majority as defined under the UGMA or UTMA, he or she has the legal right to request an accounting of how his or her money has been handled. If it has been handled improperly in the eyes of the courts, the custodian could be held personally liable.
- Income from the custodial account may be taxed to you or your child at your tax rate. If your child is under the age of 14 and receives unearned income in excess of $1,900 for 2011 (indexed each year for inflation), that

excess income will be taxed at your highest marginal tax rate. This is what is commonly referred to as the "kiddie tax." Once the child turns age 14, all income is then taxed at the child's tax bracket.

If you prefer to exercise more control over your gifts to your children than allowed under custodial accounts, then you should consider either a 2503(b) trust or a 2503(c) trust. These are both minor's trusts and are named after the applicable Internal Revenue Code section.

2503(b) Trust

The primary advantage of this trust is that the trustee is never required to distribute principal to your child. The trustee must, however, distribute all the income on at least an annual basis. Gifts to the trust do qualify for the annual gift tax exclusion, but only as related to the present value of the future income stream. For example, you contribute $10,000 to a trust for your five-year-old daughter to last for 30 years. The Internal Revenue Service interest rate assumption is 2.3 percent. Considering these facts, the value of your gift was $5,091, which qualifies for the $13,000 annual gift tax exclusion. Therefore, $4,909 is considered a gift of a future interest, and you must either pay gift taxes on this amount or use part of your lifetime applicable exclusion amount. This trust can also be structured to allow the trustee to distribute principal under certain conditions. This type of trust requires the filing of an annual gift tax return in any year that a gift is made. The trustee must also apply for and receive a tax identification number. A separate trust must be set up for each beneficiary.

2503(c) Trust

We have found that because of greater flexibility and control, clients are more willing to consider the 2503(c) trust arrangement. This type of trust allows the trustee to either distribute or accumulate trust income. The trust document can also allow the trustee to make distributions of trust corpus for predetermined reasons or at the trustee's discretion. Any income not distributed will be taxed to the trust. Income distributed to your child will be taxed at your child's tax bracket if your child is age *19 or older*. The kiddie tax rules apply for children under the age 18 or younger and dependent students under the age of 24.

The primary disadvantage of the 2503(c) trust is that your child has a legal right to all trust assets when he or she turns 21. To avoid this result, the best solution is to incorporate a "window" in your trust document. When your child reaches age 21, he or she has the right to terminate the trust and receive all assets. If he or she fails to exercise his or her right within a certain time period (usually 60 days), the child's right to take possession of the trust assets expires. The trust then continues to be managed for your child's benefit for life or until your child reaches a certain age that you choose. As with the custodial accounts and the 2503(b) trust, this trust is irrevocable. Once you have made the gifts, you cannot get your assets back. Gifts to the trust do qualify for the annual gift tax exclusion. By including a special provision in the trust, you as the grantor may be responsible to report and pay all income taxes (ordinary and capital gains). This can greatly benefit the child but is not considered a taxable gift. The provision may even be changed if paying the income taxes becomes a financial burden.

Other Tax-Free Gifts

In addition to your annual and lifetime gift tax exclusions, you receive an unlimited annual exclusion for the payment of a donee's medical expenses or tuition. We have found this to be particularly useful where a grandparent is already making maximum annual gifts to grandchildren. They can then pay the grandchild's tuition or medical costs without incurring gift taxes. For these payments to qualify for the unlimited annual exclusion, they must be made *directly* to the qualifying educational institution or medical provider. These payments are not tax deductible by the donor or donee.

If the gift you wish to make is for the specific purpose of funding education expenses, then you need to consider the Section 529 plans. Section 529 plans are thoroughly reviewed in Chapter 1.

One gift that qualifies for the annual exclusion but is still included in your estate is a gift of life insurance within three years of your death. In this case, all of the life insurance proceeds are included in your estate for estate tax purposes. For example, you decide that you want to remove your $250,000 term life insurance policy from your estate by transferring the ownership to your adult son. You do so but die within three years of the gift. The result is that the $250,000 of life insurance proceeds are included as part of your estate for the purpose of calculating your estate taxes.

Family Gifts Utilizing Trusts

Thus far we have primarily discussed outright gifts to family members. There can also be significant advantages to making gifts to family members through the use of trusts. Two primary benefits include control issues and the possibility of receiving substantial valuation discounts for such gifts. Some of the more often used trusts include the Grantor Retained Annuity Trust (GRAT), the Grantor Retained Unitrust (GRUT), and the Qualified Personal Residence Trust (QPRT).

Even without a GRAT, GRUT, or QPRT, gifts to irrevocable trusts can create additional income tax benefits for the grantor and gift tax benefits for the trust beneficiaries. On July 6, 2004, the IRS released Revenue Ruling 2004-64. The IRS acquiesced to the idea that the payment of income taxes by the grantor on behalf of his or her grantor trust will not result in an additional taxable gift to the grantor if certain trust requirements are met. This allows the grantor to shift greater wealth to future generations tax-free. If the gift trust is drafted as a so-called "grantor trust," this technique is available.

Grantor Retained Annuity Trust

A GRAT allows you to make a substantial gift to a child (or anyone) at a significant reduction or without gift taxes while you retain an income interest for a stated period of time. Because your beneficiary is only receiving the remainder at the end of the trust term, his or her interest is considered a *future* interest and not a present interest. Here's how this works:

- You, the grantor, establish an irrevocable trust in which you retain a fixed income interest. This fixed income can either be based on a fixed dollar amount or a fixed percent based on the initial asset value transferred.
- You determine the number of years the trust will last. The trust period can be any period of time. The longer the period of time, the smaller the amount of the gift to your beneficiaries is in the eyes of the Internal Revenue Service.
- You determine who the remainder beneficiaries will be (typically your children).
- You transfer assets into your GRAT.
- You receive the designated income stream for the designated term of the trust.
- At the end of the trust term, the remaining assets revert to your beneficiaries. This reversion can either be outright or in trust.

When you transfer assets into your trust, you have made a gift for gift tax purposes. To determine the value of your gift, you subtract the present value of your future stream of income from the value of your original contribution to your GRAT.

ADVANTAGES

- The primary advantage of a GRAT is that it allows you to give away a large asset while paying little or no gift taxes.
- The gift, although a gift of a future interest, represents the immediate transfer of an asset. As a result, any *appreciation* of that asset accrues to the benefit of your beneficiaries and is not included in your estate.
- As grantor, you retain the income from the trust during the term of the trust.
- You can act as the trustee of your GRAT if the trust is properly drafted.

DISADVANTAGES

- One of the primary disadvantages of the GRAT is that if you die during the term of the trust the assets revert back to your estate for estate tax purposes. For planning purposes, you will want to choose a trust term that you are likely to survive.

- The GRAT is an irrevocable trust, and, therefore, you have permanently given up the right to your principal.

- The GRAT is a grantor trust, and as such, all income is taxed to the grantor (you) whether or not it is paid to the grantor.

- Your beneficiaries' interest in the trust is a future interest and therefore does not qualify for the annual gift tax exclusion. Your only alternatives are to pay the gift taxes associated with the gift or use a portion of your lifetime applicable exclusion amount.

- The income that you receive is a fixed income and therefore may not adequately offset the future ravages of inflation.

Grantor Retained Unitrust

The GRUT, although very similar to the GRAT, has several significant differences. The key distinction has to do with how your income is determined. As discussed previously, with a GRAT you receive a fixed income. Under a GRUT, the income you receive is variable. Suppose you (at age 50) place $500,000 into a GRUT and elect a 7 percent income. The first year your income would be $35,000. If the next year the account grew to $550,000, your income would be 7 percent of the new balance, or $38,500. If, however, the account decreased to $450,000, your income would only be $31,500. If the assets that you are transferring to your trust are likely to appreciate at a greater rate than your withdrawal rate, and if you want an increasing income, then you should consider a GRUT.

Table 11.2 shows an example of how the mathematics can work for a GRAT versus a GRUT.

Qualified Personal Residence Trust

When trying to reduce the size of one's estate in order to reduce taxes, the notion of giving away one's residence rarely comes to mind. If done properly, the gifting of a residence can have significant tax benefits without limiting one's use of the residence. One of the best ways to do this is through a QPRT. This is one of those rare instances where you can have your cake and eat it too.

In working with clients who have taxable estates, we have often found that they are much more willing to give away their residence if they have the right to continue to live there, rather than giving away their investments, which often represent their security against unknown financial circumstances such as an

TABLE 11.2 Benefits Comparison of GRAT versus GRUT*

Year	Annual Distribution to Donor	Value of Remainder Interest	Year	Annual Distribution to Donor	Value of Remainder Interest
1	$35,000	$0	1	$38,150	$0
2	$35,000	$0	2	$38,673	$0
3	$35,000	$0	3	$39,202	$0
4	$35,000	$0	4	$39,740	$0
5	$35,000	$0	5	$40,284	$0
6	$35,000	$0	6	$40,836	$0
7	$35,000	$0	7	$41,395	$0
8	$35,000	$0	8	$41,962	$0
9	$35,000	$0	9	$42,537	$0
10	$35,000	$0	10	$43,120	$0
11	$35,000	$0	11	$43,711	$0
12	$35,000	$0	12	$44,310	$0
13	$35,000	$0	13	$44,917	$0
14	$35,000	$0	14	$45,532	$0
15	$35,000	$0	15	$46,156	$0
16	$35,000	$0	16	$46,788	$0
17	$35,000	$0	17	$47,429	$0
18	$35,000	$0	18	$48,079	$0
19	$35,000	$0	19	$48,738	$0
20	$35,000	$0	20	$49,405	$0
21	$0	$1,011,601	21	$0	$656,385
Totals	$700,000	$1,011,601		$870,964	$656,385

Calculations courtesy of Comdel, Inc., Crescendo Planned Gifts Marketing Software, A. Charles Schultz, President/Author, (800) 858–9154.
*Assumptions: $500,000 contribution, 20-year term, 7 percent withdrawal rate, 9 percent income return on investments, 5 percent IRS Section 7520 rate.
GRAT: $63,823 present value of gift
GRUT: $195,450 present value of gift

illness. In other cases, the residence may be one of the only available assets to give.

How to Set up a Qualified Personal Residence Trust

Under a QPRT, an individual known as a grantor irrevocably transfers his or her primary or secondary residence to a trust for a fixed period of time, such as 10 to 15 years. During the term of the trust, the grantor retains the right to use and occupy the personal residence on an unrestricted basis. At the end of the term, the residence then passes to the designated beneficiaries known as remaindermen (usually the grantor's children). At the end of the term, the grantor then leases the residence back from the remaindermen. These lease payments do not interfere with his or her ability to make annual gifts each year.

Tax Treatment

Because the remaindermen will not receive the gift for 10 to 15 years, the grantor is allowed a discount based on the present value of the future gift. The amount of the discount is determined by Internal Revenue Service tables. This allows the grantor to significantly discount the value of the gift.

> Consider Richard and Betty Franklin. Richard, age 67, and Betty, age 64, have a total estate exceeding $7,000,000. Of that, approximately $1,000,000 is in real estate consisting of their primary home and their vacation home. Their primary residence has a market value of $450,000. They want to keep the home but also want to reduce their taxes as their estate continues to grow. Richard and Betty decide to establish a QPRT and transfer their residence into the trust for 15 years. At the end of that time, the home will be transferred to their two adult children. Because the gift of the property to the trust is irrevocable, it creates a completed gift for gift tax purposes. Because the beneficiaries will not receive the property until the end of the 15-year period, it is a gift of future interest rather than a gift of present interest. Therefore, it qualifies for a discount. For federal gift tax purposes, the value of the gift, based on IRS discount tables (5 percent assumed), is only $178,109. They will use a portion of their lifetime applicable exclusion amount to avoid paying gift taxes.
>
> For the Franklins, life has changed very little. They continue to live in their home just as they always have. At the end of the 15-year period, when the property does revert to their children, they will establish a lease that requires that they pay rent to the children, which further reduces their estate. It should be noted that these rental payments do not limit their annual gift tax exclusion.

ADVANTAGES

There are many advantages to setting up a QPRT, including the following:

- In many cases, it is more palatable to give away your residence rather than cash or securities to reduce estate taxes. By holding onto your stocks, bonds, and cash, you can feel more secure about handling a significant financial emergency should one occur. However, by giving away the house while retaining the right to live in it, you do not change your lifestyle even though you make a significant move toward reducing the value of your current and future estate.

- You effectively remove a large asset from your estate at a significant discount from its current value. The Franklins were able to give away an asset worth $450,000 for $178,109.

- You remove the growth of your residence from your estate. If the Franklins' home continued to appreciate over the next 15 years at 5 percent, it would be worth $935,000. By giving their home away, they saved the taxes on the additional $485,000 of appreciation.

- You entirely avoid probate on your residence because it is passing to your heirs through the trust instead of under your will.

- At the end of the trust term, you are allowed to increase your annual gifting by paying rent to your heirs. These payments will not be included as part of your allowable annual gift tax exclusion.

DISADVANTAGES

There are also several disadvantages to a QPRT.

- If you die during the term of the trust, the value of the personal residence is included in your estate for estate tax purposes. Although this result may not be what you hoped for, it is not as bad as it seems. The property receives a stepped-up cost basis and any applicable credit amount that has been used is retrieved. In other words, for federal estate tax purposes, it is as if the transaction never occurred. You have, however, gone to the trouble and expense of setting up the trust and received no benefit.

- When you transfer the residence, the beneficiaries will receive the same tax basis as you had upon the date of transfer. However, if you had held the residence until your death, they would have received a stepped-up cost basis based on the value at the date of your death. In that case, they could have then sold the home without owing capital gains taxes.

- At the end of the term the residence may not be available for your use. Technically, the home is now the property of the remaindermen (your children) rather than your property. They must allow you to continue to live in the residence, presumably under some arrangement whereby you would be paying them rent.

- If the residence is sold, the $250,000 ($500,000 for married couples) *exclusion for gain on sale of residence* is not available because it is no longer your residence.

- If there is a mortgage on the property, any payments on that mortgage are considered a gift to the remaindermen.

Case Study

Consider a case example of how a QPRT can reduce estate taxes for Richard and Betty Franklin. In order to simplify the case and focus on the value of the QPRT, we assume that all assets except for the home did not increase in value and that the term of the trust was 15 years.

Scenario 1

The Franklins die in 2011 at the beginning of the sixteenth year with no planning.

$10,000,000	Miscellaneous assets (future growth at 0 percent growth rate)
+$935,000	Residence ($450,000 current value at 5 percent growth rate)
$10,935,000	Estate value in 16 years
−$10,000,000	Applicable exclusion amount (review Table 11.1)
$935,000	Subject to estate tax
$327,250	Approximate tax due

Scenario 2

The Franklins transfer their residence to a QPRT with their two children as remaindermen and die 16 years later.

$10,000,000	Miscellaneous assets (future growth at 0 percent growth rate)
+$0	Residence
$10,000,000	
+$178,109	Taxable gift*
$10,178,109	Subject to estate tax
$14,500	Tax due

*Discounted value of the transfer of the residence in 15 years.

As you can see from the previous examples, the potential tax savings through a QPRT can be significant. If the Franklins did not die in the sixteenth year, but lived well beyond that, the value of the tax savings would increase because the continuing appreciation of the property has been removed from their estate. They could also make rent payments to the children in addition to their annual gift tax exclusion. This allows them to continue to move more and more assets out of their estate.

Death during the Term of the Trust

As the grantor, you can receive a larger discount by creating a *contingent reversionary interest*. With a contingent reversionary interest, you state in the trust agreement that if you die before the trust term expires, your last will and testament will determine who receives the trust property.

If the grantor dies during the term of the trust, the property is included in the grantor's estate, and at that time, receives a stepped-up cost basis based on the fair market value at the date of death. Also, any applicable exclusion amount that was used to transfer the property to the trust will be revived to the benefit of the grantor. In other words, it is as if this transaction had never taken place.

Taking Advantage of Generation-Skipping Transfers

Prior to 1987, there were no laws that prevented you from leaving large amounts of assets in trust for multiple generations of family members. For example, you could place several million dollars in a trust that provided for a lifetime of income for your children and grandchildren. As long as your children did not have a general power of appointment, the assets would not be included in their estates for estate tax purposes. Passage of the Generation Skipping Transfer Tax in 1987 significantly reduced one's ability to pass money to multiple generations without a transfer tax. Although transfer opportunities have been reduced, they have not been eliminated. Therein lies the opportunity.

In the following list, we examine the rules surrounding generation-skipping transfers (GSTs):

- A skip generation refers to family members one generation removed as would be the case of a gift from a grandparent to a grandchild. If the gift is to a nonfamily member, a person is considered a skip person if they are at least $37^1/_2$ years younger than the transferor.

- The generation skipping transfer tax that is imposed is based on the highest marginal estate and gift tax rate. (Currently 35 percent for 2011 and 2012, and potentially as high as 55 percent after 2012, subject to many legislative factors. See Table 1.3, page 9.)

- There are three categories of transfers that can occur. The first is called a *direct skip*. Direct skips occur when you gift assets directly to a generation skip person. For example, a direct skip would occur if you gave $100,000 directly to a grandchild or if you gave $100,000 to a trust in which your grandchild was the sole beneficiary. Any GST tax due must be paid at the time of the transfer. The transferor can elect to pay the tax himself/herself, or he/she can elect to have the taxes paid out of the gifted proceeds. The next category of GST occurs where there is a *taxable termination*. A taxable termination occurs when assets have been placed into a trust for multiple generations of family members and the last nonskip family member ceases to be a beneficiary of the trust. For example, you place $500,000 in a trust that will provide a lifetime income for your child. At your child's death, the trust will continue to provide a lifetime income for your grandchild. When your child dies a taxable termination has occurred, and at that time, your trustee would be required to pay any GST tax due out of trust assets. The final category of skip transfers relates to *taxable distributions*. A taxable distribution occurs at the time your trustee makes a distribution to a skip person. For example, you place $500,000 into a trust for the benefit of your children and grandchildren. If your trustee makes a distribution to a grandchild (a skip person), a taxable distribution has occurred, and any taxes due must be paid out of that distribution.

So far, the GST rules do not sound very appealing. The opportunity lies in the following three exceptions to the GST tax rules:

1. *Deceased child exception*. This exception provides that if a child has predeceased you and has left children of his or her own, your gifts to that grandchild are not subject to the GST tax.

2. *$13,000 annual GST exclusion*. Similar to your annual gift tax exclusion, the GST exclusion provides that no GST tax is due for the first $13,000 per year of gifts to a skip person. This $13,000 per year will increase in future years due to special inflation indexing.

3. *$5 million GST exemption*. This important exception provides that bequests of up to $5 million can be made to skip persons free of the GST tax. This exemption is automatically applied to direct skips. It is sometimes automatically applied to nondirect skips depending upon elections made by the grantor, and, therefore, care should be taken when drafting trusts that are likely to result in nondirect skips. Note that the $5 million GST exemption is available to all individuals, therefore parent's combined exemption for bequests equals $10 million in 2011 and 2012. Gift exemptions are also $5,000,000 per donor or $10,000,000 for a donor couple for 2011 and 2012.

Case Study 1

Jeannie and Raymond Davidson would like to make a large gift to their son and possibly their grandchildren. In our discussions, we discover that their son is likely to accumulate a large estate on his own. If this gift occurs in 2011, we explain that if the Davidsons make gifts to their son either directly or in trust, substantial estate taxes will likely be due when he dies. As an alternative, we recommend that they consider a GST trust. They will use part of their (combined) lifetime applicable exclusion amount to make a tax-free gift of $1,000,000 to a trust that will provide income to their son for his lifetime. At his death the assets will remain in trust for the benefit of the grandchildren. By electing the GST exemption, there will be no estate taxes due at the son's death. Using this strategy, the parents have removed the *growth* on the $1,000,000 from their estate and have avoided future estate taxes at their son's death, thus preserving a much larger benefit for their grandchildren. Because each parent has a $5 million GST exemption in

2011, we structured their wills so as to take advantage of their remaining GST exemption at their death.

Case Study 2

Jeff and Cynthia Cooper have expressed a desire to establish a gifting program to benefit their children and grandchildren. Although their investments produce a large income for them, they are not comfortable making large lump sum gifts. They are also concerned that gifts might spoil their children. We recommend that they consider using their $13,000 annual GST exclusion to purchase a $1.5 million survivorship life insurance policy. A GST trust would be the owner and beneficiary. As a result, after the second person has died, the GST trust would be funded with $1.5 million that would benefit both their children and their grandchildren. Trust provisions would allow the trustee to make distributions to either the children or the grandchildren. In cases where life insurance is being used to leverage generation skipping transfers, it is important to file a gift tax return requesting that the GST exemption be applied to the gifts.

Sales to Family Members

There are many estate planning advantages to loaning family members money as well as sales of assets to family members. Particularly effective are installment sales and the private annuity.

Installment Sales to Family Members

Installment sales between family members are set up like any other installment sale. You determine a fair market price and then arrange repayment terms based on a market interest rate. If the sale was to include a below-market price or below-market interest rate, the Internal Revenue Service considers that you have made a gift for gift tax purposes. Advantages and disadvantages of asset sales to family members are presented in the following sections.

ADVANTAGES

- A sale of an asset to a family member removes the appreciation of the asset from your estate. Henry owns stock in his closely held business. At some point in the future, he plans to take his company public, at which point he expects the value to appreciate dramatically. Henry's son, Jake, also works in the business but owns no stock. By selling Jake stock now, Henry is able to transfer the future growth out of his estate.

- An installment sale to a family member keeps the asset in the family. Edith Thompson inherited the family farm from her parents and has a strong desire to keep the farm in the family. She sells the farm to her two children on an installment sale basis. The payments to her total $2,000 per month. Edith uses $12,000 of her 13,000 annual gift tax exclusion to give each child $12,000 toward payment of their share of the note.

- An installment sale prevents a family member from receiving wealth too quickly. Dave Adams sells his children an apartment building that he owns. The apartment building currently produces $40,000 per year of net income. The installment note requires payments of $4,000 per month for 240 months. The children have purchased a valuable asset that will increase their net worth as it appreciates but will receive little in the way of cash benefits for many years. Their incentive to fend for themselves is unhampered.

- An installment sale provides you with a continuing income stream. Not everyone can afford to give away their assets. You may not need the asset, but you may need the income it produces. An installment sale to a family member may provide the ideal solution. You remove the appreciating asset from your estate while retaining the income for an extended period of time.

- The buyer's cost basis in the property is based on the price they paid, which is presumably the fair market value. If they had received the property as a gift, their basis would be the same as the donor's basis. Buying the property will likely result in less taxes upon a subsequent sale.

DISADVANTAGES

- You have not entirely removed the asset from your estate. The value of the note receivable will be included in your estate.

- You have given up control of the property.

- You have accepted a fixed payment that will not be adjusted for inflation.

- You must recognize the gain on the sale for income tax purposes. Because it is an installment sale, taxes are due only as you receive your note payments.

- If the property is resold within two years, you may incur an acceleration of income taxes. This creates the possibility of owing income taxes without having cash to pay them.

SETTING YOUR INTEREST RATE

When you are deciding what interest rate to charge your family member, you must choose a rate that is considered a fair market rate. If you choose a below market rate, the difference between the fair market rate and the rate you charged will be imputed to you for income tax purposes. Likewise, this difference in rate can be imputed as an interest deduction for the buyer.

How do you determine what a fair interest rate is? Fortunately, the Internal Revenue Service provides you with the answer under Code Section 1272 entitled "Applicable Federal Rates." These rates change from month to month but are often less than a buyer could receive if he or she sought traditional financing. For the current Applicable Federal Rates, visit the Resource Center at www.WelchGroup.com; click on "Links"; then click on Applicable Federal Rates.

An installment sale can be combined with annual gifts to family members to magnify the power of the transaction. You sell property "A" to your son in return for a note with a market rate of interest. The note payments equal $9,500 each year for 12 years. In January of each year, you give your son $13,000 as a tax-free gift. He then uses the gift to make the note payment. You can manipulate the term of the note to make certain that the payments fall within the allowed annual gift tax exclusion. For example, if the property was valued at $100,000, and the federal interest rate was 6 percent, a 10-year term would result in payments of $13,587. By increasing the term to 16 years, you would cut the annual payments to under $13,000.

Remember that whether you give your child the money to make the note payments or simply forgive the note, you are still responsible for reporting and paying the income tax on the note interest. Although you have not received the interest, it has been imputed to you.

The Private Annuity

A private annuity is the sale of property by one family member (the annuitant) to another family member (the obligor) in exchange for an unsecured promise by the obligor to make payments to the annuitant for the rest of the annuitant's life.

ADVANTAGES

- The property and its future appreciation are removed from your estate, thus you avoid all estate taxes.
- Because this is a fair market value sale, there are no gift taxes to pay.
- You receive a lifetime income.
- The capital gains on the sale are spread over your life expectancy.
- The property is maintained within the family. This can be particularly important with a closely held business interest or family land.
- If you die prematurely (before your life expectancy), the annuity payments end immediately, and there is no remaining value in the annuity. This is unlike the installment sale in which case the note payments would continue and the present value of those payments would be included in your estate.

DISADVANTAGES

- The note payments cannot be secured by the trust property or any other asset.
- Your children (the obligors) bear the risk that you will outlive the actuarial tables.

Loans to Family Members

Unlike installment sales to family members, loans to family members offer little in the way of estate planning benefits. If you charge a below market interest rate, you will have income imputed to you, and you will have been deemed to have made a gift based on the value of the "bargain" amount. A related technique is to make a loan to a child and then use their annual gift tax exclusion to forgive all or a portion of the note payments each year. Note that this does not relieve you of your income tax liability. One possible estate tax advantage occurs if your child is able to earn a higher rate of return on your loan than you are currently earning.

Case Study

David has $200,000 in certificates of deposits earning 3 percent. David's son, James, wants to start a business that requires $100,000 of capital, but James lacks the ability to borrow the money. David loans him the money, charging him 3 percent (or the applicable federal rate, whichever is greater). His business is successful and earns on average 15 percent per year. David has effectively helped leverage his son's net worth while earning at least as high an interest as he was earning before.

Sales to Intentionally Defective Grantor Trusts (IDGT)

A sale of assets to an Intentionally Defective Grantor Trust can be an effective way to transfer the future income or appreciation from an appreciating asset with little or no gift or estate tax cost. A grantor trust is established, and the grantor must report, on the grantor's individual income tax return, all of the income, deductions, and credits of the trust. The grantor then sells assets to the trust in exchange for a promissory note. The IRS has ruled that a sale or other transaction between a grantor trust and the grantor does not result in any capital gain or loss, or any other tax consequence. The trust is ignored for federal income tax purposes. However, the assets owned by the trust are not included in the grantor's estate for estate tax purposes. Assuming the value of the assets sold to the trust appreciate higher than the value of the assets upon the sale, the appreciation escapes transfer tax. The sale of assets to such a trust is a highly complex estate planning technique. A summary of the key points is as follows:

- Such a trust is respected for gift and estate taxes but ignored for income taxes.
- Therefore no taxable gain upon sale.
- The trust should be seeded with at least 10 percent of the fair market value of the assets to be sold.
- The trust generally benefits children and grandchildren.
- Only seed money would be a gift. Normally a future interest gift could be structured as preset interests (Crummey).

- Assets are often placed in a limited liability company. The assets then qualify for discount for lack of marketability and control. This impacts the fair market value of asset.
- If the trust is not given for all or part of purchase price, it is best to pay off the balance before the death of donor-grantor.

The Legacy Trust

In thousands of discussions with clients over the past 30-plus years it has become evident that many of them have a strong desire to make certain that the assets that they worked so hard to accumulate are not wasted or lost by their children. While this desire is intuitive, the solution often is not. One solution that has received universal appeal is the legacy trust.

Let's begin by setting the context by way of an actual client meeting. During a recent estate planning review with a client, we asked the following question. "What is the divorce rate in America?" The client quickly answered, "About 50%." The next question was a little tougher. "Since you have three children whom we'll assume will all marry, what are the odds (statistically speaking) that at least one of them will have a marriage that ends in divorce?" Now the client is less certain. The answer? 87.5%! To this statistic, add the fact that America is the most litigious society in the world. Today, the common phrase is, "Sue them all, then we'll sort it out in court!" It's true that not all of these lawsuits will result in a judgment or that a judgment will be for a large amount of money, but the risks are clear. Returning to our client meeting, it appears that when you combine the risks of a divorce plus the risks of a judgment from a lawsuit, the odds are pretty high that at least one of the clients' children will face a significant event that will place their finances in jeopardy. If part of their 'finances' includes inheritance from you, your assets are simply added to the 'pot' of money, which makes the child a bigger target and increases the chances that your hard-earned assets end up in someone else's bank account. Not a pleasant thought!

What if you could do something to use your assets to benefit your children while at the same time protecting those assets from creditors, lawsuits or a divorce? Enter the legacy trust. With a legacy trust, instead of leaving your estate outright to your children you place it in a trust that has specific language that both provides financial support for your children while also including language that allows the trustee a defense mechanism in the event the child is threatened with a lawsuit or divorce.

Case Study

John and Kate Nelson are in their mid-fifties and have an estate worth $9 million. Because of the 2010 Tax Relief Act provision allowing portability of the lifetime exemption amount, no matter how their assets are divided, there will not be any estate taxes due at their deaths. They have three children in their early twenties to mid-thirties all of whom are married. Two of their children have one child each and they anticipate their other child will also have children. One child is a physician, one is on track to become a PhD professor teaching at the college level and one is a business owner. Two of the children's marriages appear very stable while one is more volatile. The Nelsons have a strong desire to ensure that their children as well as their grandchildren benefit from their estate assets. Of significant importance is making sure that the grandchildren can each afford the very best education they are capable of achieving. They also want to protect their assets from potential future legal claims against their children. We presented the concept of the legacy trust and while they loved the idea, they had a number of questions.

How Long Does a Legacy Trust Last?

The short answer is that you get to decide how long it will last. In most cases the legacy trust is designed to last for at least the lifetime of each child. The reason is that this is the best way to get the full benefit of the asset protection attributes of the legacy trust. If you said that the trust would end when the child is age 60, then those assets would forever in the future be subject to litigation risks. In fact, in the typical case, we recommend leaving the assets in trust for as long as the law allows. How long the law allows is determined by each state. Some states allow the trust to last virtually forever—what we call a "Rockefeller Trust," named after industrialist and oil magnate John D. Rockefeller who became one of the wealthiest men in the world in the late nineteenth and early twentieth century and went on to create a perpetual trust that continues to benefit his heirs to this day. Other states have a "law against perpetuities," which essentially says that the trust can last for as long as the "lives in being plus twenty-one years." Sound confusing? In our case study about the Nelsons, this means that the trust, once established at the death of the last parent, would last as long as any of the then-living potential beneficiaries including any children, grandchildren, or great grandchildren who are alive plus 21 years for beneficiaries who were not alive at the time the legacy trust first came into being. We like to refer to this as a "75-year trust," because it will often last 75 years or more, but not indefinitely.

The Nelsons decided that while they wanted a legacy trust for their children's lifetime, they wanted the children to decide where their share of the trust would go at their death. We suggested that we give the children a testamentary *general power of appointment*. This would allow each child, through his or her own will, to terminate the trust in favor of his or her chosen heirs. We further suggested that if the child failed to exercise the general power of appointment that the money would remain in the legacy trust for that child's children and grandchildren. This general power of appointment creates great flexibility, but it causes the trust assets to be included in the child's estate for estate tax purposes (see the discussion on generation-skipping transfers later in this section). This can be avoided by granting the child a *limited power of appointment*, which limits the potential appointees of the assets to someone or something other than the child's estate or creditors of the child's estate.

How Do the Children Get Money from a Legacy Trust?

You get to decide how the trust benefits your heirs. Typically, we provide that, under normal circumstances, the trust will either distribute all of the income (interest and dividends) or we'll use a set withdrawal rate such as 3 or 4 percent based on the principal balance as of January 1 of each year. In addition, we will often make allowances for distributions of principal under certain circumstances. The variations here are limitless and bound only by the imagination of the clients or their advisors. We often say to the client, "If you can figure out what you want, we can figure out how to provide for it in the trust agreement." We'll discuss some of the more esoteric ideas later in this section.

Who Would Be the Trustee?

Again, the trustee of your legacy trust can be whomever you wish. In some cases, the child will be a co-trustee of their legacy trust which gives the child a sense of having some "ownership" of the money and of the trust's operation. If you want to preserve the asset protection attributes of the trust, a child cannot be the "sole" trustee of their own trust. This is because the trust document will give the trustee a wide range of powers that allow the trustee to decide "when and if" to make distributions. If the child were his or her own and sole trustee and there was a legal judgment against the child personally, the courts could compel the child, as the sole trustee, to make distributions to himself or herself, therefore making those funds available to the creditor, soon-to-be ex-spouse or plaintiff in a lawsuit. This will not be the case when there is a separate trustee. So in the cases where the child will serve as a trustee, you'll always need a co-trustee. This can be an individual or an institution such as a trust company or a bank, which has trust services or another professional such as an attorney, accountant, or financial advisor. What is most important to remember is that the legacy trust will likely last a very long time and therefore most of the "people-trustees" will not outlive the trust so you'll want to take care in choosing a succession of people-trustees as well as an "institutional" trustee as your back-up. Having an institutional trustee in place insures that you don't run out of trustees, which would then require the retaining of an attorney to go to court and have a trustee appointed, a proposition which could be expensive and produce less than optimal results.

What if the Children Don't Like the Trustee?

When you begin discussing an institutional trustee or any trustee other than the child, there's invariably the question, "What happens if the child and the trustee don't get along?" One trust provision we recommend is giving someone, typically the trust beneficiary (or majority of beneficiaries) the power to replace the institutional or professional trustee with another institutional or professional trustee. What's important here is to make certain that the new trustee is also an institutional or professional trustee. A real case example will illustrate the reason why: One trust beneficiary became unhappy with the trustee because the trustee would not release funds when she wanted. The trust agreement allowed her to remove the trustee in favor of another trustee but was silent as to the required qualifications of the new trustee. She thought she could solve her problem of getting money out of the trust more quickly by appointing her good friend as the trustee. As the situation began to unfold, and more and more trust withdrawals were requested, we informed the new trustee of her fiduciary responsibility regarding the trust. If she failed to follow the instructions and guidelines outlined in the trust, she could become personally liable for her actions. For example, if the trust were depleted, she could actually be sued by her good friend, the beneficiary! This is something that all institutional and professional trustees understand. Having the trust agreement require successor institutional or professional trustees will often solve the problem of beneficiaries changing trustees with the expectation of having unreasonable demands met by the new trustee.

What about Having a Sibling as the Trustee?

Another idea clients will have is to make the siblings "cross-trustees." This means, for example, designating the brother the trustee of his sister's trust and the sister the trustee of her brother's trust, thereby creating very "friendly" trustees. The problem with this strategy is what attorneys call "substance over form." This means that the courts could view this as each sibling having, in effect, full power over their own trust and they could lose the asset protection attributes intended for the trust. We also run into a lot of cases where one child is highly responsible and another highly irresponsible. The client may suggest having the responsible child act as trustee over the irresponsible child's trust. In our experience, this sets up a form of sibling resentment that most often leads to conflict and a deterioration of relationships.

What about the Different Needs of the Children?

In our case study, the Nelsons pointed out that each of the children would likely have very different needs. The child who intended to become a college professor would likely need income from the trust to supplement her salary, while the physician child would likely want his trust invested predominantly for growth since he'd have no immediate income needs from the trust. The business owner child might need loans for business expansion. How would the legacy trust meet the diverse needs of these very different financial situations?

Typically this is addressed by splitting the estate assets into separate trusts for each of the children. Trust language is drawn so that it is broad enough to meet a wide range of needs or it can be tailored specifically for each child's trust.

The Umbrella Trust

We recently ran into an exception to the separate trusts strategy. In this case the client has three children, all of whom are adults. Two of the children have good jobs and stable marriages while the third child has a history of health problems that have prevented him from maintaining steady employment. His health could change in his favor and he could have steady employment or his current situation could persist. The client's estate totaled about $2 million. If they divided the estate equally, we were concerned that $700,000 may not be sufficient to fully take care of the potentially disabled child. The solution was to create an umbrella trust. Instead of creating three separate trusts, we held all of the funds in one trust with language that suggested that the trustee treat all of the children equally unless there was a compelling reason (health, for example) to treat them unequally. This gave the trustee the flexibility to focus on the individual needs of each child and allowed, if necessary, the trustee to use the full power of the trust to take care of the disabled child should that become necessary. We understand that some people may view this as unfair and our response is what's "fair" may not always be what's "appropriate."

Can the Legacy Trust be Used to Fund the Education of Our Grandchildren?

Our clients, the Nelsons, placed a very high value on a good education. It was their advanced education that allowed them to accumulate their own estate and they could see how being educated benefitted their children. They loved the possibility of using part of their estate to fund the education of their grandchildren. Would that be possible? This is a very typical request from grandparents and the answer is, "Yes." We often insert language in the trust document that provides for the use of trust funds for the educational expenses of grandchildren. We agree that one of the greatest gifts you can give anyone is the gift of the best education for which they can qualify. Another possibility within this planning point is to provide specific language allowing the trustee to transfer funds into a 529 Plan, Coverdell Education Savings Plan, or other similar plan. This would allow those funds to grow tax deferred and then make tax-free distributions for qualified education expenses.

What are the Disadvantages of a Legacy Trust?

As opposed to leaving your heirs their inheritance outright, one obvious downside is the costs involved in setting up and maintaining a legacy trust, or any type of trust for that matter. Depending on the complexity of the trust design, attorney's fees can run into the thousands or tens of thousands of dollars. Once the trust becomes effective (in the case of the legacy trust, this would typically be at the death of the last remaining parent), there will often be trust management fees, investment management fees, and fees associated with the filing of the trust tax return. In addition to the costs associated with the trusts, we find that children are not always fond of the idea of having their inheritance placed in a trust over which they have limited control. It's human nature to want to be in control and this is especially true when it comes to what children view as "their" money. If you decide to use a legacy trust, we highly recommend that you have a formal conversation with each of your children to explain the reasons you made this decision. If you're going to have a mutiny on your hands, it's usually better to find out while you're alive and can do something about it. Our experience is that a well-planned conversation tends to be received well by mature adult children. The children who react negatively often do so out of immaturity, which serves to emphasize just why the legacy trust is appropriate.

The Family Council

We have developed a concept called *The Family Council* where we will meet with the parents and children to discuss money responsibility in light of potential future inheritance. This is the perfect setting to discuss all of the benefits of the legacy trust. The Family Council is discussed in more detail in the Epilogue.

Think about it logically. If a child were to receive his inheritance outright, he only has two basic choices: He can spend it (or give it away) or he can invest it. If he spends it there are only two results: He can spend it in a way that would meet your approval or in a way that would not. If he invests it, there are only two results: He can invest it well or he can invest it poorly. In most cases, our clients are not opposed to the child spending some of the money on certain types of things like the down payment on a home or a child's education and the trust allows for this. If the child chooses to invest the money, does it really matter that the investments are being done through a trust, and one that protects the child from creditors? We would argue that the legacy trust can provide a lifetime financial safety net for your children without unduly burdening them. If fact, it can free them up to focus on things that have more meaning to them like raising their children or pursuing their careers.

Can a Legacy Trust Spoil the Children?

This is a valid concern. In too many cases we see trust fund babies never having the hunger or drive to work hard and create their own success. Think about it. When most kids graduate from college, the entry-level job opportunities might offer a starting salary of $30,000 to $50,000 per year. If that person is currently receiving $150,000 per year from their $3 million trust, what's the incentive to work? In many cases the answer is, "None." If this is a concern for you, you might consider including an *incentive provision* in your legacy trust. There are many variations of this idea but most go something like this: For every dollar of earned income, the trustee will give the beneficiary a "matching dollar." Under this provision, if our college graduate gets that entry-level job earning $35,000, he'll also receive $35,000 from his trust. And he has every incentive to work hard and move up in the organization because future raises will also be matched!

INCENTIVE PROVISION USING A ROTH IRA

A subset of this strategy is to include an incentive provision for younger beneficiaries such as grandchildren. Consider allowing the trustee to "match" any earned income by making contributions into a Roth IRA. The rules for a Roth IRA allow a dollar-for-dollar contribution of up to 100 percent of earned income up to $5,000 each year. As you may remember, you don't get a deduction for contributions to a Roth IRA but earnings grow tax deferred and distributions at retirement (age 59½) are tax-free. There are also provisions for tax-free distributions (maximum of $10,000 in a lifetime) for first-time homebuyers provided that the Roth IRA has been in existence for a minimum of five years. Let's look at the power of this simple strategy: Assume your legacy trust provides a $5,000 per year matching contribution for your grandchild from ages 16 through 22 and the money remains invested until his age 60. Assuming an 8 percent annualized return, his account value would be $830,000! And all of this was accomplished on a total investment of $35,000. Now there's a lesson in the power of saving early!

Are there Provisions that Must Be Included in the Legacy Trust?

If one of your goals is for the trust to serve as an asset protection trust, you'll need to include language giving the trustee the discretion to both make and withhold distributions of income and principal. The typical trust agreement provides that all of the income must be paid out to the beneficiary at least quarterly. Typical trust agreements also often mandate distributions of principal at certain ages. Here's a typical example in layman's terms: "The trustee is instructed to distribute all of the trust income at least quarterly. Distributions of principal will occur as follows: one-third at age 25; one-half at age 30; the balance at age 35." This arrangement provides little, if any, asset protection for the beneficiary. For example, in the event of a divorce or other legal judgment, the trust income could effectively be "garnished." Large dollar judgments could be "settled" upon the future event of the mandatory distribution of principal. Giving the independent trustee the discretion of withholding income or principal allows trust assets to be shielded from would-be legal predators.

Generation Skipping Transfers

While you're creating your legacy trust, you should consider including a provision allocating the maximum allowable transfer to a generation-skipping transfer

(GST) trust. Under current law, this is $5 million total for you and if you are married, $5 million for your spouse. Money transferred into a GST trust will not be included in your heir's estates upon their death. Let's look at an example of how this might work: John and May Moneybags die in 2012 leaving a total estate of $20 million to their two children. Their will directs that the maximum amount go to a GST legacy trust for each child. As a result, each child receives $5 million in their GST legacy trust with the balance, after paying estate taxes, going to a traditional legacy trust, which means each child has two trusts. At any child's subsequent death, any money in the GST legacy trust will not be includable in that child's estate and therefore will not be subject to estate taxes. The assets in the traditional (non-GST) legacy trust are includable in the child's estate and may be subject to estate taxes. If the GST planning is desired, the power of appointment options must be carefully examined.

In this section, we've discussed the concept of the legacy trust and the importance of using this strategy to protect your assets from possible legal attacks against your children after your death. We should note that no trust is perfectly "bullet-proof." It will be important to include language giving the trustee instructions to do everything legally possible to protect trust assets from legal challenges.

CHAPTER 12

Strategic Planning with Charities

In addition to fulfilling their philanthropic desires, most people making gifts to charities also have a keen interest in the income and estate tax benefits that come from such gifts. The income tax benefits are derived from gifts to charity made during life. Estate tax benefits can be generated when testamentary gifts are made. The maximum estate tax rate is 35% and the maximum income tax rate is also 35%. Because the applicable exclusion amount increased to $5 million on January 1, 2011, it is quite possible that no tax benefit will be derived from testamentary gifts if the value of the estate does not exceed the applicable exclusion amount. Therefore, some donors may prefer to make their charitable gifts during life to obtain a current and more predictable tax benefit. Regardless of tax benefits, more often the desire to make a significant gift to charity overshadows the donor's interest in the tax benefits.

If you want to leave part of your estate to charity, there are many strategies available that you can use to provide funds to your favorite charities while also providing estate and income tax benefits for you and your family. These strategies range from the simple strategy of outright gifts to the very complex strategies that utilize specialized trusts. Tax-exempt organizations generally include traditional charities, such as the Red Cross or United Way, as well as qualified educational institutions and religious organizations. Before making donations to any organizations, you should confirm that the group or foundation qualifies as a tax-deductible charity. A list of qualified (nonreligious) charities is available from the Internal Revenue Service (IRS) publication 78 entitled "Cumulative List of Organizations Described in Section 170(c) of the Internal

Revenue Code." This publication is quite long, so you may want to check your local library for a copy. To check out a charity on the web, go to the Resource Center at www.welchgroup.com; then click on "Links; then click on Charities-Search for Qualified Charities."

We will begin by discussing the various issues involved in outright gifts to charities, and then we will review the more complex concepts that utilize trusts.

Outright Gifts to Charities

By far the most common way to donate to charities is through outright gifts, for example, writing a check or donating items of clothing or other property. However, we often find that people make mistakes when donating assets to charities. Once you have decided to make a donation to a charitable organization, you want to maximize the benefit to both you and the charity. We examine the pros and cons of various outright gifts to charities.

Gifts of Cash

Here you typically write a check or give cash. For contributions in excess of $250, you must receive and maintain a written acknowledgment from the charity. The advantages of this type of gift is its simplicity and full tax deductibility, as well as the fact that you have removed the asset from your estate. However, you create very little leverage. You have a dollar, you give a dollar, you receive a dollar tax deduction. Depending on the type of assets, it may be preferable for you to donate some asset other than cash.

Gifts of Property

The types of property that you can give are as varied as the types of property you own. For example, you might own an old car that is in excellent condition but has little resale value. You may not want the car, but it may be of value to a charity.

If you give property such as real estate or securities, not only do you remove the asset from your estate, but you also remove the future growth of that asset from your estate. The actual transfer of your property to your selected charity can take some time. If you are giving securities that are held in a brokerage account, usually the simplest way to complete the transfer is to have your charity open an account at the same brokerage firm. You can then write your broker a letter and have him or her journal your selected securities over to the charity's account. For real property or tangible personal property, you need to have the deed or title transferred into the name of the charity. Most charities will conduct an environmental study to make sure real estate is free from liability.

Gifts of Appreciated Property

The best way to create leverage through outright gifts is by giving away appreciated property. Assume that you have made a $12,000 pledge to your church's building campaign. You are trying to decide whether to write a check for this amount or to donate the $12,000 worth of Coca-Cola stock that you bought 15 years ago for $2,000. You had planned to hold this stock as part of your long-term investment program. You are sentimental about your Coca-Cola stock and believe it will continue to be a good investment in the future. What should you do?

You should give away the stock. If you had to sell the stock now, perhaps because of an emergency, you would incur substantial capital gains taxes. On the other hand, even though you only paid $2,000 for the stock, when you give it to your church, you will receive a deduction for its full market value ($12,000). If you want to maintain the stock for your long-term investment program, you can simply buy the stock using the $12,000 cash you had planned to give your church. The result of these transactions is that you now own $12,000 worth of Coca-Cola stock with a $12,000 cost basis. Now, in the case of an emergency, you could sell your Coca-Cola stock and owe no taxes. Because your church is treated as a charity for tax purposes, when the charity sells the stock you gave it, it is a nontaxable event.

Gifts of appreciated securities and real estate are by far the most effective way to make outright gifts. For you to receive a deduction for fair market value on gifts of tangible personal property, the gift must be one usable to the charity as part of the charity's purpose. For example, the gift of a tractor to your church would likely only qualify for a deduction based on your cost basis in the tractor because it is not something that your church normally uses as part of its operations.

Gifts to Public Foundations

Like many people, you may have numerous charities that you would like to help. However, the transfer process described previously would be too burdensome for small contributions. Transfers would also not work if you may want a deduction in this calendar year but are undecided on the amount of your donations and to what charities to give. Two excellent alternatives are the private foundation or a donor advised fund of a community (or public) foundation. You are allowed to make a gift to foundations in cash, securities, or property and receive an immediate tax deduction. The foundation then holds your assets until you give them instructions on the disposition of your property to the charities you have chosen. Most of the public foundations can even provide you with information as to the worthiness of charities that you may be considering. For this service, you are charged a small fee that is usually based on a percentage of your contribution. For listings of community foundations in your area, go to the Resource Center at www.welchgroup.com; then click on "Links"; then click on "Community Foundations-Search". A more detailed discussion of private foundations is included later in this chapter.

Tax Deduction Limitations on Outright Gifts

Generally, you will receive a full tax deduction for gifts totaling up to 50 percent of your adjusted gross income (AGI) during any calendar year. If your gift is to a nonpublic charity, your deduction is restricted to 30 percent of your adjusted gross income. Gifts in excess of these amounts can be carried forward for up to five years. However, there is also a limitation on itemized deductions that must be considered, and amounts disallowed by the itemized deduction rule *are* not eligible for carryover.

Testamentary Gifts to Charities

Often people will make specific bequests to charities in their will, particularly to charities that have special meaning to them. However, if you don't need the money, you can create more tax leverage by making your donation while you are alive. Say that you intend to give a certain piece of property worth $100,000 to charity. If you leave it to charity under your will, there will be no estate taxes. However, if you give it to charity while you are alive, you not only remove it from your estate for estate tax purposes, but you also receive a current income tax deduction worth $30,000 to $40,000! Consider *lifetime* gifts if you do not need the asset.

Gifts Using Charitable Trusts

With outright gifts, you donate cash or property to a charity and receive a tax deduction. This is the only monetary benefit to you. If you are looking for additional benefits such as a continuing income stream for yourself or a portion of your assets passed to family members, you may want to consider using one or more charitable trusts. These trusts can be structured to achieve a variety of personal and charitable objectives. If you want to convert highly appreciated non–income-producing property into income-producing property while avoiding large capital gains taxes, then you might consider a *charitable remainder trust.* If you would like to see your favorite charity receive a stream of income from one of your assets, but want the property to remain in your family, then you should consider a *charitable lead trust.* If you would like to leave a lasting legacy of charitable giving for your heirs, you can establish a *private foundation.*

Charitable Remainder Annuity Trust

The charitable remainder annuity trust (CRAT) is an ideal vehicle for taking appreciated non–income-producing property and converting it into assets that can provide you or a family member with current income. Suppose you are age 70 and own land that is currently valued at $900,000. Your cost basis in the property is $90,000. You are considering an early retirement, but would need to convert assets to produce an income stream. Your first thought is to sell the property and reinvest the proceeds in income-producing assets such as government bonds. The results of the sale would be as follows:

Step 1: Determine the Tax

$900,000	Current value of land
−$90,000	Cost basis of land
$810,000	Taxable gain
× 0.15	Capital gains tax rate (based on current rates)
$121,500	Capital gains tax

Step 2: Determine the Income

$900,000	Proceeds from sale
−$121,500	Capital gains taxes
$778,500	Available to reinvest
× 0.05	Expected earnings (5 percent)
$38,925	Income earned annually

As an alternative, you should consider a CRAT. Here's how it would work. Let's assume that you are interested in leaving assets to your alma mater. You can decide what interest rate you would like to receive and whom you would like to act as your trustee. In this case, you choose 5 percent and elect to serve as trustee yourself. You have your attorney draft the document formalizing the trust. Your attorney then assists you with transferring the deed from your name as an individual to your name as trustee. Once the property is transferred, you, as trustee, sell it for $900,000. It is important that there be no prearranged sale of the trust asset before it is transferred to the trust. If that is the case, the donor will likely be responsible for the income tax from the sale of the assets.

Because it is a charitable trust, there are no taxes on the proceeds. You then place the entire sum in investments of your choosing. As trustee, you have full discretion over investment decisions. Because you elected a 5 percent payout, you will withdraw $45,000 annually for as long as you live. Not only do you increase your annual income, but you also receive an income tax deduction of possibly $400,000 (depending on federal interest rates).

This strategy is appealing, but you have two concerns. First, you are worried about your spouse's continuing need for income should you predecease him or her. Next, you are concerned about some potentially very unhappy heirs—your children. At your death, the remainder goes to your alma mater, and your children receive nothing. To resolve the spousal issue, you would set the trust up so that the income is paid over *both* of your lives. As long as either one of you is living, the trust will continue to pay $45,000 per year. The only thing this adjustment affects is your initial tax deduction. If, for example, your spouse were also age 70, the tax deduction would be reduced to $279,000 (depending on federal interest rates).

TABLE 12.1 Survivorship Life Insurance*

$900,000 (Level Death Benefit) with Annual Premium of $4,945

Year	Cash Value	Death Benefit
1	$ 1,400	$900,000
10	$ 50,000	$900,000
20	$159,000	$900,000
30	$317,000	$900,000
40	$411,500	$900,000

*Male, age 55; female, age 52.

The issue concerning your children presents a more challenging, yet solvable, problem. Perhaps the best solution would be to take your tax savings dollars and purchase a survivorship life insurance policy on the life of you and your spouse. An example of a $900,000 survivorship life policy is represented in Table 12.1. This policy should be purchased using an irrevocable insurance trust as described in Chapter 10. If your children are adults, an alternative would be to have them be the owner and beneficiary of the policy with you gifting them the cash to pay the premiums.

THE WEALTH TRANSFER EFFECT

Under the previous scenario, your goal was to convert a non-income-producing asset into one that produces income. This satisfies an income need, but what about your estate planning goals? You have removed $900,000 from your estate by way of the charitable trust and have used part of your tax savings to buy life insurance, which will be received by your children free of income and estate taxes.

As you can see, the intelligent use of a charitable trust can create what we call the "triple win." You win because you receive more income during your lifetime. Your children win because they receive a larger inheritance. And your alma mater wins because it receives a larger sum than it would have likely received under other circumstances.

However, under the CRAT, what you receive is a fixed income that does not ever change. What about inflation? The *charitable remainder unitrust* (CRUT) addresses the issue of inflation.

Charitable Remainder Unitrust

Structurally, the CRUT is set up similarly to the CRAT. You establish the trust and transfer property into it. As trustee, you then sell the property and reinvest it as you wish. You receive an income from the trust during your lifetime, and at your death, the remaining assets go to the charity of your choice. The income can be paid over the joint lives of you and your spouse if you so desire. What differs is how the income is figured. With a CRUT, you set an interest rate for purposes of calculating the amount of withdrawals that are due you each year. Although the interest rate never changes, the amount of dollars you receive fluctuates based on the changing value of the account each year. For instance, in our earlier example, you contributed $900,000 of real estate to your charitable trust, and from then on received $45,000 (5 percent) per year. The income amount never changed. Under a CRUT, you would receive 5 percent of the value of the account as of a certain date each year. If your account value increased to $1,000,000 in the second year, a 5 percent distribution would produce $50,000 for you. This results in a growing income for you assuming your total account values grow. The opposite is also true. If the account values decrease, so will your distributions. Because the account values of a CRUT must be determined each year, it is not an appropriate trust in which to place hard-to-value assets such as real estate or a closely held business interest.

Using Your Charitable Trust for Retirement Planning

If you're currently employed, you're probably concerned about retirement planning. While you're still working and earning a good salary, you should make the most of your earnings. If you are fortunate enough to have an employer-provided retirement plan, then part of the job may be done for you. Many employer plans are of the 401(k) variety. These plans are very helpful but are rarely sufficient to fully fund one's retirement. One way to supplement your retirement income is by establishing a CRUT that contains specialized provisions. A CRUT allows *annual* contributions, whereas a CRAT does not. In this trust agreement you will include two special provisions.

- As with any CRUT, you elect to receive income each year based on a set percentage of the trust's value. In this case, you should add language that says if the trust income is not sufficient to pay the percentage you elected, then the trustee will pay the *actual* income the trust produces. For example, you elect a 5 percent annual income distribution. The trust investments, however, only produce 1 percent income. The result is that only 1 percent is distributed to you. Note that this is a period of time in which you do not need additional income. You are still in your most productive earning years, and your goal is to store up assets for your retirement.
- The next provision that you include in your trust is a catch-up provision. This says any income you were owed but that was not distributed will be distributed to you when additional trust income is available.

Your initial trust investments will include assets that produce little or no income. This allows you to store income for the future. Once you are ready to retire, you (as trustee) sell these investments and reinvest the proceeds in income-producing investments such as corporate bonds and CDs. The result is that your account achieves maximum growth during your working years and then is switched to maximum income during your retirement years. Any excess income earned by your trust can be paid out to you as part of the catch-up provision. Note that the sale of the appreciated securities does not result in any taxes because of the trust's tax-exempt status.

Case Study

Assume that you are age 40 and would like to supplement your retirement program by investing $30,000 per year. You would also like to benefit your favorite charity, the Make-A-Wish Foundation. We decide to establish a CRUT with a 5 percent payout and a make-up provision. You contribute $30,000 each January and invest in a diversified portfolio of growth stocks that pay little or no dividends. As it turns out, your portfolio earns an average rate of return of 12 percent from age 40 to your age 65. This results in your account growing to $4,480,000! You now sell all your growth stocks and invest in long-term corporate bonds with average yields of 8.5 percent. As you now begin taking income, your trust agreement allows for a 5 percent payout or $224,000. But your make-up provision now allows you to take the excess earnings as well. This extra 3.5 percent excess income amounts to an additional $156,800, bringing your total annual income to $380,000. You are allowed to continue to take the excess income distributions until all prior deficits have been exhausted. Remember that each time you make a contribution, you are receiving a partial tax deduction as well. You also can set the trust up so that the income is paid over both your life and the life of your spouse.

Pooled Income Funds

One disadvantage of the charitable remainder trust is the cost involved in setting up the trust. It can cost several thousands of dollars to set one up, and you will also have annual maintenance costs of approximately $300 to $1,000 for tax returns and investment costs. Your trustee must obtain a taxpayer identification number and file annual trust tax returns. There is also the matter of trustee duties. Your trustee (often you) is legally a fiduciary to the trust and is required to follow certain rules and procedures. Failure to do so can result in legal liability. If all of this sounds like more than you expected, then you might want to consider a *pooled income fund*.

With a pooled income fund, the charity prepares all the documents and administers the fund for you (typically at no cost). You contribute property to the fund and receive *interest income units* during your lifetime or a specified period of time. Your deduction is calculated in the same manner as with the charitable remainder trust. This type of trust has several advantages over the charitable remainder trust, as well as some disadvantages.

ADVANTAGES

- The charity has undertaken the costs of establishing the trust and bears the ongoing costs of administration.
- The charity hires professional managers to invest fund assets, which relieves you of that responsibility.

DISADVANTAGES

- Because the trust has been established by the charity, there is no opportunity to customize the document to your specific needs. You are also likely to encounter less flexibility in determining your income as well as how the investments will be structured.
- All income from a pooled income fund is considered ordinary income and is therefore taxed at your highest marginal tax rate. Income from a charitable remainder trust uses a tiered rate system that allows long-term capital gains and/or tax-exempt income to flow through to you.

As a result of these disadvantages, the pooled income fund is more appropriate in cases where your intended gift is less than $100,000. A good example would be a $25,000 gift to your alma mater. The size of this gift would make a charitable remainder trust impractical because of both the initial and ongoing costs. You would, however, receive the majority of the benefits of the charitable remainder trust.

Charitable Lead Trust

With a charitable lead trust, you and the charity switch positions. The charity receives the income from the trust for a specified period of time, and the remainder interest then reverts to someone you designate (typically your child). This type of trust works well if the following are true:

1. You own income-producing property, but you do not need the income or the asset.
2. You want to divert the income to a charity for a period of time.
3. You would ultimately like to transfer the asset to a family member but pay little or no gift or estate taxes.

This trust can be set up as either an *inter vivos* (during your lifetime) trust or a *testamentary* (under your will) trust.

ADVANTAGES

- As stated previously, the primary advantage of the charitable lead trust is that you are able to transfer a large asset to your children at significantly reduced gift tax costs.

- Not only do you remove the asset from your estate, you also remove any *growth* on that asset from your estate.
- Contributions to a charitable lead trust are unlimited, whereas contributions to charitable remainder trusts limit your deduction to 50 percent of AGI if the remainder beneficiary is a public charity (30 percent for nonpublic charities).

DISADVANTAGES

- Contributions to a charitable lead trust provide you with a gift tax deduction rather than an income tax deduction unless the trust is set up as a grantor trust. The rules regarding *grantor charitable lead trust* will tend to reduce the effectiveness of wealth transfers to your children.
- Trust income is taxed to the trust to the extent that it exceeds the income paid to the charity. For example, if you set your trust up to pay 5 percent annually to the designated charity, but the trust income is actually 6 percent, the excess 1 percent will be taxed directly to the trust. In the case of a grantor trust, excess income will be taxed to the grantor.
- Capital gains are not a tax-free event as they are with a charitable remainder trust. If the trustee sells an appreciated asset, the gain will be taxed to the trust. Therefore, you will want to contribute assets that you have no intention of selling or that are not likely to appreciate in value.
- When the trust ends and the remaining assets revert to your children, this is considered a gift of a future interest and therefore does not qualify for your annual gift tax exclusion. You must either pay the gift taxes or use part of your lifetime applicable exclusion amount. Also, there are legal costs for setting up this trust, annual accounting costs for maintaining the trust, and duties that must be carried out by the trustee.

The Private Foundation

A private foundation can create a perpetual legacy of charitable giving for your descendants while accomplishing significant estate planning objectives for yourself. With a private foundation, you are, in effect, establishing your own tax-exempt organization for the purpose of benefiting charities, educational institutions, and/or religious organizations. Then, either during your life or at your death (under your will), you contribute money or property to your foundation. The income tax deduction during your lifetime is limited to 30 percent of your AGI. You may act as the trustee and designate family members as successor trustees. The trustees can be paid a reasonable income from the trust for their services. The following sections present the advantages and disadvantages of this strategy.

ADVANTAGES

- Lifetime gifts to your private foundation generate an income tax deduction within certain limitations.

- Your foundation can create a lasting memorial to your family in much the same way as the Rockefellers and Kennedys have done.

- You can use your foundation to aid a specific cause, such as child abuse, or you can provide your trustees broad discretion in deciding how to disperse charitable contributions.

- Your lineal descendants can be the trustees. This creates a lasting legacy of charitable giving for your heirs. It places them in a position of prominence in charitable circles. As trustees, they can receive reasonable income for their services.

- Assets contributed to your private foundation are removed from your estate and thus avoid estate taxes.

DISADVANTAGES

- A private foundation is a complex legal document. The costs of establishing one and maintaining it are relatively high. In addition to annual tax filing requirements, there are federal reporting requirements. Many states also impose reporting requirements. A private foundation is, therefore, more appropriate for large contributions. Many advisors suggest a minimum of $250,000 as an appropriate contribution. We normally would not recommend setting up a private foundation for less than $1 million to be given during life or at death.

- The people you would like to act as trustees, typically your children, may lack the investment management skills or general management skills to run the trust. They may also lack the interest. The trustees are fiduciaries and, as such, are responsible for their actions. Violations of fiduciary responsibilities can result in personal liability for a trustee.

- Private foundations are required to distribute at least 5 percent of the fair market value of the foundation's assets each year. The trustee must make certain that there is sufficient liquidity for this purpose.

- The federal government imposes a 1 percent excise tax on private foundation income (increased to 2 percent in certain cases).

- Over the years, Congress has switched back and forth regarding the extent of the deduction for transfers of appreciated assets to a private foundation. Sometimes the deduction is for the full market value of the gift, and other times only your original cost is deductible. For gifts during your lifetime, check with your professional advisor to determine the deduction you will receive. This will not affect gifts under your will because all assets receive a stepped-up cost basis at death.

Although the restrictions on the private foundation may sound daunting, it can deliver powerful estate planning results. Consider the following case study:

Case Study

The year is 2011. Dr. John and Mary Thompson have a taxable estate of $11,000,000, which places them in the 35 percent estate tax bracket (of course this rate may change as Congress revisits the estate tax system in 2013). Six million dollars of their estate is comprised of retirement plan assets, and the balance is made up of family farm property, which is both something they would like to keep in the family and is highly illiquid. To pay their estate taxes their heirs will need to use the money from the retirement plan. We examine the estate and income tax impact on the retirement plan at the last of the couple to die:

$11,000,000	Taxable estate
−$350,000	Estate taxes (assuming two credits)
−$210,000	Income taxes on grossed-up retirement plan distributions of $600,000 (to cover estate tax *and* income tax on distribution needed)
$10,440,000	Net to heirs from taxable estate

In order to pay the taxes, the Thompsons' heirs will need to liquidate approximately $600,000 of Dr. Thompson's retirement plan. When you use your retirement plan assets to pay estate taxes, you trigger *income taxes.* It's hard to imagine that you worked hard all your life and contributed diligently to your retirement plan only to have Uncle Sam take two-thirds of its distributions for taxes!

Now, assume that the Thompsons decide to establish a private foundation that they name "The John J. Thompson Family Foundation." They contribute their entire $6 million retirement plan to their foundation. They elect to have their children serve as trustees and give their children the right to elect their own successor trustees, presumably *their* children.

$11,000,000	Gross estate
−$6,000,000	Gift to private foundation
$5,000,000	Taxable estate*
− $0	Estate taxes (assume two credits)
− $0	Income taxes
$5,000,000	Net to heirs

*The taxable estate is reduced by the $6 million charitable contribution.

There are no estate or income taxes due because John and Mary are each able to use their $5 million applicable exclusion amount. The private foundation trust agreement allows the trustees (the children in this case) to receive reasonable management fees for their services as trustees (they must provide real services). The children will receive some income plus the pleasure of giving money to worthy charitable causes. However, they are likely to be unhappy that they receive a reduced inheritance. Hence, the Thompsons establish an irrevocable life insurance trust and place $7,000,000 of survivorship life insurance in it. As a result, when they die, the children receive $7,000,000 of life insurance income and $5,000,000 of property estate tax free plus management fees for acting as trustees of their family private foundation. The family foundation has $6,000,000, and, if it is managed well, it will grow in size and provide future descendants the opportunity to continue the family tradition of charitable giving. To pay for the survivorship life policy, the Thompsons will make annual gifts to their children who will in turn own and pay the policy premiums. Based on the parents' ages (both are age 53), the annual premiums will be approximately $15,000–$20,000 per year.

Our government has structured the tax laws in a way that encourages charitable giving. In most cases, the tax laws are merely an added benefit to philanthropists who give out of a moral sense of duty rather than tax benefit. Regardless, the tax benefits should be analyzed in a transaction to make sure that the end result is as intended. Additional tax benefits can be achieved through the use of a family limited partnership, which is described in detail in Chapter 13.

Family Limited Partnerships

The family limited partnership (FLP) or the limited liability company (LLC) have become common estate planning techniques, not unlike the irrevocable life insurance trust. Properly structured, they can be a part of your wealth preservation strategy. If Congress decides to repeal the estate tax in the future, their usefulness will be limited to their asset protection and control attributes. Until that happens, the FLP and LLC should be considered tools in your defense against estate taxes.

General Structure of the Family Limited Partnership

With an FLP, you establish a limited partnership agreement and then transfer title to certain property from your individual name to the name of the partnership. This transfer is a nontaxable event if the original property owners are the same as the original partners in the same proportion that they formerly owned the property outright. Typically, you (and your spouse) are the general partner(s), and your children and/or grandchildren are limited partners. As with any partnership, only the general partners have the right to make decisions and vote; the limited partner's role is very restricted. If, as the general partner, you decide to make a partnership distribution, all partners including the limited partners must receive a pro rata distribution. Initially, when you transfer your property to the partnership, you will retain both the general partner interest and all limited partnership interests.

Assets transferred to the FLP must be valued at the time of the transfer. As the general partner, you may then begin to transfer limited partnership interests (called "units" in the case of an LLC) to other family members through a gifting program using your annual or lifetime exclusion. Because the interests that you are transferring are limited partnership interests, a business appraiser may discount the value of the gift. For example, say you transfer farm property worth $1,000,000 to your FLP with you and your spouse as the general partners. You then want to use your combined annual gift tax exclusion ($26,000) to gift limited partnership units to your five children. You calculate that $26,000 times five equals $130,000. However, this is not correct! Because what your children will receive is a limited partnership interest in the farm land rather than the land itself, it is worth less than full value. This is because as limited partners, their rights to sell and use the property are only those granted them by the general partner and the partnership agreement. In other words, the value of a 10 percent limited partnership interest in the land is worth less than 10 percent of the whole value of the property. The result is a discounting of the value of limited partnership interests, which allows you to leverage your wealth transfers. If the land being transferred into your partnership received a 30 percent discount, this would mean that your $130,000 gifts of partnership units to your children would actually transfer $185,714 of pre-discounted land value. Now that is what we call leverage! Remember, you can make gifts every year.

ADVANTAGES

- *Control.* Control can be an advantage of the FLP *and* a disadvantage, as de-scribed in more detail below. One of the primary reasons that clients refuse to make lifetime transfers of wealth to children or other family members is loss of control. For instance, say you own 100 percent of the stock in your closely held business that you estimate is worth $16,000,000. You know that you should be transferring stock to your children and grandchildren to reduce the impact of future estate taxes. But you're frozen into inaction because you do not want to risk losing control—even to your family. As a result you do nothing. The FLP may allow you to retain *some* control of the decisions concerning your business, while also letting you address your estate tax concerns. If you are the only general partner, no one else has voting rights or decision-making authority. However, if you are the only general partner, the IRS may argue that you have *too much* control and any valuation discounts will be ignored. Therefore, it is advisable to share control of the company. In order to further reduce the risk of an IRS attack, some individuals choose to give up all control. An individual who is not ready or willing to give up half or all of the control of the FLP should be advised that the IRS may attack the entity structure if audited.

- *Leverage.* One of the primary advantages of the FLP is the leverage that is created when you gift partnership interest to your family members. Through various discounts, you are able to transfer $1 worth of property for substantially less than $1, which allows you to reduce the size of your estate much more quickly than would otherwise be possible. We will discuss valuation discounts in more detail later in this chapter.

- *Ease of transfer.* The FLP allows you to take a large asset and divide it into small pieces that can be easily transferred. You can imagine how difficult (and expensive) it would be to divide a large tract of land into pieces small enough to use as annual gifts to children. Surveys, deed and title transfers, and court filings would make transfers impractical, particularly if you planned to make transfers each year as a part of a lifetime wealth transfer program. With your FLP, you simply transfer partnership units, which involves simple mathematics once the partnership property has been valued, including the appropriate discounts.

- *Asset protection.* The FLP provides excellent protection against creditors for the limited partners. It is possible for a creditor of a limited partner to force the partner to assign his or her interest to the creditor in satisfaction of a legal claim. As an assignee, the creditor's rights are generally limited to any distributions declared by the general partner. The creditor is also treated as a partner for income tax purposes. If the partnership has income but not distributions, the creditor is placed in the unenviable position of having so-called phantom income; that is, they owe taxes but received no cash with which to pay them. This will serve as a deterrent to even the most persistent creditor.

- *Ease of establishment and simplicity of maintenance.* An FLP is relatively easy to create: All you do is prepare the partnership agreement, transfer the deed or title to the partnership name, and issue partnership certificates. Even the subsequent transfers of undivided interests in the FLP are easy. You simply amend the partnership agreement.

- *Probate avoidance.* Property held in an FLP avoids probate. This is particularly useful if you have property located in more than one state. Avoiding the probate process may save your heirs time, money, and aggravation (The FLP interest itself does not avoid probate).

- *Privacy.* Closely related to avoiding probate, an FLP provides a structure that keeps the family's business private. This is the case both during life and after your death. If you do not want the world to know what you own, how much it is worth, and who inherited it upon your death, then an FLP is an excellent choice.

- *Income benefits to the general partner.* Our clients often express the dual concerns of a continuing need for income and a need to reduce their estates to minimize taxes. They fear that if they give their income-producing property away, they will be left without the financial support they desire. The FLP can address this issue effectively because the general partner can pay him- or herself an income as the manager of the partnership. Of course, the general partner must actually be working for the FLP. This is in addition to and apart from the share of declared distributions.

- *Centralized management*. The FLP provides the benefit of centralizing the management of all assets held in the partnership. There is one partnership tax return, and if desired, there can be only one partnership bank account.

- *Continuity of management*. A significant feature of the FLP is that it can provide for continuity of management upon your death. Your partnership agreement will list your successor manager. It is particularly important that your document include a succession plan should you become incompetent due to sickness or accident.

- *Annual gifting*. Your gift of a partnership interest should qualify for the annual gift tax exclusion. Although some practitioners argue that you should include a Put right (similar to a current access to property right in an insurance trust). This helps reinforce the fact that the gift is a "present interest" and qualifies for the annual gift tax exclusion.

Now that we have made a persuasive case for using an FLP as part of your estate plan, let's look at some of the disadvantages.

DISADVANTAGES

- *Control*. As mentioned above, maintaining *some* control can be viewed as an advantage of the FLP planning technique. However, the degree of retained control should be carefully evaluated. Often times, the IRS will focus on the level of control retained by the donor (if the donor is the sole general partner or a co-general partner). If too much control is retained, the IRS may attack the valuation discounts applied to the entity. The IRS may also argue that the donor attempted to transfer property out of his or her estate (via gifts of FLP interests), but maintained too much control over the transferred property. Therefore, the IRS may argue that the donor never gave up the property and it should be included in his or her estate for estate tax purposes. This is something that should be carefully considered when evaluating how much control the original property owner should retain in the FLP.

- *Valuations*. In order for you to transfer portions of your partnership interest, the fair market value of these interests must be determined. For certain assets such as publicly traded securities, this is no problem. On the other hand, it is far more difficult to value assets such as real estate, so you will need to get qualified appraisals. A qualified appraisal does not mean that you get your friendly local real estate agent to give you an estimate of value; rather, it means hiring an appraiser who will complete detailed research as to the partnership's value and issue a written report. The appraisal will need to be completed as of the date you are making a transfer of partnership interests on the date of the partner's death. If you are making annual gifts of your partnership interests, you will need annual updates of your appraisal(s). Appraisals can be expensive, costing several thousands of dollars. Before you decide to use the FLP, you should get a sense of what the appraisal costs will be. Often you can find an appraiser who will update the appraisal annually for a reduced fee. One way to cut appraisal costs is to have them done every *other* year. For example, say you have the partnership real estate appraised in December of one year and use that value to make gifts for that year and January of the following year. Then you wait two years and repeat the process.

- *Determining discounts.* One of the primary advantages of the FLP is that you create leverage in your gifting program. Say you want to give your son a parcel of land worth $10,000. By using the FLP, the value of the transfer is $7,000 or less because you are transferring a partnership interest in the property rather than the property itself. As a partnership interest, it carries certain restrictions as to marketability and control, which makes it less valuable. How much of a discount will an appraiser apply to the property? This is an important question that is best answered by an expert in discount valuations. There are actually companies that specialize in this type of work. This is not an exact science and is subject to challenge by the IRS. If the IRS does challenge your discounts, the expert's report will serve as his or her testimony in most cases. You will want to choose someone who is qualified to do this type of work and who can issue a report that adequately defends his or her positions. As mentioned earlier, the costs of appraisals, discount valuations, and a possible legal battle with the IRS can be significant.

- *Retaining appreciated property.* With an FLP, the value of the gift of a partnership interest is based on the date of the gift. If, as the general partner, you retain a large partnership interest in appreciating property, the growth of that property is increasing the value of your estate. This can make it difficult to manage the growth of your estate, which is typically one of the primary objectives. Contrast this with other strategies such as the installment sale or grantor-retained annuity trust (GRAT), which effectively transfer all future growth to your donee.

- *IRS challenge.* The IRS is unhappy with the effectiveness of the FLP in reducing and avoiding taxes. FLPs are thus more likely to be subject to an IRS audit than some of the other techniques discussed. This is partly due to the fact that many of your assumptions are based on somewhat subjective estimates rather than exact mathematics. The IRS will particularly focus on your assumptions as to fair market value and discount valuations, which can be easily argued because there are no exact answers. To adequately defend yourself, you will want to make sure that you employ experts in the field, including attorneys, accountants, appraisers, and valuation experts.

Family Limited Partnership Rules

To be recognized as a partnership for income tax purposes, you must follow certain rules and procedures. Failure to do so may result in adverse tax consequences. Specifically, to qualify as an FLP, you must meet the following tests:

- The partnership must have a purpose other than tax avoidance. Most people cite several nontax purposes, such as centralized investment management, consolidation of control, business confidentiality, facilitating asset protection, facilitating future annual gifts, maintenance of family ownership, pooling of assets to maximize economic returns, and management continuity. It is vital that these nontax objectives be expressed clearly and precisely in your partnership documents; it is important that they be *real* objectives. Any tax avoidance objectives should not be the reason for the FLP and they certainly should not be described in the partnership documents.

- The partnership must be engaged in a business or investment activity. The partnership cannot simply be a shell for holding assets until you can transfer them to the limited partners. You must show a business purpose. Capital must be a material income-producing factor. The partnership may be subject to attack on audit if the primary income sources are fees, commissions, or other income stemming from personal services. Any partner performing personal services must receive compensation that is fair and reasonable. For example, say you place an apartment building in an FLP with the intention of transferring interests to your three children. You obviously meet the IRS test of employing capital in the production of income. If, however, you managed the apartments yourself but received no income for those services, then you would fail the second test, and the partnership income that you intended for your children to receive will be taxed to you.

- The partners must conduct their affairs in a manner that is consistent with the existence and purpose of the FLP. You must run your FLP as a true business. This means having periodic partnership meetings for making decisions and conducting business, periodic reports to the limited partners, filing partnership tax returns, and performing other functions consistent with running a business.

Discount Planning

With the help of a qualified appraiser, two types of discounts are potentially available under the FLP.

DISCOUNTS FOR LACK OF MARKETABILITY

A limited partnership interest in an FLP will normally include restrictions as to transferability, usually including a first right of refusal to the remaining partners.

These restrictions as to marketability cause a limited partnership interest to be less valuable than an outright interest in an asset. For example, think of how you would determine the value of a particular piece of property you know to have a fair market value of $100,000. You have the choice of buying the entire property outright, or you can buy a 10 percent interest in the property as a limited partner, which would mean you have no vote or input regarding any partnership decisions. You may not even know the other partners. Would you be willing to pay $10,000 for this 10 percent interest? In most cases, your answer would be no. You would want to discount the purchase price, perhaps substantially, to be enticed to buy. Fortunately, our courts take this same view. In cases where transferability is restricted, a valuation discount is usually warranted.

DISCOUNTS FOR LACK OF CONTROL

As a limited partner, you have no right to set investment policy, compel distributions, or impact any decisions regarding the partnership. The courts have typically supported the premise that this lack of control results in your interest being less valuable and have therefore granted valuation discounts for holders of limited partnership interests. This is because the law looks at the value of the interest by itself rather than as a part of the whole. This is also true of *minority* interests in a partnership or corporation. Of particular importance in a partnership is the fact that taxes are passed through to the partners whether or not distributions are made to those partners. You can imagine how unhappy a partner would be if he or she received a tax bill for undistributed income, which is often the case.

Calculating Discounts

Calculating the various discounts is a job that should be performed by knowledgeable and qualified appraisers. Discounts for lack of control or marketability are not mutually exclusive. They can be aggregated. These discounts can apply to the general partners as well as the limited partners, but typically in lesser amounts. The fact that you transfer property from your name outright to an FLP possibly creates a discount for you even if you retain the bulk of both the general and limited partnership interests. However, most valuation experts have become more conservative in this area. Typically, if a person creates an FLP and retains the bulk of both the general and limited partner interests, the appraiser is less likely to apply a significant discount. The theory being that the original property owner has maintained too much control over the property. If the original property owner only retains *some* control over the property (by retaining *some* general partnership interests), then an appraiser may apply a modest discount to the general partnership interests. This discount is typically less than the discount applied to the limited partnership interests. Some appraisers will take an even more conservative view and reduce the discount applied to the limited partnership interests if the appraiser determines that the limited partnership interest owner retains control over the entity by virtue of the fact he or she also owns some or all of the general partnership interests. We have seen examples of discounts of as much as 60–65 percent being applied. However, discounts that high can be a red flag. In most cases, discounts can range from 20 percent to 35 percent. The amount of the discount will depend up on the underlying assets owned by the entity and the degree of control given to the general partnership interest or limited partnership interest (depending on which interest is being valued). One of the most important elements in setting up your FLP is getting an appropriate discount valuation. You will want to choose someone who specializes in this field and has experience in defending his or her work. The stakes are very high if an inappropriate discount is applied and the IRS attacks the entity or the discount. A successful attack by the IRS can result in additional estate or gift taxes due (as a result of undervaluing property) or in the inclusion of previously transferred property back in the donor's estate (because he or she retained too much control). Therefore, your goal should be an appropriate discount based on defendable evidence and facts which apply to your particular FLP.

Maximizing Your Discounts

The larger your estate, the more important it will be to properly execute discount planning in FLP planning. This can be accomplished through several well-thought-out strategies.

- Only use an FLP if the circumstances are appropriate. An FLP should have a non-tax-avoidance purpose. Examine whether liability protection will be gained or other non-tax goals will be attained by the FLP planning. All of the non-tax avoidance reasons for the FLP will help the appraiser in preparing his or her report and quantifying the discount.

- Focus on the amount of control being retained. The greater the degree of control retained, the more likely the discount will be reduced. In addition, the greater the amount of control retained, the more likely the IRS will attempt to attack the entity and possibly include the entire entity in an individual's estate (despite the fact previous gifts have been made).

- Certain states have laws that make it more difficult for partners to withdraw from the partnership or otherwise liquidate their interest. This is accomplished through a requirement that the partnership have a fixed termination date. By forming your partnership in one of these states, you will receive a larger discount.

- It is important to form *and fund* your FLP *before* you make any gifts of partnership interest. People sometimes make the mistake of forming the partnership and funding it with only nominal amounts of property. They then make substantial gifts of partnership interests to family members and later transfer substantial amounts of assets to the partnership. This results in contemporaneous gifts to the family members and could be attacked by the IRS, resulting in adverse tax consequences.

- Consider adding language to your partnership agreement restricting liquidation. This provision can be substantially fortified by having a nonfamily-member limited partner, such as a charity, which must also agree to any liquidation. The inclusion of this restriction may result in a greater discount.

Recognition of General and Limited Partners' Rights

Care must be taken in structuring your FLP so that an appropriate balance is struck between giving the general partner the desired control over decisions and restricting those powers sufficiently so as to not disqualify the partnership for tax purposes. This is of particular importance where the general partner is the donee rather than the donor. Say you form an FLP, fund it with your assets, and make your son and daughter co-general partners at a 2 percent interest each. You retain a 96 percent limited partnership interest. However, you continue to make all the decisions regarding partnership business while your children act as rubber stamps for those decisions. As far as the public is concerned, you are still the one in control—the partnership contact person. This is exactly how the IRS will view the arrangement, and your partnership will likely be attacked by the IRS if audited.

Recognition of partnership income must be allocated in an appropriate manner. Each partner must receive their pro rata share, net of partnership expenses. For income tax reasons, you may want to shift a larger portion to your children who are in a lower tax bracket than you. Some advisors will draft the partnership agreement to allow this. However, doing so means you're subject to scrutiny and possible disqualification by the IRS. At the same time, the general partners must be compensated fairly for their management services. Often the general partner will work for free to make additional income available to the limited partners. At the opposite end of the spectrum is the general partner who desires a disproportionately higher income from the partnership and therefore pays him- or herself more compensation than the services are worth. Either extreme is subject to challenge by the IRS. It should be noted that what is considered fair compensation to the general partner can be a wide-ranging dollar amount. You should consider not only what the actual services are worth but other compelling issues as well. For instance, as a general partner, you are exposed to unlimited liability.

Limited partners should receive copies of partnership tax returns, and if the partnership agreement gives them any voice in management decisions, those rights should be respected. The donor should also not retain powers to unreasonably restrict a donee's right to dispose of his or her partnership interest. This is typically handled through a first right of refusal by the general partner and/or limited partners. Your agreement should not contain a set price for which the donor can buy back a donee's partnership interest. To do so might constitute a detrimental interest on the part of the donee, which is restricted in the regulations.

Minors' Interests in Family Limited Partnerships

Minors (as well as legally incompetent persons) are allowed to own interests in an FLP. A minor's interests can be held by a custodian under a UGMA or a UTMA or by a trustee under a trust account. Note that not all states have adopted the UTMA regulations, and some states may not allow a minor's account to hold a partnership interest. Extra care should be taken where the donor will also act as the custodian or sole trustee. To do so could cause the minor's interest to be includable in the donor's estate. Also, the IRS will closely scrutinize these situations to be certain that the donor is acting solely in the interest of the minor. One excellent attribute of using FLP interests for gifts to custodial accounts is that it solves the problem of transfer of control when the minor reaches legal adulthood. If you transferred securities to a custodial account, your child would legally take control of the securities based on state law (usually age 18 to 21). At that point the child could do whatever he or she pleased with the funds. However, if the asset is a limited partnership interest, their rights and control are significantly limited.

Using Multiple Family Limited Partnerships to Maximize Benefits

Some individuals may benefit from establishing more than one FLP. One primary advantage of doing so is to enhance asset protection by separating safe assets from risky assets. Safe assets would include assets such as marketable securities, notes receivable, or idle cash; risky assets include real estate, closely held business interests, or general partnership interests. By separating these asset groups, you insulate your safe assets from liability attributable to the risky assets. If you own real estate that later becomes subject to a legal award for environmental damages, your personal securities and cash would not be exposed to this suit or claim. Separating assets also allows you to fine-tune your gifting program by allowing you to maintain 100 percent ownership of the safe asset FLP while gifting limited partner units of the risky FLP. It may also be appropriate to separate risky assets into multiple FLPs for the reasons just stated. The downside to having multiple FLPs are costs in set up and ongoing administration. In addition, although we're suggesting that you consider placing your marketable securities and cash in a separate FLP, we caution you that special rules are applicable in this situation. You must avoid having your asset treated as an investment company, so you should consult with a professional advisor experienced in this important area.

Limited Liability Companies

A limited liability company (LLC) provides many of the same features as the FLP, with a few notable distinctions. One of the primary advantages is that *all* members of an LLC have limited liability for the debts and obligations of the company. As you remember, with the FLP only the limited partners enjoy this protection. The general partner has *unlimited* liability. In most other respects, the LLC enjoys many of the same benefits as the FLP, including asset protection, valuation discounts, continuity and consolidation of management, income tax shifting, and probate avoidance.

There are some disadvantages to the LLC compared with the FLP. First, the laws governing LLCs vary from state to state. You and your professional advisor will need to review your own state laws carefully. Second, in most states, a member has the right to withdraw from the company and receive the fair market value of his or her interest. This freedom of transferability can affect the size of discounts available in the LLC. Also, the complete withdrawal or death of a member can result in the dissolution of the company. In some states it is possible to include language in the company's operating agreement that satisfactorily deals with each of these problems.

The FLP can be an ideal tool for owners of closely held business interests or family farms. Often, these individuals want to have family members succeed them in the family business. Therefore, succession planning is essential in these situations. If you own your own business, Chapter 14 will provide you a thorough review of succession strategies for you to consider.

Succession Planning for the Family Business or Farm

If you are a business owner, healthcare practitioner, or farmer, you'll have to contend with special challenges as you work to preserve your assets for your heirs. To simplify our discussion, we will refer to anyone who falls into any of these three categories as a business owner. As a business owner, you're probably so involved in the day-to-day demands of running your business that you haven't really thought about succession planning. Unfortunately, too many people don't plan properly, and as a result, the value of their business is seriously diminished. A couple of typical cases show how important advance planning can be.

Case Study 1

Bill Johnson Sr. a divorcee, owned a small precision manufacturing company that had an estimated value of $6,000,000. He had spent his entire career building this successful company, which represented the bulk of his net worth. He was grooming his son Billy to take over the company when he retired. Bill Sr. also had two daughters who are not involved in the business. Unfortunately, he died suddenly, leaving his estate to the three children equally. Billy Jr. was now in business with his two sisters, and he was a minority stockholder. Although Billy's sisters had little interest in the business, they felt they deserved an income from it because, after all, Billy received a nice salary. Together the two sisters owned a majority of the voting stock, and they were able to successfully demand the income they felt they deserved. Because they did not work in the business, these income payments were not deductible by it. This story does not have a happy ending: The infighting and cash-flow problems eventually caused the company to fail. The sisters blamed Billy. After all, he was running the company.

A number of steps could have alleviated the problems in this case. One strategy would have been to have the daughters receive their share of the estate of Bill Sr. from assets other than the business. To accomplish this, Bill Sr. would have had to buy life insurance owned by a trust for the daughters' benefit or have arranged for the daughters to own the policies individually. If insurance was not a possibility, he could have considered two classes of stock—voting and nonvoting. In this way, he could have given the daughters nonvoting stock while giving Billy voting stock. All of the children would have had equal ownership in the company, but Billy would have had voting control. Another option would have been for Bill Sr. to sell the company to Billy Jr. for an installment note. At Bill's death, the children would have had an equal interest in the note.

Case Study 2

Dr. Steve Stein's dental practice has provided him and his family a good income for 35 years. Now, at age 64, he has noticed that his patient load is declining significantly each month. That is likely to continue because his current patients are all in their mid to late 60s. Also, an increasing number of his current patients are moving to retirement communities out of town, while others are dying. He seems to be surrounded by younger dentists who have thriving practices, while his profits are dropping month by month. He is ready to retire but cannot afford to because there is little value left in his practice. He has no choice but to continue to run an increasingly deteriorating practice. Finally, at age 75, he shuts his doors and sells his equipment for pennies on the dollar.

We have had an opportunity to work with numerous healthcare professionals over the years, and one of our primary objectives is to make sure that we built value in their practices. Dr. Stein should have brought in a younger dentist to the practice. Not only would the younger dentist have provided valuable new blood, but he or she would have been the perfect buyer.

Case Study 3

Horace and Martha James owned a working farm that had been in the family for two generations, and it was their desire that the farm remain in the family. Although the farm income had allowed them to raise and educate their two children, they always had to pay attention to their cash flow. Consequently, they didn't expect the farm to be worth very much and have not concerned themselves with any estate planning. However, when the Jameses both passed away, their children were in for a rude awakening. The farm was rich in timber, and the IRS valued the land at four times the Jameses' estimate. This resulted in substantial estate taxes even though the children didn't have the cash to pay the taxes. Despite the special tax provisions for farmers, the children were unable to pay the taxes, and the farm had to be sold to raise cash.

Business owners, particularly farmers, tend to underestimate the value of their businesses. This is a big mistake. For better or worse, the IRS seems particularly inclined to challenge the business values of deceased business owners. There is a lot of money at stake, and the IRS wins more than its share of these cases. The Jameses' best defense would have been a good offense. First, they could have reduced the value of the farm by using discounting strategies such as the FLP and LLC. Next, they should have considered using their annual gift tax exclusion to begin transferring undivided interests in the farm to their children at that time. Finally, they needed to monitor the value of the land and then develop a game plan that provided the liquidity to meet any potential estate tax obligation. To do this, they would have had to get aid from a qualified appraiser. This is another instance where planning ahead could have achieved the desired objective.

Special Estate Tax Benefits for Farmers and Closely Held Business Owners

One major problem shared by farmers and small business owners is that the farm or business typically represents the majority of the value in their estate. Under normal circumstances, estate taxes are due within nine months after the date of death. Because businesses and farms are by their nature highly illiquid enterprises, there is rarely cash to pay these estate taxes. Fortunately, Congress has provided a variety of special tax provisions to make it easier for the small business owner and farmer to meet their tax obligation and thus pass the assets to family members. These special provisions include the following:

- Installment payment of estate taxes.
- Special-use valuation of certain business property.

Installment Payment of Estate Taxes

Estate taxes are generally due within nine months of the date of death. If the value of your closely held business or farm exceeds 35 percent of your adjusted gross estate, your executor can elect to pay your estate taxes in installments. A 100 percent deferral of taxes is allowed for the first four years based on interest-only payments. The taxes are then paid in equal installments over 10 years. Current law also provides an interest rate of 2 percent on the first $1,360,000 (as indexed for inflation) of taxable value.

Special-Use Valuation

Imagine that you own a working farm in an outlying area of a fast-growing community. The farm has been in your family for two generations, and you want it to remain in the family. Upon your death, the IRS values it not under its current use but at its highest and best use, which is for commercial development. If it were valued as farm property, it would be worth $6,000,000, but as commercial property it is worth $15,000,000. The resulting estate tax could potentially be more than the entire farm is worth! This is not an unusual circumstance. To address this problem, current law provides special-use regulations that allow your executor to elect to value the property at its *current* use rather than its fair market value. To qualify for this election certain criteria must be met:

- The value of the property in question must represent at least 25 percent of your total estate. In addition, the combined value of the real estate and personal property used in the business must exceed 50 percent of your gross estate.

- You must have materially participated in the business five of the last eight years preceding your death.

- The property must be passed to qualified heirs who must then continue to materially participate in the business for 10 years after your death.

- Your qualified heirs cannot sell any part of their interest for 10 years after your death.

- The property must continue to be used in the same way as it was qualified for under the special-use valuation for at least 10 years after your death.

- All qualified heirs with an interest in the property must sign an agreement that requires them to pay additional estate taxes should the land fail to continue to qualify as special-use property during the 10 years following your death.

- The property is subject to a federal tax lien, which can make it difficult for the owners to obtain traditional financing or loans using the property as collateral.

This reduction in value for tax purposes is limited to $750,000 except as adjusted for inflation indexing, which is $1,020,000 in 2011. Special-use valuation is a complex area of the law, so you'll need to consult your financial advisor early in the planning process.

Valuing Your Business or Farm

Most business and farm owners have a poor sense of the value of their business. This may be because as a profession, farming can yield small profits for a lot of work. However, the IRS doesn't consider work when it puts a value on your property; you should note what the IRS thinks is *very* important. Upon your death, it is the IRS that may challenge the values your executor places on the farm. In many instances, the IRS will assume that you are going to try to lowball the value. To counteract this assumption, you will need to have qualified appraisers establish the fair market value and be prepared to defend their results. You should get a ballpark estimate now so that you can do your advance planning. Figure a worst-case valuation and then develop a plan that addresses the estate tax and succession issues. In previous chapters we discussed many ways to create discounts for valuation purposes. Other chapters outline strategies that you can use to begin transferring portions of the business or farm each year. The important thing is to develop a plan early. You don't want to die and then have your heirs in a crisis-management mode that often results in higher taxes and a greater burden on your loved ones.

Succession or Sale?

Two potentially distinct issues must be considered when thinking about the family business, the first of which has to do with keeping it in the family. If there are family members who are both interested and capable of carrying on the business, you will want to make sure that you effect a transfer that gives that person or persons appropriate control of the business. You will also want to ensure that he or she receives the business in a sound financial condition.

If you don't intend to pass the business to family members upon your death or retirement, you should structure the business in such a way as to receive its maximum value. Your decisions here will help determine the strategy that is best for you and your family.

Succession Planning: Keeping the Family Business in the Family

Take a long look at your business. Are there family members who are able and interested in continuing it? If you have a child or children who are interested and others who are not, do you have a way of dividing your estate so that all are treated fairly? You definitely want to avoid engineering a successful transfer of the family business only to have it divide the family. Let's assume that you want your business to be under your children's control. Some of the planning issues to consider are as follows:

- *Management training.* We often find situations where children are working in the family business but the parent is still making all the key decisions without any input from the children. This isn't training. If you intend to leave the business to a child, he or she has to be in the loop of business decision making.

- *Control.* If you have children who are not involved in the business, it is essential that the children who are running the business have voting control. As in the case of the Johnson family, the best solution is to make sure that the children not working in the business receive their fair share of your estate from assets other than your business interest. Although these conversations can be difficult, you should discuss these issues openly with your children so that each of them understands why you are dividing your estate the way you are.

- *Financial condition.* Try to take an objective look at your company. Is it financially sound, or is it overleveraged? In the hands of capable management, financial leverage is an important tool for growing a business. Are you the key person in that management team? How would your son or daughter fare if he or she had to suddenly step in your management shoes because of your death or disability? Make sure that you have a plan for transferring the business to your children in sound financial condition, which should be defined in terms of their capabilities, not yours. This may be as simple as providing adequate insurance on your life and a disability plan.

- *Estate taxes*. You need to determine what the business is likely to be valued for estate tax purposes. Will there be adequate liquidity to pay estate taxes? Many succession plans have failed because of failure to plan for this eventuality. Consider using some of the many strategies we have discussed in this book for reducing and transferring the value of your business and other assets.

- *Documentation*. Remember, for your business interest to be transferred, you have to have proper documentation. Do not assume that you will get around to it someday. Do it now! This can be done through your will, or it can be accomplished with buyout agreements. Consult with your tax advisor for the best method in your situation.

Maximizing Your Business's Value through a Sale

If you do not plan to leave your business to a family member, you will want to take steps to maximize its value upon your death or retirement. If you're assuming someone else will be willing to pay top dollar for your business, you have to do a lot of planning. Here are some of the issues you should consider:

- *When to sell?* Do you plan to sell your business while you are living or do you plan to wait until you die? This may sound like a strange question, but many people plan to work their entire life. Your strategy for selling during life might be very different from your strategy if you plan to wait until you die.

- *Finding a buyer*. Business owners sometimes shrug their shoulders and mutter something about someone selling their business upon their death when they're asked about what they intend to do with it. When we press a little harder for an answer, the owner often suggests that his or her spouse is probably the person who would end up dealing with the problem. Sometimes they know an advisor whom they feel they could count on to help with the sale. The truth is that none of these people are likely to be in a position to sell the business for its highest value. You are the only one who intimately understands the business, and you're in the best position to develop a plan for selling it. One solution is to find a buyer now and draw an agreement for sale in the event of your death. This may be easier than you think. Look around your business and see if any key employees would be capable of running it. Employees are often an excellent solution for a business sale. Not only do you have a ready buyer whom you can groom to take your position one day, but knowing that they may own the business one day is a very motivating factor. These employees are not likely to leave. Consider the case of the key employee who purchased and paid for insurance on the life of the business owner. The business owner had his attorney draw a buyout agreement that compelled the key employee to buy controlling stock in the company at the owner's death. The agreement also required the company to sell the stock. The owner is now giving the key employee additional management responsibilities so that he can run the company more effectively in the owner's absence. Much to the owner's surprise, the employee's management skills exceed his. He now has a ready buyer in the event of his death as well as a much more loyal and motivated employee.

What if you are not lucky enough to have a capable key employee who could buy the business at your death? Next you might consider a competitor. If one of them is reasonably friendly, you may be able to draw an agreement or at least a letter of understanding now. At the very minimum, you should sit down and write out a plan for your spouse or advisor to follow upon your death. List the people whom you think are the potential buyers, describe how to best determine the fair market value of the company, and include any other details that you feel would be useful in helping to sell your business.

- *Selling during life.* Perhaps the best way to receive full value for your business is to sell while you are still active in it, which usually allows you to receive the maximum value because you are there to assist with the transition. This does not have to be an all-or-nothing deal, particularly if you have key employees. By selling a minority interest in your company to them, you can create a loyalty that otherwise is difficult to achieve. The employees are now owners and will likely shun offers to work for competitors. You can also prepare them with both financial and management skills to take over when you retire or die. Be sure to develop an appropriate exit strategy that will allow you to get their stock back should they cease to be employed by your business. Minority shareholders can cause you a lot of problems.

Structuring Your Buy-Sell Agreement

Once you have found the right buyer for your business, you will need to structure a formal agreement that outlines all the terms. Whether your buyer is a family member or not, buy-sell agreements offer several advantages:

- If one of your goals is to make sure the family business stays in the family, a buy-sell agreement is an appropriate tool. The agreement can be structured such that all sales must be first be offered to existing stockholders (other family members) or the corporation before they can be sold or transferred to a nonfamily member.

- If structured properly, the buy-sell agreement can establish the value of your company for estate tax purposes. The purchase price for most buy-sell agreements is established by way of a formula or fixed price or is based on a required appraisal. The price *must* be established based on an arm's-length transaction, which means that the price should be one to which two unrelated parties would be willing to agree. The IRS looks closely at deals between family members to make sure that no bargain sales take place.

- The buy-sell agreement provides a ready market for the sale of the owner's interest in his or her business. Knowing the value that your family will receive for your business interest allows you to better plan your estate.

Types of Buy-Sell Agreements

Buy-sell agreements are typically classified as either *entity purchase agreements* (sometimes referred to as *redemption agreements*), *cross-purchase agreements*, or *hybrid agreements*.

Entity Purchase Agreements

With an entity purchase agreement, the company agrees to purchase your shares of stock at the occurrence of some predetermined event such as your retirement, disability, or death. This type of buy-sell agreement has several disadvantages. First, it only makes sense where there are other co-owners. Second, if life insurance is used as the funding vehicle, your company may be subject to some rather unpleasant tax consequences (for C corporations)—the alternative minimum tax (AMT). If you may be subject to the AMT, you may want to consider electing S corporation status. Also, unless the agreement is carefully structured, the proceeds could be subject to ordinary income taxes. Finally, the remaining owners are deprived of a stepped-up cost basis, which they would have received if they had purchased your shares directly. In most cases, a cross-purchase agreement is preferred.

Cross-Purchase Agreements

In a business where there are multiple owners, a cross-purchase agreement is often used in which each owner agrees to buy a portion of the interest of the departing owner's shares at retirement, disability, or death. The company itself is not a party to these transactions. This arrangement has the advantage of providing the buyer with a stepped-up cost basis in the business interest that he or she purchased. The primary disadvantage is the increased paperwork involved, especially if there are several owners or life insurance is being used to fund the purchases.

Hybrid Agreements

Hybrid agreements involve both the shareholders and the company in the buy-sell agreement. Typically they provide that upon your death, disability, or retirement, the shareholders have the first right of refusal to buy your shares. If they don't, then the company redeems your shares. In other cases, just the opposite occurs. The company has the first right of refusal to buy your shares, and if the company fails to do so, then the surviving shareholders have the right to buy them. If the shareholders refuse, the company then becomes obligated to buy your shares. This is sometimes referred to as a *wait-and-see agreement* because the buyers wait until the triggering event happens before deciding how your shares will be purchased. This allows for some last-minute tax planning to take place.

Funding the Buy-Sell Agreement

Having a buy-sell agreement is important, but your family or employees may not have the funds to buy your business interest. In a family-owned business, rarely do the shareholders or key employees have the cash to buy out the interest of a major owner. This problem is most often solved with life insurance. Premiums for permanent or cash-value life insurance can be expensive, but this is often a better solution than term life insurance, which is inexpensive initially but can become prohibitively expensive as you get older. If there are several owners who need to be insured, you may want to consider establishing a partnership to be the owner and beneficiary of the life policies. Without a partnership (or corporation), a company with four owners would need 16 separate life policies to fund a cross-purchase agreement.

Life insurance will not solve all your funding problems. For example, if the triggering event is your disability, life insurance may be of little initial value as a funding vehicle. Any cash values are likely to be inadequate to fund a buyout caused by the disability of the owner. One solution to this problem is to purchase *disability buyout insurance*. This is a special type of disability policy that provides a lump-sum payment to buy the stock of a permanently disabled business owner. The exact definition of "incapacity of a business owner" is a complicated issue that needs to be addressed with your professional advisor.

Certain other tax and cash-flow issues are critical to the ongoing financial health of your company. For example, if you were to become disabled and your company continued to pay your salary, those payments might not be deductible by your company, which would create an added drain on its resources. One solution would be to implement a *qualified sick pay plan* that establishes a company policy for providing income to disabled employees. Another problem caused by a key person's disability is that someone will likely need to be hired to complete his or her duties. This obviously creates further cash drain where the company is paying one person who is not working and another person who is.

Life insurance may also be of little value if you are selling because of your retirement. One possible solution here would be to establish a sinking fund whereby your company sets aside money monthly or yearly for this purpose. In the corporate world this is known as accumulated earnings and can spell tax trouble for C corporations. Accumulating corporate earnings for the purpose of buying out a majority owner's stock can cause the imposition of the accumulated earnings surtax, which is based on the maximum tax bracket of the individual.

Often the best solutions are to purchase insurance where you can afford it and then plan to use financing arrangements to fund the balance. For example, your agreement may indicate that insurance will be used up to a certain dollar amount (the face of the policy) and that the balance will be paid over 5 to 10 years in monthly installments at a competitive interest rate. One danger with using installment payments is that they are made with after-tax dollars. The source of these payments is typically company salaries, bonuses, or dividends from the pockets of those people purchasing your stock. If the corporation increases salaries to cover the installment payments, the IRS may declare that the owner/stockholders are receiving what it considers unreasonable compensation, and the portion that is considered unreasonable is then reclassified as dividends for income tax purposes. Dividends are not deductible by the corporation, which results in double taxation. Successfully structuring the sale of a substantial business interest can be a very complicated matter that will require thoughtful effort on your part as well as on the part of experienced professional advisors.

One Final Strategy—The Employee Stock Ownership Plan

Another viable alternative for selling your stock is to establish an employee stock ownership plan (ESOP). An ESOP is similar to a qualified profit-sharing plan except that the company contributes company stock instead of cash. Some crucial details about ESOPs include the following:

- *Employer contributions.* Just as with a profit-sharing plan, contributions to an ESOP are limited to a maximum of 25 percent of compensation. Contributions may consist of shares of company stock or cash.

- *Limitations regarding diversification.* An ESOP does not have any limit on the amount of company stock held in the plan. This differs from a typical profit-sharing plan where diversification is a fiduciary duty. One exception concerns employees age 55 or older who have 10 years or more of service with the company: They must be offered a diversification option into any of three alternative investments. The election must be offered annually over a six-year period. During the first five years, transfers may be made up to a cumulative total of 25 percent of the employee's account balance. In the sixth year, this 25 percent limit is increased to 50 percent.

- *Forfeitures.* As with most retirement plans, an ESOP typically has a vesting schedule. In other words, contributions made on behalf of an employee are not fully vested in their names until they have been in the plan for a certain period of time. If an employee terminates employment prior to becoming fully vested, his or her nonvested portion is typically reallocated among the remaining participants.

- *Financial leverage.* The rules regarding ESOPs allow a company to borrow money to buy company stock to fund the plan's contributions. The interest on these loans is a deductible expense by the corporation.

One of the primary advantages to the ESOP is that it can provide you with a ready market for your stock. If the company is a C corporation, the tax on capital gains from the sale may be avoided by reinvestment in marketable securities (stocks and bonds) within 12 months. This advantage is not currently available to owners of S corporation stock. An ESOP owning shares (even 100 percent) of an S corporation will pay no income taxes on corporate profits.

Also, under an ESOP, if the company lacks the cash flow to make a contribution, there is no requirement to do so. Because the employees ultimately will end up owning the company, the ESOP may provide additional employee motivation. Finally, using borrowed money to make stock contributions can be an effective way of raising capital for a company. One added advantage is that the stock may be sold over a number of years or in a lump sum.

Owning and running a business can be a time-consuming and demanding proposition. You put years of your life into making your business a success. To maximize the return on your efforts, you will need to develop a plan to reap the full value of your business at your death or retirement.

One common concern that we all have is protecting our assets from legal judgments. A corporation, FLP, or LLC can provide you with a certain level of protection from would be creditors. For a full discussion of asset protection, read Chapter 15, "Asset Protection Strategies."

Asset Protection Strategies

One of the most significant threats to your wealth management plan is a potential legal judgment. Our laws allow just about anyone to sue you over just about anything. Many lawsuits are unfounded but nevertheless result in settlements as less expensive alternatives to a trial. If a case does go to trial, you have a right to a jury of your peers—but will the jury really be your peers? Almost by definition, if you are reading this book, your income and/or net worth places you in the top 10 percent of wealthy individuals in this country. The typical jury is composed of people who are not wealthy and may not sympathize with a defendant who is. Remember, too, that plaintiffs (the people who sue you), have nothing at risk except their time. Their attorneys typically take their cases on a contingency basis, which means that the attorneys receive no compensation if the clients do not win. Thus, the attorneys are in effect spending their own money prosecuting the case. This can cost anywhere from a few hundred to tens of thousands of dollars of expenses as well as attorneys' time. Talk about an incentive to win a case! You may assume that attorneys review potential cases based on the merits of the facts. Unfortunately, that's often not true. Some attorneys consider the probability of winning or losing a case with little regard for right or wrong. This use of our system of justice has resulted in a litigation crisis in America. It is your responsibility to make sure that you and your family are protected as much as possible from such problems. In this chapter we will discuss the various strategies you can use to protect your assets from potential creditors. Some of them have already been discussed briefly earlier in this book; we will now review them in more detail.

The Concept of Fraudulent Transfers

Many people don't think about protecting their assets until there is a threat of a lawsuit. Then they rush around shifting assets to family members, trusts, partnerships, and Swiss bank accounts. Our legal system includes the *Uniform Fraudulent Transfers Act* to prevent this from occurring. In essence, this law says that any property transferred for the purpose of avoiding creditors represents a fraudulent transfer and can be set aside. For example, you learn that you are about to be sued, so you transfer your bank accounts and real estate temporarily to your sister, leaving you without assets. The lawsuit goes forward, and a substantial judgment is entered against you. You assume that because you now have no assets, you're judgment proof. However, the law of fraudulent transfers will allow your creditor's attorney to set aside the transfer to your sister, forcing her to transfer the assets back to you and thus fully available to your creditors. Don't think that you can make this transfer in secret. The attorneys will take your deposition, which is a legal process in which your statements are made under oath. To lie under oath is a federal offense punishable by time in prison. Rather than risking a jail sentence, you should prepare now for the possibility that you may be sued later. If you implement strategies of asset protection when you have no knowledge of possible litigation, then you can avoid the fraudulent transfer laws.

State Exemptions

Each state has enacted laws that exempt certain property from the claims of creditors. For example, in the states of Florida, Kansas, South Dakota, Iowa, and Texas, your personal residence is totally exempt from creditor claims no matter how much it is worth (although in certain bankruptcy proceedings a portion of the equity can be available to the bankruptcy trustee after a forced sale). Other states exempt various amounts of cash, cash value of life insurance, or personal property. Check with your attorney to learn the particular laws of your state.

Insurance

One obvious answer to a lawsuit is to have insurance that will reimburse you for legal fees and any judgments entered against you. Two primary forms of this type of insurance include *personal liability insurance* and business liability insurance. Personal liability insurance is typically included in your auto and homeowners insurance policy. If, for example, you are at fault in an accident and injure someone, which results in a lawsuit and judgment against you, your auto insurance coverage will pay both your legal fees and claims up to your policy limits. If someone falls down the steps at your home, is injured, sues, and receives a judgment, your homeowners policy will pay your legal costs and claims up to the policy limits. However, if the judgment exceeds the policy limits, the excess will come from your personal assets. One way to avoid this problem is through the purchase of a *personal liability umbrella policy,* which requires that your underlying auto and homeowners policies liability limits be raised to a certain level (usually $300,000 to $500,000). The umbrella policy then adds an additional $1,000,000 to $5,000,000 or more of liability protection. Such policies are usually purchased through your auto or homeowners agent and are relatively inexpensive. For example, a $1,000,000 umbrella policy may cost as little as $100 to $300 *per year.* Note that these policies cover only *personal* liability issues, not liability arising from business issues. To protect you against liability when you own a business, you should consider *business liability insurance.* (For healthcare professionals, this is known as *malpractice insurance,* and for other professionals, it may be referred to as *E and O [errors and omissions] insurance.)* This insurance is typically costly: Malpractice insurance for physicians can run into the tens of thousands of dollars each year. Many of these policies also have large deductibles, which represent the amount of money you must pay before your insurance kicks in—$10,000, $25,000, $50,000, or more. Furthermore, the insurance company will require that you use its attorney rather than your own and will likely want to settle your case even if you have done nothing wrong; that is, your insurance company will give the plaintiff money to drop the lawsuit. Unfortunately, from the public's point of view, you will have lost the case and maybe some of your reputation as well. You are not compensated for your time, anguish, or loss of income while fighting the lawsuit. Some observers have even suggested that you encourage lawsuits by having liability insurance. After all, insurance companies have been easy targets for plaintiff attorneys. Perhaps the best solution is some combination of insurance along with additional asset protection strategies.

Asset Protection for Married Couples

Being married affords you some possibilities for asset protection. We have found that most couples title the bulk of their assets jointly. We have already discussed the many reasons for not doing so; you can now add asset protection to the list. If you are at a significantly greater risk of being sued than your spouse, you should consider transferring assets to his or her name.

Tip

Some states will allow a special form of titling for real estate owned by two people called *tenants-in-common with cross-contingent remainders*. With property titled in this form, one spouse cannot sell the real estate, but both could. A creditor of one spouse will find it difficult, if not impossible, to seize the interest in property titled in this fashion. Check your state to see if this is available.

Let's review a simple example. Al Hitchcock is an obstetrician and has been married to Sue, a homemaker, for 25 years. In their community, Al is unable to purchase malpractice insurance (a reality in certain parts of our country). To protect his assets, he transfers everything except a small checking account to Sue's name. Now if he is sued and ends up with a judgment against him, his assets are protected because he no longer has any—they are all in Sue's name!

Is this strategy foolproof? No strategy is completely foolproof. You would need to be careful of the fraudulent transfer laws. Be sure to transfer the assets *before* there is knowledge of a potential lawsuit. Next, although you are protected against lawsuit, your spouse is not. Even if he or she, as a homemaker, is not likely to be sued, the possibility remains.

When we discuss the possibility of shifting assets with a client, there is often an unspoken tension in the air. The potential transferor is thinking it but unwilling to say it . . . *divorce*. What would happen if our obstetrician were to transfer all assets to his spouse and then she were to file for a divorce? The results can be quite negative, but not for the reasons that you might think. First, you need to make a distinction between separate property states and community property states. If you become divorced in a separate property state, the settlement will be based upon what is called *equitable principles*, which require the judge to look at a number of factors, including the length of the marriage, the value of separate property brought into the marriage, the value of any inherited property, and the ability of each spouse to earn a living after the marriage. The fact that you transferred your interest in marital property to your spouse will typically have little affect on how property is split upon divorce. Take the case of our obstetrician client who has been married for 25 years and whose wife is a homemaker. Even if all of their assets are the result of his income *and* they are all titled in his name, his wife would receive both a substantial property settlement and alimony in the event of a divorce. The issue here is not losing your assets to a divorcing spouse but rather receiving your share of the assets in a divorce. Let us explain. Assume that you have transferred the bulk of your assets to your spouse as an asset protection strategy. Sometime later you are sued, resulting in a $1,000,000 judgment against you, *and* you get divorced during the same time period. As part of the divorce settlement you receive $1,000,000 worth of property that can now be attached by your creditors. Transferring assets to your spouse as an asset protection strategy should only be used in stable marriages. Also, using the facts just described, if your spouse died and left you assets, those assets may become available to satisfy creditors as well. Divorce issues aside, you should know that a transfer of assets to a spouse also legally transfers the "control" of those assets as well.

Community property states present a unique challenge for couples interested in protecting assets through an asset-shifting strategy. In community property states, all property acquired during the marriage is considered to be half owned by each spouse regardless of whose name the property is in. Inherited property and property acquired prior to the marriage is typically considered separate property *so long as it has never been commingled with marital property.* Community property states include Arizona, Idaho, California, Louisiana, Nevada, New Mexico, Texas, Washington, and Wisconsin. If you live in a community property state and get a divorce, you and your spouse each keep your separate property plus one half of all community property. This sounds simple and straightforward. However, a creditor can generally attach community property to settle a judgment. If you or your spouse own separate or inherited property, it is imperative that neither of you commingle that property with community property.

It is possible to plan around the community property laws. Each spouse can sign a *transmutation agreement* that effectively separates community property into separate property. Care must be taken not to violate the fraudulent transfer laws. An agreement to retitle your home might read *"John Doe, 50 percent interest as his sole and separate property; and Jane Doe, 50 percent interest as her sole and separate property."* You might separate the assets altogether by dividing the bank account into each separate name. The transmutation agreement and the retitling of the assets are critical to a successful termination of community property.

A Word about Jointly Held Property

A quick refresher course on jointly held property may be in order. Remember that jointly held property is subject to the claims of creditors even if the claim is only against one of the joint owners. These creditors can force the sale of the property and are then entitled to up to one half of the proceeds. This joint property could be your home, and you and your family could end up in the street. Avoid jointly held property if you have concerns about asset protection.

As an alternative to joint tenancy, some states allow a form of titling called *tenancy by entireties.* This type of ownership is restricted to married couples. Property that is owned by this method cannot be attached by creditors. Let's say that you and your spouse live in a $2 million home in a state that allows you to own real estate titled as tenants by entireties. Your only other asset is your pension income of $10,000 per month, and you have no liabilities. You are sued and incur a $1 million judgment against you. Your creditors can get nothing because they cannot attach your home unless the judgment was against *both* of you. In this situation your creditors can receive nothing until there is a divorce, the property is sold, or you die. If you die *before* your spouse, their claim is forever set aside! Check with your legal counsel to see if your state allows this form of titling.

Retirement Plans

In 1974, Congress passed the Employee Retirement Income Security Act (ERISA) which provided many rules and regulations concerning qualified retirement plans. A variety of retirement plans are covered under this act including profit-sharing plans, money purchase pension plans (sometimes referred to as defined contribution plans), defined benefit plans, 401(k) plans, 403(b) plans, 457 plans, and 412(i) plans. Self-employment plans such as Keogh plans are also covered. The crucial impact of this act was asset protection for retirement plan benefits; they are no longer attachable by creditors. The only exception to this rule deals with qualified domestic relations orders (QDROs). If you are divorced, the court can award your departing spouse all or a portion of your retirement plan assets under a QDRO.

Typically, when people terminate employment to either take another job or retire, they will roll over their retirement plan to an individual retirement account (IRA) to continue to postpone taxation on their money. If you are concerned about asset protection, this may not be a good idea because IRAs are not protected retirement plans covered by ERISA. This rollover has the effect of transferring a creditor-proof asset into one that may be attachable. We say "may be" because non-bankruptcy creditor access to IRAs is governed by state law and some states do protect IRA assets. On a federal level, the Bankruptcy Act of 2005 provided limited protection to IRA funds in the bankruptcy context (up to $1.0 million of IRA funds and 100% of funds rolled over to an IRA from an ERISA plan. Therefore, the level of protection depends on whether the potential creditor is in a bankruptcy context or not. If you are changing employers, what should you do? Many employer plans will allow you to roll over your assets from a prior plan. If this is not possible, check to see if the plan of the company you are leaving will allow you to leave your assets in the plan. If it won't, you will have to roll your money over to an IRA. You can roll the account over to a qualified plan at a future date should your employer establish a qualified plan that permits this. Current law also allows you to roll your traditional IRA into an employer's qualified plan. For example, assume you have accumulated $20,000 based on your annual investments into your personal IRA account and you want to make certain it is not subject to the claims of creditors. If your employer's plan allows, you can roll your $20,000 into the employer's qualified retirement plan. It is now protected from creditors by federal law. Nondeductible IRAs do not qualify for rollover into an employer retirement plan.

What are the disadvantages to maintaining your money in a qualified retirement plan rather than using an IRA? Although an IRA may not provide absolute creditor protection (because of limits in the Bankruptcy Act of 2005 outside of rollovers and state, non-bankruptcy creditor laws), it does provide for maximum flexibility regarding investment options. Consider, for example, mutual funds. Through an IRA you can invest in most of the more than nine thousand mutual funds available today, or you can buy individual stocks, bonds, certificates of deposit, and so on. Contrast this with the typical employer-provided retirement plan that offers only a few investment choices. With homework, your opportunity to earn a higher rate of return increases with the number of investment alternatives available to you. A potentially lower rate of return is part of the price you pay for asset protection.

Life Insurance

Life insurance has long been considered an important tool for protecting the finances of American families. As such, our government has provided life insurance companies and their policyholders with favorable tax treatment. For example, when an insured person dies, the beneficiary owes no income taxes on the proceeds. Also, there is no current taxation on the earnings or growth of the policy's cash values. Many states have carried the concept of protecting life insurance policies and annuities over to the creditor protection arena as well. For example, Alabama state law provides that *cash value* cannot be attached by creditors. Other states provide similar protections, whereas still other states provide none. Some states also provide creditor protection for the cash values in annuity contracts. When it comes to life insurance death benefits, care should be exercised in choosing your beneficiary to protect the death benefits from would-be creditors. Let's say, for example, that you name your estate the beneficiary of your life insurance. At your death your estate representative is required by law to post a legal notice of your death so that creditors can file a claim against your estate. If you do have creditors, your life insurance proceeds are now available to settle their claims. You could have avoided this by having a named beneficiary. This beneficiary could be a person such as your spouse, or it could be a trust. In our practices, we have a large number of physicians as clients. We are always concerned that at their death an expatient might present a lawsuit as a way of treasure hunting, knowing that the doctor will not be around to defend him- or herself. You should check your state exemption laws to determine what protection they provide for your life insurance policies.

We should note that this beneficiary issue is not restricted to life insurance. When researching a client's case, we often find that they have made their estate the beneficiary of the retirement plan proceeds or their other employee benefits. You'll also want to consider annuities that you own. Anything that has a beneficiary designation should be reviewed. If you want your benefits to pass according to your will but also want the benefits of asset protection, consider making your beneficiary an irrevocable trust under your will. This has the same effect as naming your estate but will avoid both creditors and probate. Because the trust does not become irrevocable until you die, you retain the right to make changes any time prior to your death.

Using Trusts to Protect Assets

One way to shield your life insurance from creditors is to place your policies into an *irrevocable life insurance trust*, which is treated as a separate person for tax (and creditor) purposes. Depending on your state's laws, the cash value may already be protected, but a trust can help protect the proceeds for the benefit of your trust beneficiaries. The drawback to building up cash values in an irrevocable life insurance trust is that you have given away your money *irrevocably*. Perhaps the best way to address this problem is to add a provision in your document that allows the trustee to make distributions to beneficiaries at his or her discretion. For this to work, you will need both a friendly trustee and a friendly beneficiary. If you are married, the best choice for your beneficiary will likely be your spouse. Once this plan has been implemented, your friendly trustee can make distributions to your spouse should the need for cash arise. You have effectively shielded your money from potential creditors while maintaining reasonable access to your cash. For a complete explanation of the irrevocable life insurance trust, see Chapter 10.

Many people are reluctant to use an irrevocable trust because it is so permanent. Once you transfer assets into an irrevocable trust, it is much more difficult to get those assets back out. These trusts can also be rather expensive to set up and maintain. You may ask, "Are there asset protection benefits from using a revocable trust?" After all, this would afford you the greatest amount of flexibility. When you no longer needed the trust, you could simply revoke it. Having the power to revoke your trust is exactly the problem. If all of your assets are in your revocable trust and a creditor wins a legal claim against you, the judge can (and will) order you to take the assets out of your trust. This does not mean that use of a revocable trust cannot provide you with some needed asset protection. It just means that you will have to be a little more creative.

Case Study

Dr. Joan Spivy and her husband, John, have accumulated considerable assets. John works as a computer technician for a major corporation. Joan and John have come to us to help set up their estate plan. In addition to estate tax concerns, Joan is concerned about liability due to her anesthesiology practice. Concerning asset protection, we discussed many strategies including irrevocable trusts, FLPs, and offshore trusts. However, the Spivys like to keep things simple, and none of these more complex maneuvers appealed to them. Then we discussed a strategy that included a revocable living trust that they loved. Here's how it worked. Because Joan is at far greater risk of being sued, we established a revocable living trust in John's name. We then transferred all Joan's personal securities and real estate into the trust. The primary assets that Joan retained were her qualified pension plan assets and term life insurance. The combination of the assets would be enough to cover her applicable exclusion amount and thus fund her credit shelter trust. Although John and Joan had a long-standing marriage, Joan had expressed concerns about giving up control of her assets. To address this issue, we made Joan and John co-trustees of John's revocable living trust. This allowed Joan to retain a measure of control over the assets that she transferred to John. Now, if Joan were the subject of a substantial lawsuit, no personal assets would be exposed because they are all in John's name. The assets that remain in her name—the qualified retirement plan and the term life insurance—are not subject to the claims of creditors. Not only did this strategy address Joan's concerns, but it also removed the assets from the probate process! Now, before you assume that we have devised the perfect asset protection solution, let us point out its pitfalls. First, this plan does nothing to protect the Spivys from John's creditors. John's career makes him much less of a lawsuit target, so we are just playing the odds. Second, making Joan a cotrustee of John's trust would not guarantee that John could not run off with the money. This trust is revocable, and John could fire Joan as trustee or he could terminate the trust altogether. As added protection for Joan, the trust document would require 30 to 60 days notice for termination of a trustee. Also, when Joan transfers her assets to the trust, the title of the accounts would reflect both Joan and John's names as trustees. It would be highly unlikely that a bank or brokerage firm would close an account of this nature without both signatures. To make sure that John does not simply write a check for the account balance, the trust agreement provides for dual signatures for checks above a certain amount, say, $2,000.

Using Limited Liability Entities to Protect Assets

Conventional wisdom used to be that you could use a corporation to shield you from creditor liability. Today attorneys are concerned that a creditor may receive your corporate stock as part of a settlement and then vote that stock to liquidate your corporation in order to gain access to assets held in the corporation. If part of the reason that you are using a corporation is to provide asset protection, you should get with your tax attorney to determine if you would be better served by using another form of entity as described below. A better choice is a Limited Liability Entity such as a Family Limited Partnership, Limited Partnership, or Limited Liability Company (LLC). For purposes of this discussion, we will use the term LLC to represent any Limited Liability Entity. If a creditor seizes your interest in an LLC, depending on state law, the only thing the creditor may be able to obtain is a "charging order," which carries no right to vote. As with a trust, an LLC is considered a separate person in the eyes of the law. Just as you have your own Social Security number, an LLC (with more than one member) must apply for and receive a tax identification number. Once you have set up your LLC, lawsuits that occur as a result of your business activities will likely be limited to LLC assets, not your personal assets. We use the word "likely" because you should be aware of some important exceptions:

- First, if your LLC were to fail and you have not fully paid employee withholding taxes, the federal and state government can come after you personally. This is also true for corporations and sole proprietors.

- Second, you will be personally responsible for any loans or agreements in which you give a personal guarantee. If you obtain a business loan from a bank, your bank officer will likely require that you sign both as an LLC officer and as a personal guarantor. Often, the bank will also ask that your spouse sign personally as well. In most cases you should be able to avoid having your spouse sign unless he or she is involved in the business. As your company grows in financial strength, you may be able to negotiate the removal of your personal guarantee from your business loans. Avoiding having your spouse cosign business loans and removing your personal guarantee are prudent initiatives and are worth pursuing. One of our clients started a commercial construction company. To do so, he needed to acquire bonding from a bonding company. Initially, the company required his personal guarantee as well as a corporate guarantee to back up the bond. Today his own company is financially strong, and one of our major initiatives is to have his personal guarantee removed from the bond. The construction business can be very volatile, and the future is unknown. You always want to minimize your financial exposure.

When you conduct business for your LLC, be sure that you follow the technical procedures or you may find out that you have inadvertently given your personal guarantee. For example, when you sign an agreement, be sure to sign *John Smith, Managing Member*, not just *John Smith*. Be clear with all parties that you are doing business as a managing member of your LLC.

- If you establish an LLC but then run it like a sole proprietorship, it is likely that a creditor can pierce the LLC veil and go after your personal assets. We have reviewed many cases where people are paying their home mortgage and other personal expenses straight from their business checkbook. They have no members' meetings and no LLC minutes. Under these circumstances, if you are ever faced with liability problems, the courts will ignore your coveted LLC status.

- If you are a professional such as a physician, dentist, accountant, architect, or attorney, an LLC is of little use in providing you with asset protection. This is because lawmakers have decided that professionals should be held liable for acts of negligence. Still, an LLC may be useful when you are in practice with other owner/professionals. In some states, you cannot be sued personally for acts committed by other members/shareholder/owners. Your LLC, however, can be sued. Check with your advisor to determine if an LLC can benefit you. As a professional, you will need to employ additional strategies to protect your assets.

To best demonstrate the asset protection attributes of Limited Liability Entities, look at this example:

Amy Davis is a successful plastic surgeon who is concerned about protecting the family's substantial assets from lawsuits. She establishes the Davis Family Limited Partnership, making her husband, Jack, the 1 percent general partner, herself a 97 percent limited partner, and their two children receive a 1 percent limited partnership interest each. Amy and Jack then placed their assets into their family limited partnership, including their bank accounts, brokerage accounts, and real estate. The children also contribute to the partnership either using their own assets or monies gifted to them from Amy and Jack.

Unfortunately, her greatest nightmare comes true and she is sued, resulting in a $5 million judgment. Her malpractice insurance covers $3 million of the judgment, but now the creditors are coming after her personal assets for the balance. Unfortunately for them, she has no other assets except a limited partnership interest in the family limited partnership and minimal value in her professional corporation. Undeterred, the creditors move forward and receive a "charging order" against her partnership interest. The effect of this charging order is that the creditor now stands in her place with regard to any distributions from the partnership. Jack, being a very interested party, decides not to make any distributions. What can the creditor do? Nothing! Their charging order gives them no rights regarding management decisions, and they have no way of causing the termination of the partnership. What is worse, undistributed partnership income is taxed to the partners even though they received no money. Since the charging order places the creditor in Amy's position, they receive the tax bill! As you might imagine, this is an uncomfortable spot for the creditor who now may be more than willing to settle for pennies on the dollar.

Use of Multiple Limited Liability Entities

Under certain circumstances, it may be useful for you to have more than one LLC. Let's say that you own and operate two businesses. One is a mail-order company that sells vitamins, and the other is a dynamite blasting company. Obviously the risk of a lawsuit is much greater with the latter than the former. By using a separate LLC for each company, you shield the assets of one company from potential judgments of the other.

A Word of Caution to Directors

It is often considered prestigious to be a director of a corporation. You are treated very well, and you may even receive compensation in the form of director's fees. However, being on a board of directors can be hazardous to your wealth. As a director, you have a responsibility to the corporate shareholders. If things go wrong, you may find yourself in the middle of a lawsuit that could put your personal assets at risk. Before you join any board of directors, be sure that there is adequate liability insurance coverage and that you have a measure of control and knowledge of corporate decision making. Too often, the board of directors is considered a rubber-stamp committee for the corporation. Also, never put your spouse on your own board of directors. To do so may allow creditors to go after his or her personal assets if you have adequately shielded your own.

This warning is not restricted to directors of corporations. If you sit on the board of directors of your condominium association or local charity, you can have liability exposure as well. Even officers of corporations should be cautious. If a corporation fails to pay the payroll taxes, the IRS can trace that liability to what it considers responsible persons, which could mean you if you are an officer in that corporation. The fact that the corporation has filed bankruptcy does not remove your liability.

Foreign Asset Protection Trusts

When you think of transferring money to a foreign bank account, most people immediately think of Switzerland, which has earned a well-deserved reputation for privacy concerning bank accounts of foreigners. This privacy feature, however, is of little use as an asset protection strategy for most Americans. First, the U.S. government requires that you disclose any transfers of monies to a foreign country on tax form 1040 Schedule B and Form TD F 90–22.1. Failure to do so is a federal crime punishable by fines of up to $500,000 and imprisonment for up to five years. You will find little joy knowing your assets are safe while you are enjoying free room and board in a federal prison. Assuming that you do report that you have transferred money to a Swiss account, are your assets now safe from creditors? In a word, no. Switzerland, and most other countries, will honor judgments from a U.S. court. The result is that once you have disclosed that you have assets in a friendly foreign country, your creditors can get them. The solution here is to locate a country that is unfriendly regarding our courts, several of which have become havens for people who want to protect their assets—most noteworthily, the Cayman Islands, the Isle of Man, Nevis, and the Cook Islands. Each of these countries have turned foreign asset protection trusts into a major industry. They have passed special laws that protect your privacy, and most importantly, they do not recognize judgments from foreign countries. They also do not have income taxes on foreign accounts.

If you decide to enter the world of foreign asset protection trusts, be forewarned that these transactions are not for the timid. This is serious business involving hefty legal fees and a certain amount of risk.

The Basics of a Foreign Asset Protection Trust

The primary reason to establish a foreign asset protection trust is, of course, asset protection. To accomplish this goal, your trust will need to contain some very special and unusual provisions:

- The trust must be irrevocable. If it were a revocable trust, a U.S. judge could require that you revoke the trust in favor of your creditors.
- If you transfer assets to an irrevocable trust, you are subject to gift taxes starting at 35 percent on amounts above $13,000 per beneficiary for annual gifts and $5 million for your lifetime gift tax exemption. To avoid this trap, you need to make your trust a grantor trust, which means that you will retain some control over it, thus making the gift incomplete for gift tax

purposes. Speaking of taxes, you should know that foreign asset protection trusts are tax neutral. The income generated by the trust is taxable to you, just as it would have been if you had not transferred it. To sidestep income tax issues, grantors will often purchase private placement life insurance or annuities—contracts whose income is deferred.

- Your trust will need at least one foreign trustee. If all the trustees are located in the United States, a judge could subpoena them to appear before him or her and compel the trustee to distribute assets in favor of your creditors. This means that your foreign trustee should not directly do business in the United States. To do so would subject them to subpoena powers.

- It will be best if you are not a trustee of your foreign asset protection trust. As a trustee, a judge can compel you to cooperate.

- It will be best if you are not a beneficiary of your foreign asset protection trust. Now wait a minute! What good is a trust if you can't ever get your money? Again, if you must appear before a judge, you have a much stronger case if you are not a beneficiary of the trust. The best alternative is to have your spouse and children serve this function. Your trustee can then distribute assets to them that can be used for their or your benefit.

- Your trust agreement should require your trustee to ignore your request to send funds to you or a creditor if such a request is part of a court order. Once you have received a judgment against you and your creditor discovers that you have assets in a foreign account, the judge is likely to require that you demand release of those funds so that your creditors can be satisfied. If you refuse to do so, you can be held in contempt of court. Prison can be a lonely place, so you will want to comply with the judge's request. If you do your part but your trustee refuses to release funds, there is little else that the judge can do. We should note that there have been cases (the Anderson case, for example) where the judge held the grantor in contempt of court for failure to produce assets held in his foreign trust even though doing so was beyond the grantor's control.

- Your trust should contain a flight provision. Every now and then you will run into an extremely persistent creditor. If enough dollars are at stake, they may be willing to pursue the matter at great length. This may include pursuing the case in the country where your assets are held, or you may run into a judge that will not take no for an answer. A flight provision instructs your trustee to actually move your account to another country should the threat to your assets warrant it. Your trust agreement further instructs your trustee *not to tell you where your money has been moved*. Talk about a scary provision! The good news is that a judge cannot make you divulge information that you do not have. Often a "trust protector" is appointed to handle certain operational issues such as removal of trustee, change of situs, and so on.

If all of this sounds complicated, that's because it is. There are some potential tax consequences of transferring appreciated property to a foreign trust. Additionally, a foreign asset protection trust is a uniquely individual document that should be tailored to each person's specific facts and objectives. State laws concerning trusts vary widely and should be considered in drafting a foreign asset protection trust. Numerous groups around the country promote offshore trusts through seminars; some of these groups are legitimate, and others are not. We met with the attorney from one of these groups, which was promoting offshore trusts in the country of Panama. The group guaranteed you a 14 percent annual return that it claimed was totally safe! The prevailing rate on CDs at that time was less than 6 percent. On his business card after his name appeared the initials RIA, which stands for "registered investment advisor." To become an RIA, one must simply complete and file forms with the Securities and Exchange Commission. To use the initials in this manner is illegal because it gives the public the impression that you have somehow qualified or been approved to be an RIA. When questioned about this, he admitted that he was not an RIA at all! If you are interested in pursuing this subject, you must retain a reputable attorney who specializes in this area.

Domestic Asset Protection Trusts

If you are looking for somewhat simpler asset protection, you might want to consider a domestic asset protection trust (DAPT). Several states have passed legislation that makes it difficult for creditors to secure assets held in a DAPT from a judgment, including Alaska and Delaware. Although Delaware is best known for asset protection, Alaska provides the most air-tight legislation. For instance, Delaware allows certain classes of creditors (such as divorced spouses) to invade your trust. Alaska provides no exceptions unless there is a fraudulent conveyance. Also, Alaskan trusts do not require a termination date. DAPTs in most other states require that the trust terminate within 90 years. Other states that allow DAPTs are Nevada, Rhode Island, Utah, Oklahoma, and Missouri.

The Law of Fraudulent Conveyances applies to all trusts in the United States. If you feel you are a likely target for a lawsuit, you must transfer your assets into your DAPT *before* you have knowledge of a problem or the courts can set aside the transfer. Under Alaskan trust law, as the grantor, you are allowed to receive distributions from your trust. These distributions must be at the *sole discretion* of your trustee. As you might imagine, it is very important that you appoint friendly trustees.

In addition to asset protection benefits, DAPTs offer important estate-planning benefits. Alaska's statutes consider that transfers to a trust are a completed gift, which means that the assets are removed from your estate for estate tax purposes. This is true even if your trustee can disperse funds from your trust to you. It also means that you can use your annual gift tax exclusion and/or your lifetime applicable exclusion amount to make gifts to your trust. A word of caution is appropriate regarding this issue. Let's say that you used $500,000 of your lifetime applicable exclusion amount to make a tax-free gift to your DAPT. If your trustee distributed $250,000 of funds to you later, that portion of your applicable exclusion amount would be lost forever. Obviously, any distributions would also be available to creditors.

If you are a resident in a state other than one with DAPT laws, then a DAPT may not provide you with the creditor protection you desire. This is because the U.S Constitution requires that all states honor the judgments of other states. Be sure to check with an attorney in your state that has experience with DAPT law.

When deciding between a DAPT versus a foreign asset protection trust, you should weigh the following factors:

- *Comfort zone.* Most people are going to be more comfortable knowing that their assets are being held in a trust in the United States. We have found that something about moving large sums of money to a foreign country makes people nervous.

- *Expenses.* In most cases, you can expect your legal and administrative costs to be higher with a foreign trust. Often the costs will be significantly higher.

- *Level of asset protection.* Most experts will agree that properly drawn foreign trusts provide a higher level of protection against creditors. Foreign countries such as the Cayman Islands do not recognize U.S. court jurisdiction or judgments. From a creditor's point of view, you can imagine how discouraging (and costly) it would be to attempt to pursue a judgment in a foreign country.

- *Statute of limitations.* The statute of limitations is much shorter in countries providing foreign asset protection trusts than it is in the United States. This shorter period means that your assets are protected more quickly.

Most people who have significant wealth have concerns about asset protection. Unfortunately, we live in a very litigious society where people are all too happy to sue you for even insignificant events. Serious money is at stake here because even frivolous cases often end in settlements.

Your personal level of concern regarding asset protection will determine which strategies are best for you. We encourage you to meet with your professional advisor to discuss this issue. He or she is likely to have a good sense of which strategies best meet your needs.

Ultimately, one of the greatest factors that will impact the effectiveness of your estate plan has to do with your attitudes toward money. In our final chapter, we will explore the psychology of money and how to remove ingrained barriers to achieve greater financial success for your family.

CHAPTER 16

Personal Business Planning Issues

How important are small businesses to America? According to the Small Business Administration (SBA), they represent 99.7 percent of employer firms and employ roughly half of the private sector workers. Importantly, small businesses have generated 64 percent of the new jobs created in the United States over the past 15 years. These are remarkable statistics especially when you realize that over 50 percent of these small businesses are home-based.

Choosing the Right Entity for Your Business

For a business owner, one of the most important decisions you will make is what type of entity you will use to operate your business. Your primary choices include: Sole Proprietor, General Partnership, Limited Partnership, C corporation, S corporation, or Limited Liability Company (LLC). This chapter will focus on your various entity choices as well as some of the most important advantages and disadvantages of each entity type.

Let's begin our discussion with the two main reasons that entity selection is so important:

1. *Liability protection*. It's unfortunate but true that here in America, we live in a very litigious society. The rule of today is, "Sue everybody . . . then let's sort it out!" Part of the problem is an overabundance of attorneys and part of the problem is our legal system that encourages "lawsuit roulette" where the plaintiff (the person bringing the lawsuit) hires an attorney based on a contingency fee (you don't pay your attorney unless he/she wins the

case, in which he/she then receives 30–50 percent of the winnings). As a business owner, consider yourself as someone walking around with a bull's-eye on your back. You have become an excellent target for a lawsuit! How do you protect yourself, your personal assets, and your business? One of the ways is through the entity you choose for your business. A properly structured business entity generally can effectively shield your personal assets from a lawsuit against your business.

2. *Tax benefits.* If you are a "W2" employee (working for someone else and drawing a paycheck), your tax deduction opportunities are very limited. For most people this amounts to home mortgage interest, charitable contributions, and a few miscellaneous deductions. However if you start a business, you open the door to literally hundreds of potential tax deductions. While your primary reason to start a business should be for profits, access to massive legitimate tax deductions is certainly an excellent secondary reason. Certain types of entities will offer additional tax benefits over other types. An employee who incurs expenses to earn his/her income is greatly limited as to the deductions available, and will only benefit from a reduced percentage of the deductions.

Sole Proprietorship

Sole proprietorship is the simplest and most-often used form of business, comprising 80 percent of the businesses in America. With a sole proprietorship, you and your business are inseparable. You ARE the business. You simply decide to start your business and "presto!" you're in business! Most sole proprietors run their business out of their personal checking account, buying inventory, paying business expenses, and making deposits from sales using that account. In many cases nothing more is required. In some cases, you'll need a business license. Others may choose to establish a business name. In such cases they'll title their business as a "doing-business-as" or "DBA" and it might read something like: Stewart Welch III d/b/a Welch Fantastic Products.

When it comes time to file your income taxes, your income and expenses as well as profits or losses are filed as part of your personal income tax return on Schedule C. As such, sole proprietorships are considered what is called a "pass-through" entity. This means that all profits or losses pass through to your personal tax return. If you have no employees, you'll typically use your Social Security number as your tax identification number; otherwise you'll need an Employer Identification Number (EIN).

ADVANTAGES

Why are so many business owners using the sole proprietorship form to operate their business? The reason is because it's so inexpensive and easy to set up. In fact there are virtually no set-up activities. On an ongoing basis, operating your sole proprietorship is also very simple. You will need a system for keeping up with revenue and expenses so that you'll be able to determine profits or losses for income tax purposes but there are no other formal requirements.

A sole proprietorship is easy to open and easy to close and you can always move from a sole proprietorship to another form of entity at any time.

DISADVANTAGES

Perhaps the main disadvantage is that running your business as a sole proprietorship affords you virtually no protection from a liability perspective. If a lawsuit arises that is related to your business, not only are all of your business assets subject to claims, but all of your personal assets are fully exposed as well.

The fact that no formal processes or record keeping are required often leads to very sloppy business practices. Often the entrepreneur is born out of an idea or product. It typically starts as a small venture and then grows, sometimes rapidly, into a full-time business. The entrepreneur is often a "one-person show" and many times their business will effectively out-grow them.

When building a business, often one of the objectives is to create a "brand" or name recognition for your business. Well-known examples might include Fed-Ex or Wal-Mart. The sole proprietorship offers little in the way of name or brand protection.

BEST FIT

Even though the sole proprietorship is the most-often used form of business, it is the least attractive because of the unlimited liability exposure. It may be appropriate if:

- You have little or no personal assets thereby making you effectively "judgment-proof."
- You believe that your business is one that creates virtually no additional liability.
- You have little or no money to start your business.

If you're just "testing" a business idea to see if it has "legs," you may want to start as a sole proprietor in order to minimize organizational set-up costs and time. As soon as you determine that you have a viable business, consider adopting one of the other business entity forms reviewed in this chapter.

General Partnership

By definition, a partnership means that two or more people (or entities) have decided to enter into a business venture together. In some states, forming a general partnership does not require a lot of formality and, in fact, the agreement between the parties can be written or it can be an oral agreement. Today most states have adopted the Uniform Partnership Act, which provides a state-mandated partnership agreement for anyone who does not have a formal partnership agreement. Typically the partners decide who owns what percentage of the business (most often ownership is equal) and there's a general division of responsibility. In fact, one of the best reasons to form a partnership is to take advantage of the various partner's individual talents. One person may be the "idea person" and be great at the details of day-to-day operations while the other person is the "public face" of the business and primarily responsible for sales and promotions.

While there are no required filings for a general partnership, you are required to file a separate tax return; keep a separate set of books; and the partnership will have its own tax identification number. General partnerships are disappearing in favor of LLCs, which are discussed later in this chapter.

ADVANTAGES

One of the primary advantages of using the general partnership form of business is that it can be easy and inexpensive to set up. In addition, in its simplest form, a general partnership does not require a lot of formality to run and maintain (the books and records). A general partnership is considered a pass-through entity for income tax purposes so that any losses (or profits) will ultimately pass through to you personally.

DISADVANTAGES

The most glaring disadvantage of the general partnership form for running a business is the potential exposure to liability of both your personal and business assets. This form of business provides virtually no liability protection and in fact may increase your personal liability exposure many fold. Contrast a general partnership to a sole proprietorship. As we have discussed, as a sole proprietor, a claim against the business is equal to a claim against you personally. With a general partnership, you have all of this same liability but you are also potentially responsible for claims that arise out of the business conduct of each of your partners. Note that any partner could incur partnership debts or obligations without the knowledge or consent of the other partners and in doing so, obligates each partner. If you choose the general partnership form of doing business, you'll want to choose your partners very carefully.

Many law firms will operate as a general partnership. They will typically have a detailed partnership agreement that spells out the responsibilities and obligations of each partner as well as, a list of prohibited transactions including remedies for violation. They also will carry extensive liability insurance coverage. If you decide to operate as a general partnership, you should consider adopting a similar strategy. However, you should be aware that an agreement among partners does not bind the other parties. So, should one partner sign a contract that the partnership agreement does not allow him to sign, it still may bind the general partnership.

BEST FIT

A general partnership is a good fit for parties who wish to start a business quickly and inexpensively (reasons similar for someone forming a sole proprietorship). As with the sole proprietorship, we recommend that you carefully assess your potential liability exposure and either reduce it through the purchase of appropriate liability insurance or consider transitioning to a more protective entity type once you determine you have a viable business.

Limited Partnership

A limited partnership is a special form of partnership in which one or more persons (or entities) acts as the **general partner** and one or more parties (or entities) acts as the **limited partner**. The general partner has all the rights and obligations and risks as described previously in this chapter in the section on general partnerships. However, the limited partner has both limited risks and limited rights. Specifically, the limited partner's risk is typically limited to the amount of money he or she invested in the partnership. The limited partner typically also has no voice in the decisions or operations of the partnership, essentially being a "silent partner." A limited partnership will have its own tax identification number and you'll be required to file a separate tax return.

ADVANTAGES

Limited partners are typically 'investors,' in that their intent is to *invest in* the business . . . *not run* the business. Under this form, the investor has limited his or her liability to the amount invested so it's much easier to determine the "risk-reward tradeoff." For example, as a limited partner you decide to invest $100,000 in a real estate development project. If it all goes well, you'll benefit based on the pre-arranged split of profits and cash flow as outlined in the partnership agreement. However, if you chose to be the general partner, you may have taken on substantially greater (and often unknowable) risks for hoped-for but unknowable rewards.

As with any partnership, this is a pass-through entity for income tax purposes.

DISADVANTAGES

If you choose to act as the general partner of a limited partnership, you expose your personal and business assets to liability. As a result, you may want to consider owning your general partnership interests in the form of another entity that has greater liability protection attributes such as a corporation or LLC. This needs to be handled carefully in order to assure the benefits are achieved.

If you are a limited partner, you are not allowed to participate in management and have no say in the decisions of the partnership. If you were to violate this mandate, you could be deemed to be a general partner and then be subject to all of the liabilities previously described.

Unlike a general partnership, limited partnerships are governed by state law and as such you must register with your state's Secretary of State and comply with state law and regulations.

BEST FIT

The limited partnership form of business is best suited for a single or limited-term project such as investment real estate. It allows for ease in raising capital from investors who have no interest in being actively involved in the decisions or running of the business.

Corporations

When we think of corporations, we often think about big well-known companies such as Wal-Mart or McDonalds (big public companies). However, millions of small businesses choose to operate as a corporation for a variety of reasons.

A corporation is a separate and distinct entity created under state law. To establish a corporation, you must file an application with your Secretary of State where you'll receive Articles of Incorporation and shares of stock. You'll be required to maintain a separate set of books and file a corporate income tax return. The easiest way to think of a corporation is to think of it as a separate "person," one that has its own tax identification number (EIN). Corporations are divided into two distinct groups: the C Corporation and the S corporation. Both types enjoy what is one of the main benefits of this type of entity: very strong liability protection. This is because the corporation is considered under the law to be totally distinct from its shareholders (owners). Let's examine the pros and cons of each type.

C CORPORATION

First and foremost, a C corporation is not a pass-through entity for income tax purposes. It has its own income tax schedule. All income and expenses are tracked at the corporate level and any profits (or losses) are dealt with under a corporate income tax schedule. A C corporation will have its own EIN and you'll be required to file a separate tax return.

Advantages

A C corporation provides an excellent shield against personal liability assuming it is run properly.

If you are an owner of a C corporation, you have access to certain fringe benefit programs that are tax deductible for you such as group health insurance, group life insurance, group disability insurance, and dependent care assistance programs.

The state laws governing Corporations are well established, where some of the other entities are so new, there is not as much experience on the part of the states and the courts.

A C corporation offers a lot of flexibility for structures. For example, it allows you to create different classes of stock such as voting and non-voting shares. This can be very beneficial if you want to maintain control of the corporate decision-making but would like to transfer some of the ownership (and future growth) to children. Or you may have key employees you'd like to reward with ownership so that they will participate in the company's future growth but do not want them to have a 'legal' voice in the management of the company. Other strategies include the ability to issue stock options, preferred stock, warrants, subordinated debt, and convertible notes.

If your vision is to eventually take your company public or that you may want to raise capital from venture capitalists, the C corporation is an excellent platform from which to launch your strategy.

Disadvantages

The costs of setting up and running a C corporation are significant. And if you are doing business in states other than the state of registration (home state), you will be subject to additional registration requirements, which can be costly. Many states charge initial and annual fees for corporations registered in their jurisdiction and other fees such as a franchise tax or share's tax.

The regulations and procedures that you must follow are quite onerous. Failure to follow these rules and regulation could jeopardize your corporate status resulting in many potential negative consequences, including the loss of personal liability protection.

A C corporation is not a pass-through entity and any losses cannot be deducted on your personal income tax return. In fact, as an owner of shares in a C corporation, you may become subject to **double taxation**. This occurs when the corporation distributes money to its shareholders. First the corporation paid taxes on its profits when earned, and then the shareholders must report distributions as a dividend. This double taxation can also occur upon the liquidation of the corporation. One way shareholder-employees (owners) attempt to avoid this double taxation is to pay themselves a very high salary (thereby reducing profits). However, the IRS may attempt to attack this strategy on the basis that a portion of your salary is "unreasonable" and thereby force the corporation to declare the unreasonable portion as profits subject to the corporate taxes and the distribution to you has to be treated as a dividend (i.e., double taxation).

Best Fit

The C corporation is ideal if:

- You desire a very high level of personal liability protection.
- You do not need a pass-through entity so that losses can be deducted against your personal income.

- Your long-term strategy is to seek venture capital for your company, or you want to be able to issue stock options, warrants, specialized debt instruments, issue different classes of stock, or take your company public.

S CORPORATION

To establish an S corporation, you make a special election (an S election under the IRS code) that transforms a regular C corporation into a pass-through entity. As a result, you retain the substantial liability protection attributes of the C corporation but losses (and profits) "pass through" to your personal income tax return. This eliminates the possibility of double taxation as with a C corporation. One possible exception is that if you are going from a C corporation to an S corporation, you may encounter taxation related to retained earnings of the C corporation. An S corporation will have its own tax identification number and you'll be required to file a separate tax return.

Advantages

Just like the C corporation, the S corporation provides excellent personal liability protection since the S corporation is deemed to be a separate entity (i.e. a separate person) under the law.

In addition, any losses (or profits) pass through to your personal tax return. There is a lot more flexibility in moving money in and out of an S corporation.

Finally, if in the future the pass-through attributes are no longer needed and you decide you'd like any of the additional opportunities offered under a C corporation, conversion from an S corporation to a C corporation is very easy. It's worth noting that making an S election only affects the taxation of the corporation and does not affect the legal structure under state law.

Disadvantages

Like a C corporation, the costs of setting up and maintaining an S corporation are quite high in relative terms. You must follow strict regulations and procedures. Failure to do so could jeopardize your corporate status resulting in many potential negative consequences.

Unlike a C corporation, an S corporation has restrictions as to the number of allowed shareholders (100); the capital structure (only one class of stock is allowed, however, voting and non-voting rights are allowed); and the type of shareholder (only individuals who are also U.S. citizens or residents, estates, or certain trusts).

Best Fit

An S corporation is a good fit if you seek strong personal liability protection but desire to have any losses (or profits) pass through to your personal tax return. Additionally, you may want to choose the S corporation if your long-term strategy is to convert to a C corporation in order to take your company public, attract venture capital, create different classes of stock, or utilize any of the other benefits of the C corporation.

Special Note for C and S Corporations: We have mentioned the onerous requirements related to these types of entities. A short list of those requirements includes:

- Filing a Certificate of Incorporation with your state's Secretary of State
- The adoption of a set of bylaws
- The election of a Board of Directors
- Annual meetings of the Board of Directors and shareholders
- Recording of the minutes of the annual meetings of the Board of Directors and shareholders
- Adherence to the capital structure requirements as well as maintaining evidence of such
- Maintaining separate books and records for the corporation as well as maintaining separate bank accounts

A breach of these requirements can jeopardize your corporate status and open you to a host of negative consequences, one of which is a *piercing of the corporate veil* as discussed later in this chapter.

LIMITED LIABILITY COMPANY

LLCs are relatively new entity structures were introduced in the 1990s. You may also hear this entity type referred to as a Limited Liability Entity (LLE), which is used to encompass both the LLC and Limited Liability Partnership (LLP). They are creatures of state law, which is an important point because this means the laws that govern them can vary from state to state. However, today most states have adopted the Uniform LLE Act which offers consistent standards for this entity type. In many ways, the LLC represents a cross-section of some of the very best attributes of each of the entities we have discussed. Like a sole proprietorship, partnership, or S corporation it is a pass-through entity allowing you to deduct losses personally. Like a C or S corporation, it provides an excellent shield against personal liability. Like a partnership, it provides excellent flexibility including the ability to specifically allocate income and losses. Finally, while not as easy and inexpensive to set up and maintain as a sole proprietorship or partnership, an LLC is much less costly and complex than a C or S corporation. Owners of an interest in an LLC are called "members" versus shareholders in a corporation or partners in a partnership. An LLC will have its own tax identification number and you'll be required to file a separate tax return. If there is more than one owner of an LLC, for income tax purposes it is treated as a partnership, unless the owners 'elect' for it to be treated as a corporation.

Advantages

LLCs are typically highly flexible allowing their members many alternative options for managing the operations (control of decision-making), allocating income and losses, and distribution of cash. Most are structured similar to a partnership but you can set up a single-person LLC—which is treated like a sole proprietorship for tax purposes—or the LLC can elect to be treated as a C corporation or S corporation.

As already stated, LLCs are most often set up as pass-through entities allowing losses to flow through to your personal income tax return. They provide excellent personal liability shielding similar to C or S corporations.

LLCs are relatively inexpensive to establish. They are somewhat more costly than a sole proprietorship or partnership but typically much less costly than either a C or S corporation.

Disadvantages

While the costs to establish an LLC are relatively modest, the ongoing requirements are similar to that of a C or S corporation. You must run your LLC as a separate business in every respect including annual meetings, maintaining appropriate records, separate bank accounts, etc. Failure to do so will jeopardize your LLC status with potential consequences similar to that of a corporation.

An LLC may not be the best choice of entity if you ultimately plan to take your company public or desire to issue specialized securities such as preferred stock, stock options, or debt instruments. Converting from an LLC to an S or C corporation is relatively difficult and expensive and essentially requires that you liquidate the LLC with all of the resulting tax consequences.

Because LLCs are established under state law versus federal law, the rules and requirements can vary from state to state. You'll need to become familiar with the particular requirements of the state in which you wish to operate.

Best Fit

The LLC may be the best choice of entity if you are seeking a relatively inexpensive way to start a business that has strong personal liability protections and very flexible options for operating your company. With an LLC, you get many of the advantages of a general partnership while enjoying the protections offered by a C or S corporation.

SINGLE-MEMBER LLC

The single-member LLC is a subset of the LLC that allows an individual an alternative to the sole proprietor form of doing business. Again, it's important to emphasize that the single-member LLC is governed by state law not federal law so the rules, regulations, and protections can vary by state.

Advantages

Compared to the sole proprietorship, the single-member LLC potentially provides a higher level of personal liability protection (depending on your state's laws). The single-member LLC is easy and inexpensive to set up.

It is also a pass-through entity and income and expenses are reported directly on your individual income tax return. Some states allow you to use your Social Security number as your tax ID number but most require a separate EIN. A separate EIN is always required if you have employees.

Disadvantages

The effectiveness of the personal liability shield has come under question with the single-member LLC. For example, in June 2010, the Florida Supreme Court allowed the liability shield of a single-member LLC to be pierced.

As with a regular LLC or corporation, you must follow the rules, regulations, and procedures in order to minimize the risks of having the LLC's veil of protection pierced.

Best Fit

The single-member LLC may be ideal for the beginner entrepreneur who is seeking to keep costs of set-up low and desires a higher level of liability protection than is offered under a sole proprietorship.

Closing Thoughts

Following the Rules, Regulations, and Procedures

One of the biggest mistakes we find that entrepreneurs make is that they are sloppy when it comes to following the rules, regulations, and procedures required related to corporations and LLCs. They'll fail to have annual Board of Directors meeting . . . "Hey, it's just me and my wife!" They'll fail to keep minutes of board meetings. They'll pay some personal bills from the business. Then when a crisis arises in the form of a lawsuit, they realize that these shortcomings allow opposing attorneys to attack the business in an attempt to break the corporate shield and attach personal assets (i.e., pierce the corporate veil). The best solution is to systemize the required processes and have a double-check system whereby someone (your CPA, attorney, or financial advisor) makes certain all books and records are properly maintained.

PIERCING THE CORPORATE VEIL

If you choose to run your business as a C corporation, S corporation, LLC, or single-member LLC you *must* run it as a completely separate business. Avoid the trap many entrepreneurs fall into by using their business as their "personal checking account." We have observed many cases where the owners of these entities will pay country club bills, mortgage payments, and other personal bills directly from the business checking account. Still others fail to observe the procedural requirements such as the annual meeting of the Board of Directors (who are often spouses) as well as keeping minutes of board meetings, etc. As a result, when a crisis arises such as a judgment in a lawsuit or a challenge by the IRS, they are an easy target for lawyers or IRS agents to pierce the corporate veil and have their corporate status set aside opening them up to personal liability. We repeat, "You must strictly follow the rules and procedures!"

DOING BUSINESS IN MULTIPLE STATES

If you plan to do business in multiple states make certain you understand the various requirements of each state. A number of states require some form of registration (and fees) and failure to follow their rules and regulations could void the normal protections offered by corporations or LLCs and open you up to fines and penalties or personal liability if you become subject to a lawsuit.

PERSONAL SERVICE PROVIDERS

Under the law, certain professionals are denied protections related to their personal services to others afforded by the use of an entity such as a corporation or LLC. Examples of such professionals might include: doctors, attorneys, accountants, architects, financial advisors, engineers, and veterinarians, or others who are licensed by a state or agency with licensing power. The legal reasoning is that these professionals should be held to the highest standards of service and should be held personally responsible when their actions cause harm. While the legal entities discussed in this chapter do provide benefits and liability protection for instances of claims arising from other than personal services, personal service professionals will need to seek additional measures to protect their personal assets from claims arising from litigation. The first line of defense is always best practice methods and procedures backed up by appropriate professional liability or malpractice insurance. More in-depth strategies might include the use of specialized trusts or the transfer of assets to a spouse or other family members. For more information about this topic, seek the counsel of an attorney or financial advisor who specializes in asset protection.

USE OF MULTIPLE ENTITIES

One strategy you may want to consider is the use of multiple entities whereby you group assets into two categories:

1. *Risky assets*. These are assets that tend to attract the highest level of liability. Examples might include real estate such as your home, commercial property, apartments, or raw land; farm or mechanical equipment and vehicles; or business assets. Within your risky assets category, consider

multiple LLCs. For example, set up an LLC for your farm property and a separate LLC for each of your rental properties.

2. *Non-risky assets*. These are assets that by and of themselves attract very little liability and might include stocks, bonds, and bank accounts.

By segregating assets, your intent is to isolate a legal judgment within the particular LLC where the liability arose and not put your other assets at risk. Yes, this strategy does multiply your costs of set-up and maintenance but should you receive a judgment, you'll think it was well worth the time, effort, and costs.

Importance of a Business Plan

Research indicates that about 25 percent of start-up businesses fail within the first three years; 50 percent fail within the first five years; and by year ten, 70 percent of these businesses have closed their doors. Why are the failure rates so high? Based on over 30 years of observing businesses and entrepreneurs, we find the reasons fall into one or both of two categories:

1. *Inadequate capital.* When starting a business, most entrepreneurs significantly underestimate how much capital will be needed to sustain the enterprise. Many will assume that their savings will be more than enough only to realize they'll need to place a second mortgage on their home to "get them over the hump," only to realize they'll need to borrow from family and friends, only to realize they still need capital and have no place to turn.

2. *Poor management skills.* Most start-up businesses begin with a "good idea" for a product or service and the individual-turned-entrepreneur launches the business making himself or herself the CEO, COO, Director of Sales, and Chief Bookkeeper. In many cases they will meet with initial success only to realize they lack the skill set to adjust to a growing business. Often they are unwilling to relinquish control of aspects of the business or delegate responsibilities in an effective manner. This "one-man-band" mentality places an artificial lid on growth and profitability and many entrepreneurs wake up one day to find out that they own a job, not a business; a job that requires very long hours for very little pay.

We have found that the solution to these problems is two-fold:

1. *Start with a business plan.* Whether you are thinking about starting a business or already own one, if you don't have a business plan, make creating one a top priority. Without a doubt, we have found that the companies that develop a business plan and then use it as living, breathing, ongoing guide are the most successful businesses.

2. *Put together a team.* We have found that the fastest path to ultra-success is realized by putting together a team of people whose strengths and talents complement your own. These team members will fall into three categories:

a. *Professionals.* Professional team members might include an attorney, CPA, or Certified Financial Planner. Unless you are an accountant by trade, don't attempt to do your own books in addition to running your business. Play to your strengths, delegate to your weaknesses. Even if you think you 'can do it all,' focus your time and efforts on the highest payoff activities and delegate the others.

b. *Consultants.* One of the best strategies for accelerating your success is to be mentored by someone who has already achieved the level of success you desire. Sometimes you'll be lucky enough to find someone who will mentor you for free. Most of the time, you'll need to pay for their coaching and advice. Be willing to pay. It will be the best money you can spend. The ideal consultant is someone who is a patient and good teacher. Ask around, they are not hard to find.

c. *Business team members.* Don't be the "Lone Ranger." That is, the independent soul who believes, "I don't need anyone's help! Win or lose, I did it MY way!" This mentality significantly increases your risk of failure. As part of your business build an organization chart based on where you see the business five, ten, even fifteen years into the future. Once built, adopt a mentality that you'll interview anyone seeking a job that might fit in one of your organization chart slots. Keep a file of "A" prospects and be prepared to hire them away at a future date if you're not prepared to take them on right now. However, be willing to "hire early," meaning, take a chance that highly talented people will bring value to your organization that is beyond what you must pay them. After all, that is your goal for every employee (for them to bring more to the bottom line profits than they cost). This is the essence of leverage . . . people leverage.

Ultimately, owning and running your own business can be a highly rewarding experience both from a financial and an emotional perspective. It is a great feeling knowing that you used your ideas and skills to solve problems for others, making their life better because of your help.

Dealing with Parents and Their Money

To properly plan your estate, it is important that your professional advisor has an understanding of the size and intended disposition of your parents' (and adult children's) estate. If their estate is large and will be left to you, the strategies employed in your own estate plan may need to be altered significantly. Likewise, if your parents' estate is small and there is a chance they may require your financial support, you need to know this. Unfortunately, discussions about money between parents and children rarely happen. Children who bring up the issue feel as if they are fortune hunting. Parents rarely take the opportunity to discuss money issues with their children. As you might imagine, the result is typically a lack of multigenerational planning, which can cause higher estate taxes and/or undesirable or inefficient transfers. The solution is obvious. We need to get the children and parents together to talk about money issues.

There are several ways to accomplish this. One of the best strategies is to use a professional advisor. Tell your parents you have retained a professional advisor to help you develop your estate plan and that the advisor has said you should coordinate your planning with that of your parents. See if your parents would be willing to meet with your advisor. Often, it's preferable that you not be at this meeting. Another alternative is to see if your parents will give permission for your advisor to meet with their advisor to discuss the coordination of multigenerational planning for the family. And in all seriousness, giving your parents books like this one may provoke some thinking on their part about their plans.

If your parents are truly unwilling to discuss money issues, make sure you do not make the same mistake. Embrace the concept of *The Family Council* and use it as a forum to discuss money matters with your own children.

The Family Council: A concept we developed to help families facilitate discussions about money in general and the family's finances in particular. Periodically (annually or at least every two to three years), family members come together in a meeting that is facilitated by one or more of your professional advisors. Working with the advisor(s), you prepare an agenda ahead of time. You decide how much of the details of the family's finances you want to discuss. Some parents prefer to withhold the particulars of how much they are worth and who will receive what, whereas others want their children to know all of the details. What is important is that you begin to transfer your values concerning money management to your children.

Once children start school, they are old enough to begin learning basic money concepts. Remember, your children are eventually going to inherit large sums of money. Our experience is that children who inherit money but haven't received any guidance from their parents are left to make their own choices—all too often the wrong ones—about managing their money. The money is spent on new cars, travel, or bad investments. On the other hand, if parents give their children advice regarding money, the majority of the time the children will embrace that advice. This is true even if the advice is bad advice! The conversation may go something like this: *"My daddy told me that I should hang on to this railroad stock because it had always been good to him and his daddy before him."* Even though the railroad stock represents 90 percent of their investment portfolio, they are reluctant to sell. Again, the Family Council meeting could include your financial advisor who can properly facilitate discussions about money and investments.

As you can see, estate planning is a complex subject involving a multitude of decisions and possible strategies. To do it well, you will need the assistance of one or more professional advisors who have extensive experience in estate planning matters. If you are not certain how to find a qualified advisor, feel free to contact one of us, and we'll be happy to refer you to someone in your area. Good luck, and may God shine His glory on you, your family, and your finances!

Professional Advisors

Estate planning is full of intricate details, so you should consult a professional advisor rather than trying to do it yourself. Choosing the right advisor is vital to your financial well-being. To select the right advisor, consider the following:

Experience. Each advisor you choose should have significant experience in his or her field. We strongly believe that *no* professional advisor should have unsupervised client responsibility until they have apprenticed under an experienced advisor for a minimum of three to five years. Experience is the foundation of all competence.

Competence. Although having an advanced designation is no guarantee of competence, it is an indication of a commitment to staying on the leading edge in one's field. The following are designations worth noting. Each requires the completion of one or more competency examinations as well as ongoing continuing education:

- *Certified Financial Planner*™ *or CFP*®. To be a Certified Financial Planner™ (CFP®) certificant, you must meet education requirements, pass a rigorous national exam, complete 30 hours of continuing education every two years, agree to abide by a strict code of ethics, and have three years of experience in the financial planning field. If you are seeking someone to help you with your overall financial game plan, you should seek out a CFP® certificant.

- *Certified Public Accountant.* All Certified Public Accountants (CPAs) must pass a series of national exams that test competency. CPAs must also complete 40 hours of continuing education work each year. They must also agree to abide by a code of ethics. For tax planning, we recommend that you use a CPA.

- *Accredited Estate Planner (AEP).* This designation focuses on education specifically related to the estate planning field. Five years of experience in estate planning is required to become an AEP. Designees must also complete 30 hours of continuing education during each 24-month period.

- *Estate Planning Law Specialist (EPLS).* This is the newest designation for lawyers. Passing a comprehensive examination is required along with peer recommendations.

- *Chartered Financial Analyst.* The Chartered Financial Analyst (CFA) designation is associated specifically with the securities field. To be a CFA, you must initially pass three difficult national competency exams, have three years of work experience in the field, complete continuing education each year, and abide by a code of ethics.

Compensation. When choosing your advisors, be sure to find out how they are compensated. Knowing the compensation upfront will avoid any misunderstandings in the future. Most attorneys and accountants charge hourly fees. Ask what the hourly rate is and get an estimate of the amount of time the person expects to spend on your case. Require that the person notify you immediately if he or she anticipates spending more hours than the estimate. He or she should also provide you with an itemized bill. Some accountants and even a few attorneys are now being compensated based on commissions from the sale of securities or other financial products. An extra measure of care should be taken on your part if your attorney or accountant recommends products to you in which they would receive a commission.

Financial planning professionals are typically compensated in one of three ways: fee only, fee plus commission, or commission only. If you work with an advisor who receives commissions from the sale of financial products, you should insist on full disclosure of the source and dollar amount of all commissions being paid. Any reputable advisor will be happy to accommodate this request.

Chemistry. Ideally, when you choose a professional advisor, you will select someone with whom you will work for the rest of your life. However, it's not unusual to find a competent advisor with whom, for some reason, you do not click. Most professional advisors will meet with you initially without charge. This first meeting is used to determine the scope of the work to be performed. You should also use this first meeting as an opportunity to determine if the advisor is someone with whom you feel you would be happy working with over the long term.

If you want a referral to an advisor, contact us and we will be happy to provide a referral.

Sirote & Permutt, P.C. Sirote & Permutt is a full-service law firm of 115 lawyers. Of these lawyers, 14 practice as estate planners and probate lawyers. Six of the 14 are fellows of the American College of Trust and Estate Counsel. The principal office is in Birmingham, Alabama, with other offices in Mobile and Huntsville, Alabama and Pensacola, Florida.

The Welch Group, LLC. The Welch Group, LLC, provides fee-only wealth management services to affluent families throughout the United States. Our sister company, Fee-Only Planning Professionals, LLC, provides fee-only financial advice and investment management services to young professionals and executives nation-wide.

If you would like additional information about our services, contact us at:

Harold Apolinsky, Esq., EPLS
Sirote & Permutt, P.C.
2311 Highland Avenue South
Suite 500
PO Box 55727
Birmingham, AL 35255-5727
(205) 930-5122
hapolinsky@sirote.com
www.sirote.com

Stewart H. Welch III, CFP®, AEP
The Welch Group, LLC
3940 Montclair Road, Fifth Floor
Birmingham, AL 35213
(205) 879-5001
stewart@welchgroup.com
www.welchgroup.com

Craig M. Stephens, Esq.
Sirote & Permutt, P.C.
2311 Highland Avenue South

Suite 500
P.O. Box 55727
Birmingham, AL 35255-5727
(205) 930-5246
cstephens@sirote.com
www.sirote.com

Estate Planning Terms

Abatement   The reduction of bequests when the assets of an estate are insufficient to pay all taxes, expenses, and bequests in full.

Ademption   When property listed in a will is subsequently disposed of prior to death, thus preventing the beneficiary from inheriting the property.

Administrator   The person or institution appointed by the court to administer or settle the estate of a deceased person who dies intestate.

Alternate Valuation Date   The date six months after your death (in most cases). Your estate representative has the option of valuing your assets as of the date of death or as of the *alternate valuation date* if certain criteria are met.

Annual Gift Tax Exclusion   Everyone can give away assets or cash up to the *annual gift tax exclusion* amount to as many people as they desire each year free of gift taxes. For 2011 the annual gift tax exclusion amount is $13,000. For subsequent years the amount is indexed for inflation.

Applicable Credit Amount   A tax credit allowed by the federal government against taxes due on gifts or transfers from your estate, and for 2011 and 2012 the Applicable Credit Amount is $1,730,800.

Applicable Exclusion Amount   The dollar value of assets that you can give to a nonspouse either during your lifetime or at your death free of estate or gift taxes. For 2011 and 2012, the dollar value is $5,000,000 for estate taxes and gift tax purposes.

Beneficiary   A person who is designated to receive benefits under a will, trust, or insurance policy.

Bequest   Property left to a person or organization under a will or trust.

Bypass Trust   See *Credit Shelter Trust*.

Codicil   An amendment to a previous will. A *codicil* is executed with the same formalities as a will.

Community Property   Nine states (Arizona, California, Idaho, Louisiana, Nevada, New Mexico, Texas, Washington and Wisconsin) have *community property* laws, which, in general, state that all property acquired by either partner in a marriage is considered owned one-half by each partner.

Contingent Beneficiary   A person or organization that is a beneficiary only upon the occurrence of some contingent event. For example, "I give Jean Daily the sum of $5,000 only if she is married to my brother John Daily at the time of my death."

Credit Shelter Trust   (or *Bypass Trust*)   A trust established under your will to take advantage of the *applicable exclusion amount*.

Curtesy   See *Dower*.

Custodian   A person or trust company responsible for the care and management of property for a minor. The relationship is a *fiduciary* relationship.

Decedent   The person who died.

Disclaimer   When a person disclaims benefits received from a *decedent*. If the *disclaimer* is timely (usually within nine months of receiving the rights to the property), irrevocable, the person never received any benefits from the property, and all other requirements are met, then there will be no tax consequences to the disclaiming person.

Domicile   The state in which you have your permanent residence.

Donee   A person receiving a gift.

Donor   A person making a gift.

Dower   (female); **Curtesy** (male)   Some states have laws that give your spouse the right to receive a certain portion of your estate (usually one-third to one-half) even if he or she is left out of your will. Also referred to as an *elective share*.

Escheat   State law that requires the estate of a person who dies without a will and without heirs to revert to the deceased's primary state of residence.

Estate   All of the property you own at your death (your *gross estate*).

Estate Taxes   Transfer taxes imposed by our federal government (and our states in some cases) for the privilege of giving your property to your heirs.

Executor   The person (or institution) you name in your will who will be responsible for settling your estate at your death.

Fiduciary   A person or institution occupying a position of trust. Fiduciaries are held to high standards of accountability by our courts.

Five and Five Power   A provision common in a trust agreement giving a surviving spouse the noncumulative right to withdraw annually the greater of (a) 5 percent of the trust corpus or (b) $5,000. The exercising of such right does not cause inclusion of the trust assets in the estate of the surviving spouse.

Generation Skipping Transfer Tax (GSTT)   A tax imposed on transfers of assets (either through gifts or your will) to a "skip" generation (a grandchild, for example). For 2011 and 2012 the first $5 million of transfers are not subject to the GST tax.

Gifts   The transfer of property to another person or organization without receiving anything of value in return.

Gift Tax   A tax imposed on the transfer of assets made during a person's lifetime. Note that the tax is due on gifts in excess of certain limits.

Grantor   A person who establishes and transfers property to a trust. Also called a *settlor*.

Guardian   A person responsible for the care of a minor (called *guardian of the person*) or a minor's property (called the *property guardian*).

Heir   A person entitled under state law to receive assets of another person who died without a will.

Holographic Will   A will that is completely handwritten. Many states recognize holographic wills only under certain circumstances.

Incompetent   Someone who has been judged by a court of law to be incapable of managing his or her financial affairs.

Inheritance Tax   A tax imposed by some states on heirs who receive an inheritance.

Inter Vivos Trust   A trust created during your lifetime rather than under your will. Also called a *living trust*.

Intestacy Laws   The laws of each state which determine who will receive the assets of a person who dies without a will.

Intestate   To die without a will.

Irrevocable Trust   A type of trust that cannot be revoked, changed, or amended. This type of trust is often used to remove assets from one's estate.

Issue   Your direct descendants, such as children, grandchildren, and great-grandchildren.

Joint Tenancy with Survivorship Rights   A way of titling property whereby at the death of one joint tenant the remaining joint tenant(s) automatically receives the deceased person's interest.

Joint Will   A single document that serves as the will for two people (usually a married couple).

Legacy   A gift of property under a will. The recipient of such property is called a *legatee*.

Legacy Trust   Typically a lifelong trust, and often a multi-generational trust that contains asset protection attributes.

Life Estate   The right to use property during one's lifetime. At death, that person's rights terminate.

Living Trust   See *Inter Vivos Trust*.

Living Will   A document that declares the level of care you desire should you become medically incapacitated. Generally, it states that you do not wish to be kept alive by artificial means.

Marital Deduction   The law provides that a married person may leave (or gift) an unlimited amount of assets to his or her spouse free of estate and gift taxes. This typically results in a postponement (rather than elimination) of the estate or gift taxes.

Marital Trust   A trust set up to receive assets that qualify for the *marital deduction*.

Minor   A person who is not legally considered an adult (age 18, 19, or 21 in most states). Minors cannot legally enter into binding contracts.

Non-Contest Clause   A provision in a will that provides that any person contesting the will shall have no rights to any assets under the will. Also known as the *in-terrorem clause*.

Nuncupative Will   An oral will. Many states do not allow oral wills at all; other states allow them only in extreme circumstances such as imminent death.

Per Capita   A distribution that is divided equally among the named persons (or their descendants) who have survived the testator. For example, you leave $100,000 to be divided per capita among your two sons and two daughters ($25,000 each). If one of your daughters predeceased you but had two children, your surviving children and two grandchildren would each receive $20,000.

Personal Property   All property other than real estate.

Per Stirpes   A distribution that is divided among named persons *or their descendants* should they predecease the *testator*. For example, you leave $100,000 to be divided among your two sons and two daughters ($25,000 each). If one of your daughters predeceased you but had two children, your surviving children would each receive $25,000, and your deceased daughters' children would each receive $12,500.

Power of Appointment   A right given to a person allowing them to designate to whom someone else's assets will go at the occurrence of a specified event.

Power of Attorney   A document executed by you that gives another person (your *agent*) the right to act on your behalf. A *power of attorney* can be written to include very broad or very limited powers.

Primary Beneficiary   The person (or persons) who will receive property under a will, trust, or insurance policy.

Probate   The court-supervised process of transferring one's property at death to his or her rightful heirs.

Probate Property   All property of a deceased person that is subject to *probate*. Certain property such as joint tenancy property is not subject to probate.

QDOT   Legally referred to as a *qualified domestic trust*. This is a spousal trust that allows non–U.S. citizen spouses to receive assets qualifying under the *unlimited marital deduction*.

QTIP Trust   Legally referred to as a *qualified terminable interest property trust*. This spousal trust allows you to control the ultimate disposition of the assets in the trust. Your spouse receives all income from the trust during his or her lifetime. This trust can qualify for the *unlimited marital deduction*.

Real Property   Land and fixed improvements such as buildings, trees, and fences.

Residue   The portion of your estate that remains after all specific distributions have been made. Also known as the *residuary estate*.

Revocable Trust   A type of trust that can be changed, modified, amended, or terminated at any time by the grantor during his or her lifetime.

Rule against Perpetuities   A complicated section of the law that prohibits leaving assets in trust indefinitely while avoiding taxes. Basically, the law states that funds can be left in trust for the lifetime plus 21 years of any beneficiary living at the time the grantor establishes the trust. Beyond that time a severe penalty is imposed.

Settlor   A person who establishes and transfers property to a trust. Also called a *grantor*.

Spendthrift Provision   A provision in a trust that prevents trust assets from being pledged, assigned, or otherwise used as collateral for a loan. The purpose is to protect the assets from the beneficiary's creditors.

Sprinkle Provision   A provision in a trust that allows the trustee the discretion to distribute trust income among the beneficiaries as the trustee deems appropriate. The distributions can be uneven (excluding some beneficiaries in favor of others), or the trust income can be accumulated.

Stepped-Up Cost Basis   The tax basis of appreciated property steps up to fair market value on the date of death. For example, if you own a stock that is worth $40,000 for which you paid $10,000 (your tax basis), you have a taxable gain of $30,000. If you died, the tax basis steps up to the fair market value of $40,000, and an immediate sale would result in no taxable gain.

Taxable Estate   The portion of your estate that is subject to federal and/or state taxes. From the gross estate you subtract funeral and administrative expenses, debts (including certain unpaid taxes), charitable contributions, and the marital deduction (if applicable).

Testamentary Trust   A trust that is created under your will that will take effect at your death.

Testator   One who dies having made a valid will.

Trust   A legal arrangement whereby one person (the *trustor*, *grantor*, or *settlor*) places assets under the management or supervision of another person or institution (the *trustee*) for the benefit of a third person (the *beneficiary*).

Trustee   A person or institution that manages and administers a trust.

Unified Credit   See *Applicable Credit Amount*.

Unified Gifts/Transfers to Minors Act   State laws that provide a method of holding assets for minors.

Unlimited Marital Deduction   A provision in the law that allows a married person to give or leave an unlimited amount of assets to his or her spouse free of gift or estate taxes.

Will   A legal document that details how your estate is to be distributed upon your death.

IRS Life Expectancy Table

The following table, referred to as the Single Life Expectancy Table, is used for determining the life expectancy of an individual for the purpose of determining Required Minimum Distributions (under Section 401(a)(9) of the Internal Revenue Code.

Single Life Table

Age	Life Expectancy
0	82.4
1	81.6
2	80.6
3	79.7
4	78.7
5	77.7
6	76.7
7	75.8
8	74.8
9	73.8
10	72.8
11	71.8
12	70.8
13	69.9
14	68.9
15	67.9
16	66.9
17	66.0
18	65.0
19	64.0

Single Life Table (*Continued*)

Age	Life Expectancy
20	63.0
21	62.1
22	61.1
23	60.1
24	59.1
25	58.2
26	57.2
27	56.2
28	55.3
29	54.3
30	53.3
31	52.4
32	51.4
33	50.4
34	49.4
35	48.5
36	47.5
37	46.5
38	45.6
39	44.6
40	43.6
41	42.7
42	41.7
43	40.7
44	39.8
45	38.8
46	37.9
47	37.0
48	36.0
49	35.1
50	34.2
51	33.3
52	32.3
53	31.4
54	30.5
55	29.6
56	28.7
57	27.9
58	27.0
59	26.1
60	25.2
61	24.4
62	23.5
63	22.7
64	21.8
65	21.0
66	20.2
67	19.4
68	18.6
69	17.8
70	17.0
71	16.3

(*Continued*)

Single Life Table (*Continued*)

Age	Life Expectancy
72	15.5
73	14.8
74	14.1
75	13.4
76	12.7
77	12.1
78	11.4
79	10.8
80	10.2
81	9.7
82	9.1
83	8.6
84	8.1
85	7.6
86	7.1
87	6.7
88	6.3
89	5.9
90	5.5
91	5.2
92	4.9
93	4.6
94	4.3
95	4.1
96	3.8
97	3.6
98	3.4
99	3.1
100	2.9
101	2.7
102	2.5
103	2.3
104	2.1
105	1.9
106	1.7
107	1.5
108	1.4
109	1.2
110	1.1
111+	1.0

Index

and retirement needs, 48, 49
transfer fees, 112
will provisions, 76, 77
Motorcycles, transferring to living trust, 119
Moves out of state and need for reviewing will and estate plan, 96
Multiple entities, use of, 234, 235
Multi-state businesses, 234
Mutual funds, 18, 25, 26, 28, 33–35, 44, 46, 53, 54, 125, 149, 213

N
Nevada
community property law, 67, 68, 212
domestic asset protection trusts, 221
New Mexico, community property law, 67, 68, 212
Nodeathtax.org, xiii
Nominee partnership, 116
Noncitizen spouse, 108
Notary public, 111
Nuncupative will, 73
Nursing home care, costs of, 141, 142.
See also Long-term care insurance (LTC)

O
Oklahoma, domestic asset protection trusts, 221
Oral will, 73

P
Partnerships
contract liability issues, 226
family limited partnerships. *See* Family limited partnerships (FLPs)
general partnerships, 225–227
limited partnerships, 216–219, 223, 227–228
living trust, nominee partnership, 116
tax identification number, 226, 227
tax returns, 189, 191, 194, 226, 227
Uniform Partnership Act, 225, 226
Patten, Dick, xiii

Patterson v. Shumate, 213
Payment on death (POD) accounts, 69
Perpetuities, rule against, 166
Perpetuities clause, 85–86
Personal liability insurance, 209, 210
Personal loan guarantees, 146, 216, 217
Personal messages, included in letter of instruction, 90
Personal property
bequeathing, 76, 77, 94
transferring to living trust, 119, 120
Personal residence
creditor protection, 209
exclusion for gain on sale of residence, 157
homestead exemption, 118
ownership interests, 68, 69
Qualified Personal Residence Trust (QPRT), 152, 154–159
title to, 64–68
will provisions, 77, 94
Personal service providers, 234
Phantom income, 188
Piercing the corporate veil, 233, 234
Pooled income funds, 180, 181
Postmortem planning, 63, 66, 103
Pour-over will, 120
Power of appointment
general power of appointment, 104–106, 159, 166
general power of appointment trust, 105, 106
limited power of appointment, 139, 166
Power of attorney
durable power of attorney, 12, 87, 97, 109, 111, 114, 115
durable power of attorney for health care, 88
general power of attorney, 87
limited power of attorney, 87
springing power of attorney, 87
use of in estate planning, 14, 16, 65, 67, 75
Private annuity, 163